I Really Should
Have Stayed Home

I Really Should
Have Stayed Home

The Worst Journeys
from Harare to Eternity

Edited by
Roger Rapoport
& Bob Drews

RDR Books
Oakland, California

I Really Should Have Stayed Home

RDR Books
4456 Piedmont
Oakland, CA 94611
Phone: (510) 595-0595
Fax: (510) 595-0598
E-mail: info@rdrbooks.com
Website: www.rdrbooks.com

ISBN: 1-57143-081-4

Library of Congress Catalog Card Number: 99-074652

Associate Editors: Anne Hagen and Kim Klescewski
Proofreader: Joanna Pearlman
Cover Photograph: Robert Holmes
Cover Design: Jennifer Braham
Text Design: Paula Morrison

Distributed in Canada by General Distribution Service
325 Humber College Boulevard, Toronto, Ontario M9W7C3

Distributed in England and Europe by Airlift Book Company,
8 The Arena, Mollison Avenue, Enfield, Middlesex, England
EN37NJ

Distributed in Australia and New Zealand by Astam Books Pty Ltd.,
57-61 John Street Liechardt, New South Wales 2038

Printed in Canada

Dedicated to
Dan, Jonathan and Elizabeth Rapoport

Table of Contents

Disasters That Can't Wait to Happen

by Roger Rapoport

Since the publication of *I Should Have Stayed Home,* RDR Books has grown to become the world's largest purveyor of travel horror stories. Indeed, copies of our travel series have been spotted all the way from travelers on the slopes of Kilimanjaro to kayakers in the Yukon to backpackers in Thailand.

Chronicling travel misfortunes and missteps has become our passion.

Translated into numerous languages, *I've Been Gone Far Too Long, I Should Have Stayed Home* and *After the Death of a Salesman* have tickled funny bones from the South China Sea to the Bay of Fundy. But our mission is not to make light or to make fun. It is to make people laugh, and in that there can be a serious message and a serious mission. Just imagine: author royalties from these books have underwritten the relief work of Oxfam in the Third World. So someone who writes about finding a bushmaster in their bidet can use the proceeds to provide safe drinking water in Africa. Not only have our books given readers around the world a chuckle, our own problems have made headlines. Who would have believed that during a signing for *I Should Have Stayed Home* in Denton, Texas, thieves were busy out in the parking lot stealing my rental car with boxes of books, underwear, sports jacket, camera, checkbook and most important of all, my laptop with the manuscript for *After the Death of a Salesman.* And as our offices have become a magnet for travel disaster stories around the globe, we've developed a motto here at RDR Books: "Have a great trip, but if anything goes wrong, we want to hear about it."

This volume is the fourth in our travel horror series. In it, we are pleased to introduce a number of new writers. As you've seen, there's nothing quite like a trip from hell to establish the literary gifts of a promising newcomer. Our books have generated a great deal of interest from people who want to know what it is about travel that lends itself so brilliantly to the literature of the damned. In the process, they themselves have sometimes become contributors.

In my line of work I have an opportunity to study this issue closely. The reason why we are blessed with so many fine stories is simple enough. In our quest to go everywhere and do everything, we've learned that we, the inexperienced, are condemned to confront the impossible dreams foisted upon us. I doubt any of the copywriters responsible for all this false advertising can even spell salmonella. Whenever I tell the story of my latest travel disaster my wife always shakes her head and says, "You're such an optimist." Have you ever noticed, for example, that when you want to simply change a flight, the airline wants $75, but when they mess up and throw your schedule out of whack, there just doesn't seem to be anyone around to give you that $75 back? If you're lucky, as I was recently in the Minneapolis-St. Paul airport, you'll be given a $7 food voucher at 3 A.M., only to find that every restaurant in the building is closed.

I keep dreaming that someday a new airline (not run by accountants) will just charge everyone the same price to go to the same destination instead of offering dozens of fares based on the fact that in a near-monopoly market it's easier to exploit confused customers.

I keep looking for a soapbox where I can preach against so

many of the wrongs that have led to the disasters that make this book so much fun. Of course that would make it impossible to publish these wonderful volumes. But every time I read another travel horror story, I think about what could have been done to prevent disaster. I suspect that the only way out is to stay home. And that would be a shame.

Some of our correspondents, their tales told here, have gone from bad to worse. Take the traveler who wrote a devastating story for us about the perils of traveling in Asia. He ended up accepting tainted baklava from an acquaintance in Turkey and woke up in a hospital a day and a half later minus his wallet. Understandably he didn't want to write about the positive side of the experience: He emerged from the hospital with both kidneys intact.

As the damage toll rises, I wonder if the concept of safe travel is becoming an oxymoron.

My own theory is that the tendency of large companies to run their organizations on automatic has made even the simplest travel transactions difficult. My banker recently told me about a large rental car company that takes customers' ATM cards and keeps entering the same charge over and over again. In the heightened security of airports where left luggage is confiscated, it is my impression, from personal experience, that theft is on the rise. At least that's what I keep telling the claims department of my insurance company. And, as more and more flights are routed through congested hubs, the transportation system seems to be run by sleepwalkers. At this writing Washington's Reagan Airport has responded to the crush by operating without ground radar. Another great example is jammed LaGuardia Airport in New York, where airline schedules are being downsized with the help of a landing slot lottery.

What a perfect metaphor for what travel has become. This

was brought home to me recently on a takeoff from the San Francisco airport. The front wheels of our Airbus had just left the ground when the tower canceled our takeoff due to conflicting traffic. The pilot applied the brakes at 100 percent and in just a few seconds we went from 150 miles per hour to a screeching halt. It was half an hour before the brakes cooled to the point where we could get back onto the runway for a second takeoff. Commenting on the series of delays and problems that had preceded our aborted takeoff, my seatmate looked at me as we began our second takeoff roll and said, "I have a funny feeling about this flight." The fact that everything went perfectly from that point forward was little consolation to the passengers who had been screaming less than an hour before when the pilot hit the brakes.

And so we have become conditioned to the reality that a Bon Voyage is any trip that doesn't end up in the newspapers or a travel horror book. Hardly a day goes by without callers from remote places like Harare, the capital of Zimbabwe, asking us if we are planning yet another volume of travel disasters. As long as misery loves company, you can count it.

Take Time to Watch the Bugs

by Cameron M. Burns

As I LAY SLEEPILY on the bed of our Manuel Antonio bunga-low, watching the Costa Rican trees sway gently outside the open door, a blood-curdling scream echoed from the closet.

It wasn't the normal kind of cry I knew my wife was capa-ble of, a fairly simple girlish shriek or something along those lines. No, this was something much more sinister, a deep, deranged howling kind of moan, one that grew in volume and tone until it reached a crescendo as an unnerving, Banshee-like wail.

I pulled my heart out of my throat, and leapt from the bed. Had she found a body? Had a trap door opened in the ward-robe floor revealing a pit of deadly vipers? Had she sliced off her legs shaving?

The answer came almost instantly as Ann ran towards the open door and flung her blue cotton T-shirt outside. I watched in astonishment as a stick-like creature flattened itself out on the concrete sidewalk, then ran down the path. It was a scor-pion, and one of the proudest specimens I'd ever seen. Some 8 inches in length (when it flattened out to run) it was a light translucent brown, with bluish-black claws and pincers.

On the walkway outside our room, a small crowd of gar-deners, hotel maids and fellow tourists had quickly gathered. One of the gardeners, a fellow named Jose (Jose No. 1, for this story), spotted the fleeing scorpion and promptly stepped on it, smashing the poor creature's body into a creamy pulp. He squatted down and studied it for several minutes as the crowd dispersed. Then he looked up at me: "Muy Peligrosso!"

He shook his head several times, to indicate that Ann had narrowly escaped with her life. He looked me in the eye, and with the middle and index fingers of his left hand curled like the fangs of a tarantula, he stabbed at the palm of his other hand: "ESSTINGA!!!"

Jose No. 1 stood up and using his boot wiped the remainder of the pulpy scorpion body from the sidewalk and into the garden. With that, he turned and walked away.

It took me several minutes to find someone who could speak English, and after a trial-by-fire sort of interrogation, I learned that this particular model of scorpion was not found locally. It was from the central highlands of Costa Rica, the mountainous region that makes up the spine of this small Central American nation. After much gesticulating and back-and-forth translation, we all agreed that this fellow's particular trip to Manuel Antonio from the mountains had likely been in our luggage. And this particular type of scorpion, Jose No. 1 assured me, was deadly.

Ann and I had planned our trip to Costa Rica in the summer of 1994. It was to be our honeymoon, and rather than travel with a tour group, we had opted to fly to San Jose, then pick out whatever "mini" adventures appealed to us on a day-by-day basis. That is, perhaps, the greatest appeal of Costa Rica: the country's ability to host numerous adventures, even if they're scheduled one day after another. It's a small country—just 200 miles from the Nicaraguan border to the north and Panama to the south—and it's possible to drive across the entire nation in a single day. In 1949, the forward-thinking nation did away with its army and invested a healthy chunk of the savings into social services and education. Indeed, education officials from Europe regularly study the Costa Rican system.

But it's perhaps the area of nature where Costa Rica shines brightest. More than one-quarter of the entire country has been set aside and preserved in its natural state, in the form of national parks or preserves. Its wildlands are a botanical wonderland of flora and fauna—an estimated 9,000 species of plants, 1,200 varieties of orchids, 800 species of ferns, 850 species of birds, 10 percent of all the world's butterflies and 5,000 different species of grasshoppers. The weirdest number we found, however, was that half the mammal species in Costa Rica—over 200—are bats. So, my new bride and I went. But we had little idea all of these adventures would be shared by Costa Rica's vast population of arachnid.

Our first adventure was a three-day stint touring Tortuguero National Park. Our guide, Alberto, pointed out the spectacular waterfalls and canyons, the lush forest and the exotic birds. Halfway through the park, Alberto produced a jar from inside his backpack. It contained a bright yellow, highly venomous eyelash viper. The driver pulled over, and Alberto, in showmanship fashion, released the creature into the grass at the edge of the road.

"This little fellow was in the courtyard behind my apartment," he explained. "I wanted to make sure he returned to the forest. They are extremely dangerous, so stand back please."

Next stop was a banana processing facility, along the road to Limon. Here, Alberto pulled out a bunch of green bananas, then immediately dropped the bunch to the ground. An enormous green tarantula crawled out from the bunch and reared up, ready to strike. "Very dangerous," he said.

We moved on to Tortuguero, where we toured the fabulous canals and observed sloths in Tortuguero's trees. Our visit concluded with a hike up Cerro Tortuguero, an 800-foot hill offering views into neighboring Nicaragua. Near the top of

Cerro Tortuguero, we came across a mosaic of spider webs adorning the bushes and trees on the side of the trail. Our guide, Jose (Jose No. 2), studied the intricate webs, and pointed out the tiny, delicate creatures sitting at the epicenter of each web. Ann and I collectively shivered. There were a dozen webs in an area the size of my closet.

"Peligrosso?" I asked pointing at the maze of webs.

"No se." Jose No. 2 shrugged and wandered off down the trail.

Our next adventure took us down the Pacuare River on a rubber raft. We spent two days bouncing down rapids and through eddies, stopping occasionally for a meal, or a side trip to examine flora, fauna and geologic wonders. We spent our only night on the trip in a rustic jungle bungalow, the kind of place that was crawling with insect life. We spent a few minutes sweeping the nooks and crannies of the wooden hut free of critters, especially the few that looked like they might make a break for our bed in the night.

In the morning, as our rafting guide, Manuel, loaded the boats, there was another evil-sounding shriek. This time a Dutch woman, another tourist on the trip, had spotted one of the biggest spiders any of us had ever seen. She screamed and ran back up on the beach. The rest of us stood waist deep in the river and wondered if Costa Rica had piranhas. The spider, we were informed when Manuel caught it, was a "Jesus Christ" spider. With a body the size of a silver dollar and eight long legs that gave the animal a 7-inch span, this particular spider had the remarkable ability of running on water. I mean, not just moving across water, the way spiders do. This thing was capable of maintaining a flat out gallop for hundreds of feet at a time. Hence the name, Jesus Christ.

This impressive arachnid had apparently been hunting on

the river's surface, then frightened by our arrival on the beach had taken refuge in one of the boats. Manuel checked the rafts inside and out and declared them free of spiders and fit for continued white water action.

I don't know how ready the rest of the crew was for continued white water action, but we carefully climbed into the rafts and checked them thoroughly. According to entomologists, spiders are found all over the world in vast quantities. Over 1 million of them can be found in a typical one-acre grassy field, and they've been found as high as 23,000 feet in the Himalayas. There are about 2,500 different species in North America, and an estimated 34,000 species worldwide. No one knows exactly how many species of spider Costa Rica has, but by the time we had mounted the yellow raft, we were guessing that the natural distribution process had favored Central America.

A few days later we were bound for Arenal, a sleepy village in the Central Highlands surrounded by farms and coffee plantations. Having ridden the bus from San Jose (patron saint of all the Joses in Costa Rica, hence their natural prolific distribution in Central America) to Tilaran, thence by taxi cab to Arenal. Of course, we had wanted to go to Volcano Arenal, not Lake Arenal, thus the desperate Spanglish confusion when the bewildered taxi driver dropped us off at a lone motel in the middle of nowhere at 2 A.M. We were shown to rooms that were alive with insect life. Hundreds of cockroaches scurried back and forth across the floor. Moths buzzed around the lights like Japanese kamikaze pilots. Creatures of all shape, size and bodily configuration scurried across the bed. Ann, who's not a great fan of insects, held herself together pretty well until she ventured into the shower. A gargantuan cockroach sitting on the water taps sent her straight towards me with a plea of getting her out of there. She was ready to have my head, which

I told her was somewhat ironic since the females of many species of spiders eat their mates soon after copulation is complete. "In fact," I said cheerily, "with some species, the female mates, eats the male, then carries the babies around on her back until she dies. Then the babies eat her."

"Wonderful," Ann said.

We spent the night huddled together in a single cot, waving a rolled up magazine at the various flying predators, occasionally hitting one, occasionally being attacked and bitten or stung, or whatever it was they were doing.

The next morning we caught a bus to La Fortuna, the village we'd really meant to visit, which sits below the famous volcano. I found us a room at a tiny downtown hostel (only a few spiders under the bed, but some weird-looking beetles on the window), and we wandered through the village taking in the sights. We enjoyed a festive lunch at the town's best restaurant, and that night visited the volcano and swam in hot springs near its base.

The following day, after inquiring about the next bus out of town, Ann and I found ourselves with a full day to kill. So, at the advice of some locals, we signed ourselves up for a three-hour tour of the Venado Caves (Cavernas de Venado).

Our guide to the caves, named—what else?—Jose showed us the entrance: a narrow limestone hole in a small rocky wall, with a fast stream issuing from the portal. To our astonishment, the rock walls around the mouth of the cave were covered with spiders. Not only the large Jesus Christ spiders, of which we'd become so fond on our rafting adventure, but also other species no one knew anything about.

We looked at the mouth of the cave, then, with raised eyebrows, at Jose No. 3. He winked, then ran through the entrance and into the cave. "No problemo."

I went next, and Ann, reluctantly, came third. Inside, our cheap plastic flashlights illuminated the walls of the cave. The spiders, it seemed, were only congregated around the entrance. Inside, our only problem was bats, which were everywhere. One flew into my mouth.

We roamed through the caves, from chamber to chamber, and examined the fantastic stalactites and stalagmites, which dominated the bigger rooms. After several hours, we ran back out the entrance, and congratulated each other that we were alive.

We took a taxi back to Fortuna and cleaned up for the bus ride back to San Jose. There, we loaded up our belongings and caught a bus to the Pacific coast, more specifically, to Quepos and Manuel Antonio National Park.

Somehow during the next few days—as we journeyed from La Fortuna to San Jose to Manuel Antonio—our friend the 8-inch scorpion came with us. Whether he thought he was hiding in a safe spot, or whether he was some rare, migratory species of backpack-dwelling scorpion, we'll never know. All Ann knows is that when we arrived in Manuel Antonio, she hung her wet T-shirt up, which happened to be inside out, in the closet. In the morning, she took the garment from its resting-place and began to turn it right side out. That's when she discovered her hitchhiker and her evil wailing began.

Of course, had her shirt been right side out to begin with, she would have put it on straightaway. She'd never have flipped it right side out and discovered the scorpion waiting inside. I shudder to think of the noise she might have made.

Once we'd both calmed down, we spent the morning going through every scrap of clothing we'd brought to Central America—dumping it on the floor, jumping on it repeatedly, smashing it with our fists and ultimately throwing it all into the shower for a thorough rinsing. After much frightening packing, we flew to San Juan, and the Hotel Don Carlos, where our new "Anti-Scorpion Packing Process" was repeated in the bathroom. Clothes were stomped on, screwed into tight balls, then flung into the shower where they were rinsed thoroughly.

We flew home the next day. My new bride told me that next time we planned a trip to the tropics, it would be to sit on a warm beach and sleep in a clean hotel; no jungle adventures, no spider riddled caves, no roach motels. In other words, none of my adventurous crap. Of course, Ann and I are still married, and occasionally she reminds me of our creepy-crawly honeymoon.

The United States boasts some 40 different species of Scorpionida Arachnida, only one of which is deadly. There are some 1,400 species worldwide, many of which can produce a neurotoxin which destroys the nervous system, ultimately causing death. Whatever species our hitchhiking friend was, no one in Manuel Antonio seemed to know and we'll likely never find out.

We like to think of him as our adventure guide, so we called him—what else?—Jose.

Night Train to Luxor

by Brooke Comer

My friend Delia lives without visible means of support (in other words, she is a writer, like me) in luxury apartments in Bombay, New York and Cairo. She is a world traveler, thanks partly to assignments from film and travel magazines and partly to the largesse of her male, jet set friends.

One winter when we were both in Cairo covering the International Film Festival, she invited me to a party that began at midnight at La Parisienne, a bellydance joint in Giza near the Pyramids. I had spent an exhausting day chasing an Egyptian producer whose scorn for Hollywood might be rooted in jealousy, but was scorn nonetheless, and who seemed to think that wasting hours of my time convincing him to do an interview for a Hollywood magazine would avenge his splendid but under-financed productions. In short, I was too tired to make the party. I didn't hear from Delia for three days, which is not unusual, but when I did she was surprisingly tanned, which *is* unusual, as December in Cairo is not the season for sunbathing.

"You should have come to this party," she told me.

"When did it end?" I envisioned a few guests still sleeping it off on the floor of La Parisienne, possibly under sunlamps.

"It's still going on."

It turns out the host was a sheik whose parties never last less than a week. When La Parisienne closed, he'd piled all the guests (Delia included) and the most voluptuous bellydancers into his private 747 and flown them away to one of his villas in the warmer climes of Bahrain.

"Was it fun?" A stupid question, especially considering the relative tedium of the film festival.

Delia assured me that her last three days had been better spent than mine, though she did have a few criticisms regarding the quality of travel to Bahrain (she'd been flown back to Cairo first class on Gulf Air and was still sublime with caviar and smuggled Stolychnya). The interior of the sheik's private plane was done in fuzzy purple and orange velvet paisley and the only onboard audio consisted of an elevator version of the Doors' song "Light My Fire." Due to a lack of seats, she'd had to spend the entire flight sitting on the host's lap, which might explain why he had later invited her on a luxury Nile cruise line that he owned. She'd accepted the cruise on the condition that I was invited too. "He also owns a publishing company, and he's looking for writers, so it's strictly business," she assured me. "And I told him I wouldn't go without you."

I imagined the sheik locking us all into the honeymoon suite and declined. But Delia does not take no for an answer and insisted on calling him so he could assure me that his motives were legitimate. She seemed surprised, and a little disappointed, to learn that he had no intention of accompanying us on the cruise because he had no recollection of having extended the invitation. But Delia, using the same tenacity with which she'd extracted his cell phone number the first night she met him, pressed the sheik for two stateroom suites and assignments to write about the trip for the English-language magazines that he also owned. Hiring outsiders to do an in-house job was clearly a favor that brought some interesting perks along with it: the Nile cruise and a byline in a trade magazine read exclusively by oil executives in Saudi Arabia.

But our free trip wasn't entirely free. The sheik-publisher

wouldn't reimburse our travel expenses to Luxor. Most passengers on Egypt's luxury cruise lines fly from Cairo to Upper Egypt, but plane tickets were out of our price range so we chose the night train.

I liked the sound of it. Night train to Luxor had the ring of a film noir and suggested mystery, the thrill of danger. It also had the ring of sold out. When we went to the train station to buy our tickets, we were told there were no more seats available from Cairo to Luxor. There were, however, plenty of seats from Cairo to Edfu, the next stop after Luxor. When we got back to our hotel, Delia found a fax under her door from the sheik's office telling us that the locks, where the boats were boarded, were closed at Luxor anyway and we should buy tickets to Edfu, where we'd board the cruise ship instead.

"Isn't that lucky," Delia marveled.

The afternoon prior to our evening departure, Delia plied me with thimble-sized cups of Turkish coffee. "One of us has to stay awake at all times," she instructed. "Sleeping on this train is like inviting a murderer into your bedroom. And we're targets because we're Americans." Delia's eyes glittered. Targets were recognized and she loved recognition.

Our route, she told me, ran through the mother lode of fundamentalist Egypt, the small villages that were home to American-hating spies, scouts and suicide bombers, some or all of whom might try to board and destroy our train. It had happened before. She could show me articles on the Internet. Bombs had exploded. Lives had been lost, American blood shed. "We can't trust anyone," she said darkly.

I considered parting with the extra $350 it would cost to fly from Cairo to Luxor, but at 10 o'clock there I was, boarding the train and letting the porter stow my bag, which I was sure would be removed by mistake in the early hours of morning and left in the sand at a desolate station in Abydos or Dendara.

We were the only women in our car, which, Delia hissed at me, was a bad sign. But the other passengers appeared to be benign businessmen, and our seats were spacious enough to sleep in, even though Delia insisted that sleep on this train would be suicide. To help keep us awake, a video monitor attached to the ceiling blasted the 10-year-old film *Wall Street,* dubbed into loud Arabic. There was no audio control short of smashing the screen out, which Delia suggested might happen when one of the fundamentalists disguised as a businessman figured out the film's capitalist-imperialist message.

Our tickets included a meal of gray meat and yellow rice, served with a cold boiled potato and bread. We could buy tea, Cokes and bottled water from little boy vendors walking the aisles in a trance-state, possibly a result of sleep deprivation.

Delia curled up with a flask of Dewar's and watched the movie. I practiced closing my eyes for short periods to see if I could fall asleep. I could. I woke up sometime later to a blood-curdling scream. Delia had apparently also fallen asleep and while she was sleeping an Egyptian dwarf had taken a seat on her lap. He sat with his hands on her shoulders, his legs wrapped around her waist, his face buried in her neck, which he appeared to be kissing passionately. He did not resist her violent efforts to oust him from his perch and did not look victorious, ashamed or even mildly wicked. His gaze was reproachful, righteous and stern, as if he was the one who had been molested while sleeping. He was dressed impeccably, like every other man in our car, in a dark suit and tie, and when he jumped onto the floor he dusted his hands and walked away, frowning.

"You disgusting idiot," Delia shouted at him. "May Allah spit on your unworthy ancestors. May you come back in your next life as a worm!" She turned to me. "That was so Fellini, don't you think?"

No one else in our car paid any attention to the dwarf incident. We rolled on through the night, stopping at the small towns Delia had warned me about, but no one came aboard. The movie ended, but the sound did not cease, a loud buzz replacing the soundtrack. The businessmen began to snore and so, finally, did Delia. I would have slept too but I was distracted by the sparks hissing in the blue light bulb just above my head. I envisioned myself asleep while the bulb burst into flame and fell, setting my hair on fire.

I was so busy looking up; wondering if there was a switch so I could turn the light off without electrocuting myself, that I didn't notice the flood until my toes were wet. There was a small bathroom at the end of the car, which you stepped down about four inches to enter. That was a good thing because even when we left Cairo, water was collecting on the floor. I'd been mildly reassured that the overflow came from the sink, and not the toilet, due to a faucet that wouldn't turn off. Apparently the waters had risen sharply because pressure suddenly sent the door slamming open and flooding the aisle. I pulled the bag I'd been resting my feet on up onto the seat.

The train staff, who'd been so attentive when it came to selling us little bags of nuts, hard candy and water in unsealed bottles, had disappeared. I woke up Delia, who was not happy I'd interrupted her sleep. She rubbed her eyes and looked at the water. "It's nothing. Haven't you ever ridden a train before? This happens all the time on Amtrak." She went back to sleep.

I wanted very much to sleep too, but I couldn't. Blue sparks flew above my head like fireflies. Outside, in the gray light, we sped past palm trees, deserts and small towns of stick shacks dominated by mosques. My body ached with fatigue. This may have been fundamentalist turf, but I didn't fear them. I envied them. After all, they could sleep.

Finally I did too, only to be awakened by the sharp kick of a little boy holding a pot of coffee in one hand and a stack of cups in the other. The sun was shining. The light bulb above me was completely black; had it burned itself out? I touched my hair. It was still there. Only patches of water remained in the aisle, leaving behind a distinct and unpleasant smell.

I took a coffee cup, and the child began to scream.

"He wants you to pay him first," Delia translated. She was already awake, her coffee balanced on one knee, talking to a swarthy man with a pockmarked face in the seat behind her who rested a thick hand on her shoulder. I gave the boy an Egyptian pound (about 25 cents) and he poured my coffee.

The conductor announced that we were approaching Luxor, at least, that's what I think he said. I only understood "Luxor."

Delia began to gather her bags, and I reminded her that we were going on to Edfu. She shook her head. "No, we'll get off here. Sayed is so generous, he's offered to drive us straight to the boat. It'll be much more fun." She pointed to the pockmarked man, who blushed and smiled. "He's in the fruit business," she whispered. "A big wholesaler."

"Isn't Edfu out of his way?" I asked. "Isn't it at least 30 miles from Luxor?"

"His brother works in Edfu. He's going there anyway."

The porters were vigilant about protecting our stored bags after all. They didn't even want to give them to us in Luxor because our tickets said that our destination was Edfu. When Delia gave them five pounds and they looked dubious, I decided they must be honest if the bribe made them uncomfortable. Then she handed them another five pounds and they not only ran to find our bags, they carried them to Sayed's car. Or rather, to his truck.

Sayed's truck had a wide bed and high, wooden sides, creating a space that was filled with green and gold melons. The tiny cab could accommodate only one person—the driver. Sayed made it clear that one of us was welcome to sit on his lap and help him drive, and he was disappointed when we chose the other option, to ride in back with the melons. It turned out to be a long way to Edfu under the Upper Egypt sun, which got a lot hotter at this time of year than the northern sun in Cairo. It also turned out that Sayed had no idea how to get to the Edfu lock; his brother had never worked there. His brother lived in Newport, Rhode Island.

It is impossible to sleep on unripe melons. The side road— or perhaps it was the main road—which Sayed chose was full of ruts and potholes and surely didn't help. The melons bounced underneath us.

Delia had slept well on the train and was not tired. "This is what it's like to be a melon," she said. "Aren't you glad we got off the train? I told you this would be more fun."

It was high noon before we finally found the Edfu lock, and while Delia hurried off to make sure our ship had not sailed, I faced the task of informing Sayed, who was under a serious misimpression, that he would *not* be joining us on the cruise. The look of dazed shock on his face when that reality finally hit home was nothing compared to the horror in Delia's eyes, when we arrived breathless, heavy luggage in tow, at the walkway to our ship. The staff was lined up to greet us by the ornate, gold leafed door, white-gloved hands extended. At the head of the line, indicating he played a prominent role onboard, stood the dwarf, unmistakably the same diminuitive fellow that Delia had knocked off her lap. If he recognized her, he gave no indication. She, however, refused to shake his hand as we passed through that glorious portal.

Pass the Anteater, Please

by Claudia R. Capos

FOR MANY TRAVELERS, Thanksgiving Day is fairly predictable. Ham or turkey with the relatives, followed by family chitchat or football games on TV. But not for me.

Over a period of 10 years, I traveled to the most far-distant countries in the world annually to celebrate Thanksgiving Day and to eat the most non-traditional Thanksgiving dinners I could find. Over time, this custom took me to, among others, Hobart, Tasmania, the stomping ground of swashbuckler Errol Flynn; Katmandu, Nepal, the Himalayan home of the Abominable Snowman; and Nairobi, Kenya, the last outpost of civilization in the heart of safari country. I even sailed up the Ganges and down the Amazon to add more twists to my annual celebration.

At each stop, I tried to choose a dining spot that reflected the history and culture of the country I was visiting. I also attempted to select (and to eat, if humanly possible) the kind of indigenous cuisine that modern pilgrims would most likely serve for their Thanksgiving Day feast.

Sometimes the gastronomic rewards of my Thanksgiving Day forays were worth the effort, not to mention the considerable airfare. Other times the whole experience left me longing for all the traditional fixings. And, of course, it wasn't always easy trying to order Thanksgiving dinner in countries where people didn't know what Thanksgiving is all about.

The first year I celebrated Thanksgiving on Bali, one of the most enchanting islands in Indonesia. Even now I can still picture the blazing red sunsets over Kuta Beach and smell the heavy perfume of the tropical flowers. On Thanksgiving Day, I found a small open-air restaurant with a canopy of palm leaves that seemed perfect for the occasion. When I asked the Balinese waiter if he had turkey on the menu, I hit a snag.

In response to his look of bewilderment, I tried to explain that a turkey was something like a big chicken, and I demonstrated by flapping my arms and gobbling. Everyone else in the restaurant paused for a few seconds, their forks frozen in midair. For a minute, there was a flicker of recognition in the waiter's eyes. He soon returned carrying a very large platter.

As it turned out, he was close. But, as they say, no cigar. It was a platter of grilled turtle rather than grilled turkey, the former a delicacy of the Balinese.

A new-found friend from New Zealand, who was also vacationing there and had offered to celebrate Thanksgiving with me, said she thought the turtle tasted a bit like grilled goat, kind of chewy and well spiced. I didn't argue the point since I'd never sampled grilled goat either. At least the meal was edible.

There have been times, however, when it wasn't.

One Thanksgiving, I booked a jungle cruise down a 350-mile stretch of the Amazon River from Iquitos, Peru, to Tabatinga, Brazil. The minute I stepped aboard the Rio Amazonas, a converted banana hauler that was to be our "Love Boat" for four days, I buttonholed the cook and requested he prepare something special, something very Amazonian for my Thanksgiving dinner. I specifically asked for piranha, thinking what an ironic twist it would be to end up eating man-eating fish for Thanksgiving instead of the other way around. But luck was against me. One of the crew members told me when I sat down at the table on Thanksgiving Day that we would not be entering piranha waters until the next morning. That meant my plate of pan-fried piranha would end up becoming a belated Thanksgiving dinner.

But the crew did not disappoint me that Thanksgiving night. They brought out a covered dish and set it in front of me with great fanfare. Off came the lid, revealing half of a grilled anteater that had been captured by a local Indian tribe, former headhunters as I later found out.

More precisely, it was half of a very old anteater that had been burned to a crisp. It was shoe-leather tough and I found I couldn't cut it, chop it, tear it apart, bite it or chew it. Even dousing it with the locally made hot sauce, which was guaranteed to burn a hole in your stomach lining, didn't help. Fortunately, the meal included other Amazonian trimmings such as potatoes, rice and bananas, so I didn't go hungry.

Selecting just the right restaurant, one that reflected the history and culture of the country and served indigenous foods, was an important factor in my Thanksgiving Day quest. One year I headed Down Under and made my way to Tasmania, a strange apple-shaped island off the southeastern shore of Australia. Tasmania was originally settled as a penal colony, and among the top tourist attractions today are the Colonial Convict Museum and the ruins of the Port Arthur prison complex. In view of the island's dubious history, I thought the logical choice of dining spots would be the Ball and Chain Restaurant in Hobart, the birthplace of actor Errol Flynn.

I wasn't disappointed. The dank-as-a-dungeon dining room was done up in 19th-century penal colony decor, complete with iron bars, rough-hewn wooden tables and even a pillory for customers who didn't pay their bills. The waiters and waitresses were dressed in period prison garb, and the background music was a motley collection of Australian beer drinking songs. I passed up the "penitentiary chicken" and the "condemned man's reprieve" and decided to go with a gigantic Tasmanian crayfish served up mornay style with a cheese and wine sauce. It more than lived up to its billing that night.

Although I had originally planned to celebrate Thanksgiving the next year in Monrovia, the capital of Liberia (for some reason, the idea struck my fancy even though Liberia's only real claim to culinary fame is baked barracuda), the timing turned out wrong. Instead, I ended up in Nairobi, Kenya, on Nov. 24 searching for some restaurant that served native African food. There were virtually none except the African Heritage Cafe on Kenyatta Avenue. I later learned why when I persuaded the chef, a tiny lady with thick glasses named Mamatin, to prepare a sampling of indigenous dishes especially for me.

To be perfectly honest, there is only so much you can do with corn, beans and potatoes. Even under the most skillful direction, it will never qualify as haute cuisine. In the end, the names of the dishes—"viesi," "boga," "gatheru," "irio" and "skuma wiki"—turned out to be much more interesting than the ingredients.

At times, the place rather than the meal itself was the real attraction for Thanksgiving.

One year while visiting Easter Island, which is famous for its monolithic carved statues but not for its restaurants, I enjoyed a Thanksgiving picnic under the palms at Anakena Beach with my tour companions. It was at that same idyllic spot back in 450 A.D. that Hotu Matua, the island's first self-proclaimed king, landed with his seafaring settlers. Centuries later in 1955, Norwegian explorer Thor Heyerdahl set up his rustic camp on Anakena Beach and began his extensive excavation of the island.

Our Thanksgiving meal that day included much of the

same fare—chicken, bread, fruit and juice—that both Hotu Matua and Heyerdahl could very well have eaten when they were on Anakena Beach themselves.

Have I ever broken my Thanksgiving tradition by eating American food? No, but I have been tempted.

In Jerusalem I came very close to hunkering down with a big juicy burger, French fries and a shake at a McDavid's fast-food restaurant. Fortunately, my better sense prevailed and I decided to go to the Hahoma, the only kosher restaurant in the old Jewish Quarter of the city back in 1984.

In this case, selecting the main course was simple: St. Peter's fish, which is found only in the Sea of Galilee, was the perfect choice. There is a legend behind this particular fish, I discovered. In Biblical times, the Romans heavily taxed the people of Capernaum, and on one occasion when there was no money, St. Peter directed the villagers to lower their nets into the sea.

The fish they caught turned out to have a gold coin in its mouth, which saved them from the ravages of the Roman tax collectors. This legend also explains why St. Peter's fish is always served with its head on.

As luck would have it, my fish was short on gold coins that night, so I had to ante up the shekels to pay for my Thanksgiving dinner all by myself.

Finding a suitable restaurant in Old Malacca, a weathered seaport on the western coast of Malaysia, proved to be much more difficult. After having been ruled successively by the Chinese, Portuguese, Dutch and British, the city should have been able to offer at least a modicum of good Occidental and Oriental cuisine. Guess again.

The driver of my trishaw (a three-wheel bike with a passenger seat in front) was panting by the time he finally dropped me off in front of the Lim Tian Puan, a Chinese restaurant, one rainy Thanksgiving night. We had been circling past small, dirty-looking street cafes for nearly an hour and I figured the Lim Tian Puan was probably my last prospect for a decent meal. I was ushered into the dining room by a Chinese woman and seated at a small table draped in a red cloth. No one around me, including my waitress, spoke anything but Chinese. However, the menu items had English translations, so I was able to make my choices without wild guesswork.

I passed up the shark's fin with scrambled eggs in favor of spiced teochew duck, the restaurant's specialty, bean curd with crabmeat and fried rice. After a moment's hesitation, I added steamed-pig's-brain-with-chicken-leg soup to my order. In Asia, just about any plant or animal part is considered fair game for the dinner table, and I was curious to see how the cook would handle that combination.

Half an hour later, my food arrived. The waitress smiled as she ladled my gray soup broth with whole chicken feet floating in it out of the pot into my bowl. I decided to start with something more palatable looking and took a spoonful of the bean curd with crabmeat. It looked, and tasted, a little like tiny pillows of soggy foam rubber.

The spiced teochew duck was excellent and reminded me of the pressed duck I had enjoyed in Chinese restaurants back home. The fried rice, flavored with bits of egg and scallion, was also worth a second forkful.

But the soup stopped me cold. I asked the Chinese woman who had seated me how I was supposed to eat it. She gestured for me to nibble the skin off the chicken feet but not to eat the bones.

I fished out a chicken foot and pulled off a piece of tough yellow skin with my teeth. That first bite convinced me I didn't want a second.

When the waitress wasn't looking, I deftly tossed all the chicken feet from my bowl back into the pot on the table and continued spooning up my soup broth, hoping I wouldn't encounter any recognizable pieces of pig's brain.

A few minutes later, the waitress came by, spotted my bowl sans chicken feet and dutifully scooped a few more out of the pot into the bowl. As soon as she wasn't looking, I threw them back into the pot.

By the time the meal was over, the chicken feet had made at least 10 jet-propelled trips back and forth, leaving the waitress somewhat mystified about the remarkable qualities of my soup pot and its bountiful contents.

It was one Thanksgiving, probably the first and hopefully the last, where I didn't bother to ask for a doggie bag.

A Wacky Little Place Called Belgium

by Brian Abrahams

Petit pays, petites gens. (Small country, small people.)
Leopold II, King of Belgium

WHEN YOU'RE OFFERED a job in Europe, you don't turn your nose up and say: "But which *country* in Europe?" It's Europe! It's like cheese—Gouda, Swiss, Brie, Velveeta—it's still all just cheese—how different can cheese be? Well, in Belgium, the de-facto capital of the new Europe, you may want to turn up your nose at the smell of the cheese *and* at the country. It's a nation about which much could be said, but no one bothers.

We were getting persistent complaints from customers that product shipments were arriving empty. The upside of this was that it dramatically reduced the instances of defective parts. The downside was that customers wouldn't pay for computer drives they never received. The warehouse workers were carefully vetted, and we decided they were honest. Around this same time the police contacted us to say that they were investigating computer hardware thefts by employees of our shipping company, and they asked if we would help set up a sting.

They took the standard shipping packages and made tiny marks inside. The product was shipped to an invented customer and when the packages were opened the product was gone and so were the marks inside the package. So the shipper guy had been opening the packages, taking the drives out, and then sealing new empty packages to send to the customers, making it look like we were committing the fraud. The guy was nailed and our Belgian manager gave an affidavit acknowledging what had happened. For reasons known only to the police, despite the hard proof they had the authorities decided they were finished with the suspect at that point and never charged him.

He was not finished with us, however.

One night not long after the sting, a Molotov cocktail was hurled through the window of our warehouse. The interior was pretty much of a wipeout, including other computer hardware that our management company handled. As with the theft, the Belgian police never charged anyone with the arson and we had to move our office to another location. We also moved our product warehouse to Shannon, Ireland, as far from Brussels as possible. The lawsuits against our management company went on for years.

Bureaucracy and frivolous legislation also can run amok. I encountered my own nightmare of stupid Belgian laws in just trying to be a good father. In the never-ending search for child entertainment and recreation, my wife mandated a weekly father-son swim not long after we'd settled in. Not wanting my 2-year-old to be the hydrophobic child I was, I agreed. With a community pool close to our house I thought it would be pretty painless.

Before even getting moist I ran into the usual Belgian rules. The admission clerk informed me that all swimmers had to wear bathing caps. Men, too. Like in 1920s-era movies with flappers swimming at the Jersey Shore. Not owning one, I had to rent their white and powder blue striped cap. I looked like the kid at summer camp who had something wrong with him but was there under a special program and got harassed for two weeks straight. But that was just the start.

It's also a Belgian regulation that the *only legal swimwear* in a public pool is a Speedo or Speedo-style bathing suit. This isn't just a bad idea, it's the *law*. If God is in the details, so is the Belgian legislature. I later learned that this lawmaking was in response to people working out or playing tennis in shorts and then jumping into the pool in the same shorts. So what? It happens in the States and there have been few outbreaks of typhus or cholera at suburban country clubs. And as an American I have a more frequent acquaintance with shampoo, soap and water than the average European so I posed little threat to the public health of Belgium. On the other hand, all the Belgians, who bathed once a month whether they needed it or not, were getting to jump into the pool no questions asked.

I glared at the woman behind the desk. A Speedo. The bikini-cut, thin, show-all-you've-got kind of swimwear. Worn only in the U.S by egomaniacs with all the right equipment and the body to show it off. I waved my hand in front of her face and said the suit would be no problem. I figured that like so much of the red tape in Belgium, squeezing around it would be understood and accepted.

Then my son and I went to change. Instead of a locker room as we know it in America, they had little enclosed changing spaces out in the middle of a big tiled room that vaguely *resembled* a locker room. Each person got their own space, which was great, but they were the size of a skimpy broom closet, which wasn't so wonderful. There wasn't room for me, my son, our coats, clothes, etc. and still room to change. So I had to change, before and after swimming, standing in the aisle between these rows of cubicles which is essentially wide open to public view, including the young female attendant less than five feet away. (Not in a direct line of sight with me of course, unless she got up to stretch her legs. It was the fastest dressing/undressing I have ever done. Do they have a MAN in the

WOMAN'S locker room? I want THAT job.)

Finally we made it into the pool. I rolled up my shorts underneath to create a sort of Speedo-style look. There was a huge lap pool and a four-foot deep child's wading pool. We had just started to walk into the wading pool when two lifeguards came from across the other side of the building and asked me to leave as they pointed at my bathing suit. I asked them in half-mime, half English, with a little *s'il vous plait* thrown in, to please let me stay, it was my first time, I didn't own a Speedo, etc. Faced with packing my disappointed son back in the car, I did the best groveling I have done in a long time, including my special puppy dog eyes, which probably look more pathetic than anything else. But if there's one thing that the French and French Belgians love, it's a groveling American. They conferred with each other in French for a minute and one of them motioned for me to follow him.

He reached into a bottom desk drawer in the lifeguard office and pulled out a little scrap of lycra.

"Everyone has worn this," he said, handing it to me. I guess I wasn't the first ignorant American to think he could get around the rules. It was wrinkled, faded, sheer and in lousy condition—more the rumor of a swimsuit than the actual article. However, it was change into it or no swimming for my son. I ignored the stare of the lifeguard and looked down at my son. I REALLY, REALLY didn't want to wear a Speedo, but we had been building up the excitement for the pool for two days and we were barely wet. I looked up again, certain I saw the lifeguard trying to stifle a laugh. Or maybe it was a yawn. I looked at my son's puzzled expression. I couldn't let red tape keep him out of the pool, even though this remnant of fabric made even a Speedo look generous. We went into the bathroom to change. There was no way this loaner suit had ever seen a washing machine. I prayed that the most recent occupants had good hygiene.

I'm not exactly ... how would you say ... svelte. Belgian chefs are the best in the world and savoring their offerings had made me rather ample. Not obese, just in need of a good six-week aerobic program. And this suit showed every hair, every pore, EVERYTHING. I thought about drowning myself right then to end the misery, but then my toddler would have to drive home. I'm sure I looked like some kind of circus attraction with the floss-like suit and striped bathing cap. The Stay-Puft Marshmallow Man in a nylon G-string and carnival hat. I tried to refocus by recalling a previous experience that was more humiliating. None came to mind. So I pictured my son winning a high school swim meet and me not there to see it because I was dead of a stress-induced heart attack. Conscious of a group of fully dressed parents, mostly mothers, in the balcony above watching a swim class, I took a deep breath and made a break for the water, yelling for my son to follow me.

Four feet of liquid in a children's pool doesn't provide much cover. I curled into a ball, comforted knowing that tears would be mistaken for water droplets. Even when my toddler got in and out of the pool, I didn't go out after him. There was a Belgian couple there with a toddler the same age and whenever their son got out of the wading pool they dashed out and grabbed him in fear of his falling into the big lap pool. I just screamed "YOU GET BACK IN HERE RIGHT NOW!!!! NOW!!!!" They couldn't understand why I wasn't going after him. The suit was so thin and sheer that I kept grabbing at it to see if it was still on.

Now Belgian bodies are nothing to brag about. Their love of heavy traditional sauces, beer, chocolate and almost anything fried has left many of them as aerobically challenged as me. (In fact, I've never seen more obese lifeguards. If there will be any CPR done at that pool it will be to save the lifeguards from heart attacks.) However, there were enough thin and toned swimmers to stoke my shame. I thought about staying in the pool until the lights went out, which seemed like a good strategy since I was starting to shrink and shrivel anyway. But eventually my son insisted we go home for lunch, crying that he was "hungry." I tucked him under my arm and made a brilliant broken-field run for the locker room, ignoring the yells in French and Flemish to stop running. Having been all but naked in the middle of a community pool, taking the last bit off in front of the female attendant was nothing for me now.

For once I successfully reached a child-rearing goal—my son loved the pool. So each week I had to repeat the terrible ritual. I did buy my own suit, the largest one that would slip under the statute, but small enough that I burned it when I returned to the U.S.

No need for a souvenir of my humiliation.

Something in the Air

by Zona Sage

IT WAS SHORTLY after takeoff that I first noticed a sickening smell. "Do you smell that?" I asked my companion.

"Yes, what is it?" she scrunched her face in reaction to the odor.

"I don't know. Smells like bad kim chee, something like that?"

"No, I think methane, something chemical."

We were wedged into seats in the five-seat across middle section, with seats in front and in back of us. When the seats in front reclined, the jaws-of-life were necessary before we could get out to go to the bathroom. There was little room to move, much less to escape the awful smell invading the air.

The odor came in waves, getting worse at times. As the cart rolled down the aisle for our dinner, I mentioned the problem to the flight attendant: a tall, thin man with a curious tiny, devil-like beard. I imagined him more at home in a black cape than his uniform.

"Yes, madam. We are aware of the problem. We believe that some passenger has brought cheese aboard and has it in an overhead bin. We'll check on it after dinner."

We could have expected something like this, after all. With no carry-on luggage to stuff into overhead bins, we had postponed the inevitable moment when the economy passengers would be stuffed into the storage areas they called our seats. With too many hours in transatlantic flight ahead on the fully booked flight from Paris to New York, we had savored the last few moments of wiggle room in the waiting area. We might have delayed even longer, had we known what awaited us on the flight.

Security was very tight at the Paris airport; especially flying an American airliner, terrorist concerns abounded. We submitted to a full security interrogation with passport and tickets before we were allowed to get into the ticket line to check our luggage. Where had we stayed? What had we done? How well did we know each other? Did we bring anything in our luggage at the request of anyone else? Had we packed our own suitcases?

After the ticket counter, we had to pass yet another security checkpoint with passports and boarding passes before we could ride the futuristic escalators that crisscrossed in see-through tubes in open space.

We cleared another security point (passports and boarding passes again) in order to proceed to our boarding gate. When we boarded the plane, we had to present our passports and boarding passes again. Even as we walked into the jetway that fed us onto the plane, uniformed personnel approached each of us separately. "May I see your passport?" "Did you buy anything at a duty-free shop?" "What did you buy?" "Do you have it with you?" I confessed to a small purchase of cologne and was released and allowed to board the plane at long last. I had never been through such tight security.

On the plane, hours went by. A disaster movie had played to conclusion: the Earth had escaped annihilation when Robert Duvall sacrificed himself and his crew to crash into the oncoming meteor. The subsequent disaster called dinner had also played to conclusion, and I had survived that as well, possibly because I chose not to eat the melange of pasta and melted plastic. ("We apologize to those passengers whose food trays may have overheated.")

For some reason the stench had abated during dinner. After dinner, however, the malevolent odor returned and a huge nauseating wave attacked my senses. More people were complaining to the flight attendants about the stench. I stood by the galley with some other concerned passengers, trying to figure out what the smell was and where it was coming from. A gaggle of uniforms went up the aisles, placing their hands gingerly on the outside of the metal doors to the overhead compartments, as if feeling the temperature of the contents. "That's one test for it," I heard one say to another. A test for what? Was some vital airplane fluid leaking out, were we going to burst into flames? I returned to my seat and put on my seat belt. Would we have to prepare for a crash landing? On my way back to my seat I noticed a Buddhist nun sitting peacefully right behind me, completely oblivious to the fuss and fury all around her. Ah, the bliss of a life devoted to more ethereal concerns.

"There, there it is, do you smell it?" One of the flight attendants was standing next to me in the aisle, talking to another. "God, it's horrible."

She was tall, with full wavy blonde hair and red lipstick. She seemed to be one of the senior flight attendants and was maybe in her late-30s. She looked down at me. "Are you American?"

"Yes," I replied, thinking, "Oh no, is terrorism involved?"

"May I whisper in your ear?" She knelt down. "Do you think it could be the gentleman in front of you?"

I was taken aback. The older Asian man? Why would it be him? The flight attendant, on her knee at my side, didn't wait for my response. She bent forward slightly and sniffed at the back of the man. She looked at me, shook her head and got up.

The situation was obviously serious by now because a man from the cockpit was called upon to assist in tracking down the problem. After sniffing up and down the aisle, he was soon at my side. "Yes, I can smell it, " he told the female flight attendant who was apparently leading the search and destroy mission. "One of the flight attendants told me he thought it was cheese in an overhead bin up ahead," I volunteered to them, trying to be helpful. A search commenced of the overhead bins, as one by one they were opened and the contents sniffed. No, it wasn't that.

"Excuse me." The petite, elegant Asian woman to my left was leaning toward me, talking very low. "I think the Vietnamese nun behind us, you know, she has brought on durian." Durian! The scourge of Asia, durian is a huge, spiky fruit whose delights among its devotees drive its price up to great heights. Its reputation as an aphrodisiac helps some overcome the one big drawback to the fruit—its stench. Although its virtues are extolled, no one will deny the horrible smell, which has been compared to rotting flesh. Some have said eating durian is like eating strawberries and cream in a filthy outhouse. The smell is so horrible that signs are posted in hotel rooms and public conveyances throughout Asia—No Durian Permitted.

I turned to the flight attendant at my right. "Have you traveled in Asia?" I asked her. "Yes, why?" I spoke only one word in reply—"durian."

She recoiled. "My God, you're right! Durian!"

I relayed that the meek Buddhist nun directly behind me was suspected of having the dreaded fruit. The flight attendant went straight to the task.

"Durian?"

The nun turned over the contraband that she had succeeded in carrying through innumerable security checks—a large plastic container of the King of Fruit, as its fans call it. The flight attendant held it out ahead of her as she went forward with it. When the attendant returned without the dreaded package I plied her with questions.

"She said it was medicine, made from durian, that friends had given her," the flight attendant said. "She had it stored in that plastic container and was eating it throughout the flight. So, whenever she took some out and ate it, the smell increased. She must have taken a dinner break, and then was back at it."

I wondered about the "medicinal" purposes of a fruit famed as an aphrodisiac. According to an Indonesian saying, "When the durian comes down, the sarongs go up." Was her "medicine" related to the blissed out state she seemed to be in?

We made the rest of the flight free from the noxious attack on our nostrils. But believe me, I am writing those folks at the Paris airport.

They are just not strict enough with those security checks.

Food Fight

by Marius Bosc

RETURNING FROM FRANCE to San Francisco, my wife, Joyce, and I stopped in New York to see friends. One evening we decided to treat ourselves by going to a Chinese restaurant on the Lower East Side.

When Joyce and I arrived the place was full, which seemed to be a pretty good endorsement. After our food arrived, I tried my lo mein and didn't particularly care for the taste of the noodles so I called our waiter over and told him so. To my astonishment, he replied that if I didn't like the food to "leave." I thought that rather odd, but replied "no" and figured I would wait for the others at our table to finish their meals. All of a sudden, the waiter came over and slapped me across the chest. I was surprised, but not too much to return the favor and slap him back.

Then all hell broke loose. He grabbed the chair with me still in it and swung it so that I went twirling across the room like a ballet dancer. Like an old Western saloon movie scene, people got up screaming and running out of the restaurant while four or five waiters came at me with their fists.

After my arms gave out trying to fight back, I was knocked to the floor, where I was surrounded and kicked as I lay on my back and tried my best to fend off the blows. Finally I took refuge underneath a pile of tables, only to look up and see a young waiter with a pistol pointed at my head.

I kicked away the gun, and at that point, to my ultimate relief, the police came and broke up the melee. Joyce and I were taken to the local precinct, where we found the waiters, chef, owner and his lawyers on one side of the room slowly filling out forms for court. It was only at that point that some-one asked if they could take me to a hospital to check out my injuries, and so we went, under armed guard.

The adventure didn't stop there. When the nurse prepared to give me a tetanus shot, I told her I was allergic to some types of medication. She scoffed and called me a "big baby," while the man on the table next to me was heaving.

I survived the hospital to return to the precinct, where a policeman told me I'd have to go to court in a month. Explain-ing I was a visitor from San Francisco, I asked if I could just drop the charges. His answer: No, because he'd spent the last hour typing out the complaints.

What to do? I took matters into my own hands, went across the room and told the restaurant owner I would drop the charges if he would. The entire restaurant party looked relieved, including the waiter whose hand I had kicked, which now was the size of a small melon.

The owner and I shook hands, dropped the charges and we all left. On the way out, the owner slipped me some money. The next time I returned to New York, I noticed that the restau-rant was boarded up.

Snowed In

by Carol Nicholas and Pete Wiley

April showers bring May flowers . . . unless of course you're in Buffalo, Wyoming.

Each year the fraternity of traveling salesmen and truckers ceremoniously remove their snow tires, store their chains and prepare for their spring, summer and fall tours across America.

Since it was already springtime, April 14 to be exact, I followed the tradition and packed away all linkages with winter. The studded snow tires and chains were relegated to the back of the garage, and I managed to find my favorite fishing lures and pole and stored them in my trunk just in case an opportunity might present itself.

On this particular tour I had scheduled seminars and interviews across Idaho, Utah and Wyoming. Everything was going as planned until about midway into the tour. Just as I was leaving Utah it began to snow. As I crossed into Wyoming it got worse and soon several hundred fellow travelers and I found ourselves in the midst of one of Wyoming's worst spring blizzards.

Wyoming highways are treacherous enough in the winter when everyone is prepared for the ice, wind, snow and freezing temperatures. But when you're caught off guard it's pure mayhem.

Misery may love company, but I discovered I had more company than I bargained for. Just a few miles ahead, traffic came to a halt as the Wyoming state patrol temporarily barricaded the highway to Gillette and rerouted all the traffic into Buffalo.

With visibility at about zero and the temperature falling way below zero, I sought shelter for the night. Unfortunately I seemed to arrive way at the end of the line and all the deluxe accommodations in Buffalo were already taken. Every hotel displayed its NO VACANCY sign and the overflow crowd was being assigned more spartan accommodations anywhere warm including the public library, city hall and the Buffalo High School gymnasium.

As I pulled into a truck stop, I overheard the patrol telling a few of the truckers ahead of me they had some good news. There was one more motel in town that they were going to reopen for this emergency. There were only five rooms available, but it sounded great to me, especially since I was #4 on the list.

Another car pulled in right behind me and immediately took the fifth and last unit. Right behind him came Mac, driving his 18-wheeler and desperate for a place to stay. Since we were both traveling alone and the unit I was assigned had bunk beds, Mac and I ended up roommates for the duration of the storm. This gave new meaning to the term "Odd Couple."

Neither one of us wanted the top bunk, so we carefully disassembled the bunk beds, giving us each a twin bed squarely on the ground. We found an old soda pop case and stood it up between the beds for a nightstand. That, unfortunately, took all the extra floor space in our compact room.

We did have a kitchenette complete with an efficiency stove and mini refrigerator. But the best part was the color cable TV sitting on the kitchen counter. Meanwhile, outside, the temperature continued to fall, the winds continued to howl and the snow continued to drift.

Being an optimist, I moved my car so I would be headed out and ready to go as soon as the storm broke. Being a realist, I headed for the grocery and stocked up on crackers, cheese, pretzels, chips, cookies and pop.

Mac had the same idea, so we had our kitchenette about as well stocked as any mini mart.

As I was putting my groceries away, Mac pulled a plastic bag out of his jacket and began rolling a cigarette. I thought to myself, now here is an authentic cowboy. But when he lit up, the smell was really strange. It wasn't like the usual thick cigarette odor you smell when you enter a truck stop or tavern, but I admit I wasn't a tobacco connoisseur. I'd never smoked a day in my life. I had so many allergies I didn't dare add nicotine to my list.

As the evening wore on I wasn't sure what bugged me the most about Mac, his incessant talking or that peculiar cigarette smell. The TV was my only escape, so I sat glued to its tiny screen trying to ignore Mac's constant chatter.

The next day was just as bad. The blizzard wasn't showing any signs of letting up, so as Mac kept yakking, rolling and smoking, I found myself caught in a vicious cycle. It seemed the more he smoked, the more I ate, and the more he yakked, the more addicted I became to that little electronic box in our room.

Three days later, I couldn't take any more. The highway patrol finally opened the road to Gillette but still had a traveler's advisory for the area. I figured it couldn't be any worse outside in the elements than it was inside with Mac.

It turned out, of course, that those strange-smelling cigarettes were marijuana. Plus, during our stay I gained 10 pounds and was definitely on overload in the junk food department with enough sugar and salt intake to last me a lifetime.

So before the patrol could change its mind, I packed my

bags and was back on the road. It didn't take long to see why the travelers' advisory was still in effect as I slowly made my way across town toward the main highway. Finally I recognized the truck stop and knew I was near the freeway entrance. Since the highway was just now being reopened, all the truckers were lined up hoping to get on their way, too.

With only a half-mile to go, a snowplow pulled in front of me and I continued at a snail's pace behind him. With such miserable road conditions you would have thought that having a snowplow be your own personal escort would have been a piece of luck. But unfortunately, as the snowplow scooped the snow from its rather narrow path, the wind simply sent it spraying right back in its trail and into my path.

With my tires spinning and me going nowhere, I jumped out and headed down the road toward the truck stop. All of a sudden I heard a strange noise above the howling winds. It was a weird, unfamiliar sound. But the sight was even more weird and unfamiliar. From out of nowhere appeared at least 100 head of cattle stampeding directly toward me.

Now a track star I'm not, but for just a few seconds I must have done a pretty good imitation of my favorite cartoon—the "Roadrunner." I literally flew across the road, up and over the snowdrifts and dove into a ditch.

After what seemed an eternity, the noise level finally returned to normal. All I could hear was my heart pounding enough for admission to any of the cardiovascular emergency rooms in the country.

I peeked over the snowdrift to see if the way was clear. Whatever had apparently spooked the cattle must have disappeared. I could see them about five blocks past me, huddled together and seemingly out of their stampede mode.

I climbed back up the main road and headed for the safety

of the truck stop. My heart was still racing. The wind was still howling. And lo and behold, that weird but now familiar loud thundering sound was echoing in my ears.

I thought, "No! My ears are playing tricks on me." But it was no trick. About three blocks behind me, the cattle had made a U-turn and were stampeding one more time directly toward me. After my initial rehearsal, I was even better on my second nosedive into the ditch.

Nothing in my life experiences had prepared me for this. I discovered later that the cattle belonged to three trucks parked near the truck stop. To keep the cattle from freezing to death during those four days of subzero temperatures, the truck drivers had unloaded them so they could move around to keep their circulation and body heat up. And that's how we ran into each other.

As they pounded past me a second time, I assessed my situation. (1) My car was still stuck and needed to be towed. (2) My hand was throbbing. I had managed to sprain my wrist, twist my ankle and rip my slacks as I performed my two nosedives. (3) I had just barely escaped two stampeding herds of cattle. For a fleeting moment I thought about good old pot-smoking, incessant-talking Mac, relaxing in front of the TV in our cozy motel room across town and wondered if I'd made the right decision.

My dad always used to say, "If you can't beat 'em, join 'em." So, with a quick assist from the truckers my car was out of the drift and I took my honorary place in the truckers' lineup. After adjusting the heat and windshield wipers to their highest settings, there was nothing to do but wait. I watched my hundred buddies pound up the ramps taking their assigned positions in the three cattle trucks. Then I pulled in safely behind them and we all moseyed out of town.

The Ugly Californians

by Randy Pruitt

I SHOULD HAVE TAKEN it as a bad omen when my wife's California relatives phoned at 3 A.M.

"Say, what side of the road do you guys drive on over there?" asked Fred, an uncle on her mother's side.

"Over there" was Germany, our home for three years while I worked as a reporter for *The European Stars and Stripes.* Fred apparently didn't know that Europeans drive on the right, or that there was an eight-hour time difference between Europe and California.

Fred followed up with the announcement, "We're going to come to see you," meaning he and his wife, Edna.

It wasn't a complete surprise. My wife, Bernadette, who had been researching family history, had told him she'd located distant relatives in the Carpathian Mountains in far-eastern Slovakia. The idea was to pay the relatives a visit. So, we set a date when we would pick up Fred and Edna, both 67, at the Frankfurt Airport.

It wasn't too reassuring when they got off the plane to see Fred wearing a $2,500 Rolex and two flashy diamond rings. Edna immediately announced she was hungry and inquired if a McDonald's was nearby. Another bad sign.

We spent the night at our home in Zwingenberg, not far from Heidelberg. Edna spent the time telling us what she couldn't eat.

"That's why I'm sticking to American food," she declared. Bernadette and I eyed one another warily. Didn't she realize

41

where we were headed?

The next morning Bernadette fixed some sandwiches and packed some canned U.S. food obtained through the commissary. I got behind the wheel of Fred's rental Escort and aimed it toward Pilsen, in the Czech Republic, our destination for the day.

"I'll give you some tips for driving on the Autobahn," I volunteered.

"You haven't seen anything," Fred scoffed. "Have you ever driven on the L.A. freeways?"

I confessed I hadn't. "But you've got speed here," I explained.

Edna, from the back seat, touched my shoulder and laughed sweetly. "Oh, but they drive 80 and 85 in L.A.," she said.

I had to smile. While we were talking, Germans were zipping around us faster than that. Our own speedometer read 80.

Four hours later, Fred got behind the wheel. Hitting 85, he swung into the left lane to pass his first vehicle. He stayed left. In seconds, a Mercedes was riding our bumper, its headlights flashing.

"He wants to pass you," I informed Fred.

"I know what he wants," Fred growled. "I'll teach him to blink his lights at me."

My groan was audible. "You can't drive in the left lane over here. It's for passing," I informed him.

Fred wouldn't budge. "I'll move over when I'm damn good and ready," he said.

I explained the rules of the Autobahn. Grudgingly, Fred pulled into the right lane.

Fred, I soon discovered, didn't mind breaking other rules of the road. Although it's illegal to stop on the Autobahn, Fred frequently pulled over to videotape the scenery. He continued to balk at giving up the left lane. I think it galled him that even at 100 miles an hour, he wasn't King of the Road. Other drivers' fist shaking only amused him.

As Fred gained more driving confidence, he took more chances, darting in and out of traffic. For the first time, it occurred to me that we might not make it back alive. I was reminded of the German joke about an Autobahn fatality. The victim's tombstone inscription read, "I got here first." The silence in the car was deafening at one point and I wondered if all the passengers were praying. I know I was.

Bernadette and I are from Oklahoma. Something lying just under the surface always works its way to the top when you get Californians and Oklahomans together. It's not pretty.

I suspect Californians, particularly those well off, don't like to be closely confined with Okies because we remind them of their dirt-poor past. I still have visions of a California uncle visiting each summer and of how he always wore a suit, even around the greasy garage run by my dad and grandfather.

He also brought along miles of home movies. Sometimes he'd run things backward so I got to see my California cousins go from swimming pool to diving board. I forget what movie stars lived down the block.

Fred apparently associated us with *The Grapes of Wrath.* He began by asking a lot of "friendly" questions. He registered surprise when we assured him Oklahoma now had everything from Baskin-Robbins to Wal-Mart.

"Ah, but do you have Safeways?" Fred asked as if to stump us.

"Yes, and flush toilets, too," my wife replied.

"I didn't mean it like that," he snapped.

Around noon, Edna was the first to suggest lunch. Bernadette got out the sandwiches.

"I don't want one," she whined. "I want something hot." I ticked off the list of things Edna had told us she couldn't eat. Salty, sugary, boiled, sautéed, fried. It didn't leave much. We stopped at a Gasthaus to watch Edna wolf down a schnitzel the size of a catcher's mitt and a mound of salty fries. She washed it all down with two liters of beer.

In Pilsen, I'd made arrangements for us to have coffee at the home of Milos and Jitka Konecny. Milos had acted as my translator on several occasions.

"Don't try to impress them," I advised Fred. The Czech couple, both engineers, were very well educated but lived modestly. Fred's expensive watch and diamond-studded rings only added to my apprehension.

We weren't there five minutes before Fred let it slip his house had three bathrooms. Seconds later he deftly worked in his two new cars. I was relieved when we left for our hotel. I drove since I knew the location. Ongoing construction prevented me from driving right up to it.

"Looks like we'll have to park a few blocks away and hoof it," I said. "I am not walking," Edna declared. I could tell she meant it.

So, getting dirty looks from workmen, I violated a half dozen laws and maneuvered up to within a block of the hotel. Bernadette and I pointed Fred and Edna toward the front door and promised to return.

"It's tempting to leave them here," I told my wife as we looked for a parking space. The thought produced my first smile of the day. "I'm going to owe you," she said. "For the rest of my life," I responded dryly.

We returned to the hotel to find Edna in the lobby in a huff. "They took my passport!" she wailed.

I explained it was the custom for many hotels to keep passports.

"I talked to Agnes Hobbs before I left and she said to never give up your passport," Edna rattled on, frantic. According to Agnes Hobbs, an American passport offered the protection of a bulletproof vest. At that point, I didn't want or care to know who Agnes Hobbs was.

"Wait here," I instructed Edna.

Minutes later, I returned with their passports.

"It's okay, Edna. I gave them ours."

Her eyes widened. "Aren't you afraid?"

I shook my head and dredged up a smile. If the next two weeks were anything like today, I was more frightened of life with Fred and Edna than any secret police that might be lurking about.

"Are these the Carpathian Mountains, Bernadette?"

Every time we saw mountains Fred asked this question and laughed. It was his version of kids climbing into a car and immediately asking their parents, "Are we there yet?"

The joke was getting old.

It was one day later and we were deep in the backwaters of Slovakia. The narrow two-lane road was twisting, treacherous and Fred was showing me a driving technique. Rather than stay on his side of the highway to steer around curves, he was cutting across the centerline at an angle. "It makes driving easier and it saves wear and tear on the tires," he said proudly.

"Yeah, and it could get us killed," I responded.

He slapped my knee and laughed. "Oh, Randy, I'm not gonna have a wreck."

Fred ignored traffic signs and posted speed limits. He made turnabouts when and where it suited him. Clearly, he was 67 going on 17.

It all caught up with Fred at an intersection with flashing

lights. He shot through it at the same time a Skoda bore down on us. Rubber screamed followed by an ear-splitting crash.

"Damn!" Fred grunted.

We climbed out. Fortunately, no one was hurt. The Escort had sustained only a basketball-size dent to its left, rear side. The Skoda was a different story. Its front end was crushed. Fluids of all sorts gushed onto the pavement.

The Slovak driver leaped out, shaking his fist. Fred didn't appear amused as the beet-red Slovak pointed to a sign showing he had the right of way. As if on cue, it began drizzling. Fred, looking mortified, stood in it while he waited for a policeman. I almost felt sorry for him.

After the burly cop arrived, the situation got even more awkward. All our vehicle papers were in German. The policeman spoke only Slovak. Fred spewed English non-stop.

Fred suddenly revealed to me he didn't get auto insurance at the airport. "But I think my company back home will cover me," he whispered.

"I hope so," I muttered, eyeing the crumpled Skoda again.

At this point, Fred whipped out his AARP (American Association of Retired Persons) card and handed it to the policeman.

"For Pete's sake, Fred, you're in Slovakia, not Los Angeles," I said. "He can't read it, and if he could he certainly wouldn't know what the AARP is."

Suddenly, Fred pulled out a thick folder of traveler's checks and gestured, grinning. I winced. Either Fred was trying to pay for damages or he was offering the cop a bribe.

Using sign language, the cop made it clear he wanted us to follow him to headquarters. I drove, keeping all worries to myself.

Fred followed him inside where he signed papers he

couldn't read. He paid a fine of less than $5 and was allowed to leave. The wreck cost us three hours.

To everyone's relief, I drove the rest of the afternoon. I spent much of it lecturing Fred on driving in Europe, not caring if he liked it or not.

He got out his video camera and began filming through the bug-splattered windshield. "We had a holdup back there," he said into the microphone as his camera ground away. "Randy had an accident."

He waited for laughter, but none came.

He cleared his throat. "I guess I'd better set the record straight. I had that accident . . . but I think if Randy had been watching it wouldn't have happened."

I ground my teeth and dreaded the next 12 days more than I have ever dreaded anything.

"Say, Bernadette," Fred asked suddenly. "Are these the Carpathian Mountains?"

We found a luxury hotel that evening. We needed it after the day's events. Fred took in his luggage but left his video camera lying on the front seat.

"You'd better carry it up to your room," I told him.

He shrugged it off with a wave of his hand. "Why? I have faith in my fellow man."

Alone in our room, Bernadette and I conferred. She was stressed, too. Edna, she revealed, had been slapping her on the arm each time she wanted to get her attention or make a point.

"It's starting to hurt," Bernadette said, showing me her bruises.

"Well, it can't get any worse than this," I said to cheer her up.

"It can if he drives," she countered.

I agreed. We were contemplating our limited options when

Fred phoned from his room. He now wondered what he'd signed at the police station. I advised him to find someone at the front desk that speaks English.

"Have them read your copy of the accident report," I said. Fred asked about dinner, but I told him we weren't hungry.

On the road the next morning Fred revealed that he had admitted fault in the accident by signing the papers. A young girl at the hotel had translated everything and had even called the police station in his behalf.

"I hope you tipped her," I said.

Fred glared at me, indignant. "Of course, I gave her five."

"Good, five American dollars will go a long way here."

"No, I gave her five crowns," Fred explained. "It's the same thing, isn't it?"

I shook my head. "Hardly."

At approximately 30 crowns to the dollar, Fred had rewarded the bright, helpful girl with about 15 cents.

For future reference, I tried to explain the country's currency system, but Fred got out the video camera, which miraculously had survived the night in the car. Again, he began filming through the windshield. This, I was learning, was his way of tuning me out.

"I'll drive when you get tired," he volunteered.

I'm never getting tired, I thought, although I knew that sooner or later I'd have to give him the wheel.

It wasn't long before Fred began to criticize my driving. My slow cruising speed especially annoyed him. He kept looking down at his Rolex while I marveled at the horse-drawn wagons, the farmers working in fields, the campers gathered around lakes. When we neared the village where his father came from, I came to a crawl at an odd, unmarked intersection.

"Why are you slowing down?" he demanded.

"Just to be safe," I explained.

"Well, nothing's coming," he snapped.

At that instant, I fantasized stopping at the nearest train station where, after handing him the car keys, Bernadette and I would book passage back to Germany. I had a hard time letting go of the idea.

We found the relatives in a tiny village that had only two businesses: a pub and a shabby "hotel."

"I'm not staying there!" Edna screeched.

"We'll find something nearby," I said.

Milos had notified the relatives that we were coming and arranged for a translator to be present. We found them in a neat, two-story house. They appeared thrilled to see us. Instantly, we felt like celebrities. Nosy neighbors of theirs strolled by to gawk at the Americans and utter consoling things about the new car with the big dent.

Everyone was all smiles except Edna. Among this pleasant peasant stock, she was clearly out of her element. She wore a scowl that needed no translation.

"I'm not going to drink that stuff," she said brusquely when offered a glass of vodka.

Quickly, I interceded. "They want to drink a toast to your health," I told her. At that moment I hoped everyone was drinking to her mental rather than physical well-being. She held the glass but never brought it to her lips.

Fred, on his third toast, appeared to be in heaven and we were happy for him. He repeated Slovak sayings he'd learned as a child, winning over his hosts' hearts and minds.

That's when Edna took me aside and whispered conspiratorially. "I don't think he's related to these people. I think we should leave."

She said she would convince Fred we needed to leave in

the morning. I was to do likewise with Bernadette. Then, she proposed, we'd drive straight back to Germany where it was "more civilized." I told her to forget it.

Hours later, the relatives asked us to spend the night.

"I'm not staying here," Edna protested loudly. "We're going to find a lovely hotel."

Fred looked crestfallen.

"We'll go to the hotel and you can stay," I suggested to Fred.

"No," Edna said firmly.

That settled, we agreed to return tomorrow for some more family history and a big dinner.

The only accommodations we found in a nearby city was an old Soviet-style hotel that was falling apart. It probably had 500 rooms, but we seemed to be the only guests. Outside, a dog barked all night long. I hoped Edna was happy.

Our hosts must have spent two weeks' wages on our dinner. Food and liquor were everywhere and we were encouraged to "Eat! Eat! Eat!" as we moved throughout the house, our glasses never empty.

Edna, though, sat alone, clutching her purse, a frumpy hen guarding her nest. Any offer of food or drink to her was met with a near snarl.

"She should never have come," Fred confided at one point.

Suddenly, I felt sorry for him. He was finally adapting to the foreign landscape. Last night, he'd even driven sensibly to the hotel.

Bernadette took notes as the translator outlined the family tree. One relative, it was revealed in hushed tones, fled to Argentina after the war. We decided to wait until later to tell Fred of the Nazi skeleton in his closet. After dinner we all drove to the family cemetery with Edna griping all the way.

On the drive back toward Germany, Edna came up with a

new plan, one Bernadette and I fully endorsed. She revealed she had a nephew who was stationed with the U.S. military in Germany. He lived near the Czech-German border. It was decided that Bernadette and I would accompany them to the nephew's. From there, we'd take a train back to our home. We were ecstatic, but we felt sorry for her nephew.

Nearing the nephew's house, Edna developed an abrupt change of plans.

"I've decided not to see him right now," she announced. "Let's go back to your house."

"But why not?" I inquired. "We're just a few miles from his house."

"I'll see him later," she said. "I want to do my laundry first."

"But you can do your laundry at your nephew's," Bernadette explained. "I'm sure his wife wouldn't mind."

"No!" Edna said stubbornly.

"Look, your nephew lives five hours from our house," I said. "That means 10 hours of extra driving just for some laundry."

"I don't care. I want to do my laundry first," she insisted.

Fred's sigh was loud. Her plan didn't make any sense to him either.

Back at our house, it became apparent that Edna had changed her mind again. She'd now decided not to see her nephew. "I want to stay here and relax," she said, plopping down in my easy chair. That evening, she refused to take a tour of our village or even a leisurely drive to a nearby castle. She made it clear she didn't want to leave the house.

It was Snuggles that got Edna off her duff. Snuggles was our black poodle mix that we were getting ready to retrieve from the kennel. Fred and Edna were unaware of him until we picked him up and brought him home.

Edna's distaste for dogs was something she couldn't hide. She refused to pet him and eyed him with disdain when he curled up on the sofa.

"Do you ever tie him up outside?" Fred asked. It was clear that Edna had put Fred up to asking what was, to us, an impertinent question. Dogs simply aren't tied up in Germany.

Well, we could take Edna's bad habits, her rudeness, her bossiness, but when it came to Snuggles it was too much for Bernadette.

My wife quickly gathered up some maps and outlined a route that included the historic city of Rothenberg.

"Here," she said, handing them the materials. "They even have a McDonald's."

Fred and Edna looked taken back, but Bernadette was adamant. "It will do you good to get out by yourselves," she added.

Suddenly there were questions about getting lost, about finding a hotel, about the language.

"You'll do fine," Bernadette said as she practically pushed them out the door.

We didn't see Fred and Edna until the day before they were to depart.

While they were gone we enjoyed ourselves immensely. Me, Bernadette and, of course, Snuggles.

One Too Many Nights in Tunisia

by Claudia R. Capos

DIMLY LIT CORRIDORS with puke-colored tile walls should have been warning enough when we walked into a private health spa in northern Tunisia. Things only got worse when we met Dr. Kilani, a lascivious chiropractor whose eyes took on a peculiar metallic gleam when he turned a fire hose on full blast and directed it at your naked private parts.

In retrospect, the Station Thermale was a far cry from the likes of Canyon Ranch and the Golden Door, where American glitterati go for spa treatments and "life enhancement" programs. Had we been smart, we would have packed our bags immediately and headed home the next day. But Doug and I were determined to sample the exotic offerings of Tunisia during our vacation. That's the whole reason we booked a week in a timeshare hotel in Korbous, a remote village tucked away on the country's rocky northern shore.

At the time, Libyan strongman Col. Muammar Khadafy was rattling his sabers. With his usual bravado, he announced he was closing the Libyan border with Tunisia on the eve of our departure. The possibility of some fireworks erupting between the Libyans and the Tunisian-based Israeli agents who, Gadhafi claimed, were infiltrating Libya made us a bit uneasy. Nevertheless, the lure of camel jockeys and their Arabian Nights mystique overcame our usual sense of prudence. Scrimping on expenses, we jumped at a bargain basement $600 round-trip fare from Chicago to Tunis aboard JAT airlines, which at that time was the Yugoslavian national carrier.

On most other airlines, the flight to Tunisia would have taken around eight hours. Ours ended up dragging on for two and a half days. Flat tires, endless delays, chain-smoking passengers who filled the cabin with thick brown smog and trays of food resembling garbage-disposal detritus indelibly ingrained the JAT flying experience in our memories.

Midway through our flight, we deplaned for an eight-hour layover in of all places, Belgrade, Yugoslavia. Eager to do some sightseeing, we begged for transit visas from one of the airport's iron maidens and crammed into a slightly dinged Renault with a couple of fellow JAT passengers, who were meeting their relatives. Together we headed into the mind-numbing utilitarian dreariness of Belgrade, where concrete-block government buildings tower like massive tombstones and the luckless populace is housed in high-rise human filing cabinets. After an hour on our own, Doug and I hailed a taxi for what should have been a five-minute, 45-dinar ($4 U.S.) trip from Saint Sava, a cavernous Serbian Orthodox church, to the Three Hats restaurant in the cobblestone-paved Skadarlija district. Our surly dark-haired taxi driver grunted unintelligibly to everything we said. We never were completely sure whether he even understood English. However, our driver rightly surmised we had no clue about the difference between then-Yugoslavia's old currency and its new currency, which was 10 times the value of the old. He quickly relieved us of the 454 dinars in new currency (roughly $40 U.S.) we had gotten at the Belgrade airport money exchange. Stranded in the middle of the city, which exudes just about as much charm as the stalags along the Trans-Siberian Railway, we barely were able to scrape up enough dinars to take us back to the airport in time for the second leg of our flight to Tunisia.

In Tunis, we rented a car and drove to our timeshare hotel,

La Residencia-La Kirbira, in Korbous. That was no mean feat, given that nearly all the road signs in Tunisia are written in Arabic lettering and the final stretch of roadway leading to Korbous is little more than a one-lane dirt track. A torrential downpour that evening made it nearly impossible to see more than a few feet in front of the car. La Residencia proved to be a nondescript cinder-block hostelry, which attracted a fair number of holiday revelers from Libya. We fervently prayed none of them were practicing terrorists. At the reception desk, the clerk woodenly informed us that our timeshare company had failed to mail a confirmation, so there was no record of our room reservation and no suite available for our weeklong stay. Our wallets were considerably lighter by the time we convinced him to overlook these technicalities and give us a room key.

As it turned out, the austere hotel lacked most conventional amenities, including an operative shower. What's more, the interior walls were paper-thin, something I discovered one morning while recovering from a sleepless night of traveler's distress. Greasy odors from morning meals, which other guests were cooking in their rooms, rekindled wrenching memories of the ill-fated fish dinner I had consumed 12 hours earlier at a seafood restaurant in the town of Hammamet. In between frantic trips to the bathroom, I also realized it was possible to hear simultaneous conversations being conducted in two or three different rooms up and down the hallway. I could only speculate about what other guests thought of the cacophony coming from our quarters.

During a day trip to the ruins of Carthage, Doug and I were accosted by one of Tunisia's self-appointed "tour guides" while we were poking through fallen marble columns and broken mosaics. These long-robed, burnoose-draped panhandlers lurk around heavily trafficked archeological sites, such as Carthage, Dougga and Thurburbo Majus, in the hopes of latching onto unwary tourists. Like dog fleas, they pester their victims with such unswerving persistence that most hapless visitors end up paying them something just to go away. In this instance, Achmed, or whatever his name was, had a special deal. Just for us. Glancing furtively over his shoulder, he pulled out a soiled, wadded up handkerchief and unwrapped it, revealing three ancient-looking metal coins. Through partially rotted teeth, he confided in halting English that he had found the coins buried in the ruins. His initial asking price was $50 U.S., but Doug was able to whittle that down to $12.

Smugly, Doug tucked the precious little treasures into the pocket of his jeans. A few days later, while making our way through the labyrinth of streets in Tunis' central souk, we stumbled upon a shop that was selling huge mounds of these "ancient coins" for pennies apiece. They were all newly minted.

An ongoing obsession with preserving our youthful good looks prompted us to sign up for a 12-dinar water massage and steam bath at the Station Thermale, one of several private health spas in Korbous. On past vacations, I had indulged myself with mud packs in Mexico and mineral baths in Hungary, but I had drawn the line at the Gerovital injections offered in Romania.

Station Thermale was housed in a large whitewashed building with a tower on the edge of Korbous. The exterior had a time-weathered gray patina, and the inside resembled a few of the Third World medical clinics we've ended up in from time to time. Ancient tiles hugged the walls like nicotine-stained dentures, and we wondered what kind of molds and fungi had taken up residence in recent decades. Doug and I were greeted by a barrel-chested chiropractor wearing a big white lab coat. His name, he announced, was Dr. Kilani. His hands were the size of oven mitts. When he broke into his sycophantic smile, which he did quite often, his thick black mustache partially framed a double row of pearly white teeth. Eager to get started, Dr. Kilani led us to separate dressing rooms.

When he was alone with me, he didn't mince words. "Take off your clothes and get into the tub," he instructed, his eyes boring into every crevice. Fortunately, I had brought along a two-piece swimsuit, which I donned quickly before lowering myself gingerly into a feed trough filled with tepid, murky water. Dr. Kilani's countenance soured visibly when he returned some minutes later.

On the massage table, I clung tenaciously to my dignity, and my trusty swimsuit, as the good doctor smeared my legs, arms, body and neck with some sort of odorous cream and began digging his knotty fists into my flesh. I ached for days.

Afterward I joined Doug, who had taken Dr. Kilani's missive seriously by stripping to his birthday suit. We both were anticipating a muscle-soothing Tunisian water massage as we stepped into a large vacant spa room.

Instead, Dr. Kilani stood 15 feet away with the nozzle of a fire hose in his hand. Taking aim at me, he turned the water on full force, first hot and then cold. He was hoping, I'm sure, to disengage both pieces of my swimsuit with the jet stream.

When Doug's turn came, the good doctor cranked the water pressure up a notch and zeroed in on his target. The impact nailed Doug to the wall behind him where he flailed like a frog pinned to a dissection tray.

For a few breathless moments, I thought the family jewels might well be dethroned. Above the whoosh of water, I shouted at Dr. Kilani to stop. Finally, he cut off the flow, put the hose down and disappeared without a word.

Both Doug and I scurried back to our dressing rooms, threw on our clothes and made a beeline for the exit. We never set eyes on Dr. Kilani again.

Our return flight to America on JAT airlines was scheduled to depart from the Tunis airport at 2 A.M. To kill time, Doug and I treated ourselves to a romantic farewell dinner in the white-linen accented restaurant at the Abou Nawas hotel, which afforded a spectacular view of the sea and sandy beach.

Around midnight, we set off for the airport in our rental car. After a few miles, we were flagged down by armed military police. They gestured for us to pull off on the side of the road. We were apprehensive at first. Then true desperation set in. Incisively, Doug stomped on the gas pedal. The frail car, its four-cylinder engine knocking loudly, rocketed past the roadblock, leaving the police cursing and waving their fists in the air. We both slunk down in our seats, hoping they wouldn't shoot.

Shaken, we arrived at the airport where we encountered a barroom-brawl scene from a spaghetti western. Drunken passengers, who had been chugging Slivovitz all night, were slugging it out at the ticket counter. Epithets in a variety of foreign languages exploded in the air. Some passengers used their suitcases as battering rams to shove others out of the way. Elderly tourists toppled like empty pop bottles.

The melee continued until we all boarded and found seats. Within a few hours, the plane was heading homeward, and the movie *Honey, I Shrunk the Kids* was showing on the pull-down video screens. Truthfully, I cannot remember to this day how it ended.

The Orient Distress

by Nadine Michele Payn

IT WAS 5 P.M., and we were giddy with anticipation as we dragged our luggage along the crowded concrete platforms of the Bucharest de Nord train station. We squeezed past parting lovers, families with assorted packages, Gypsies in bright paisley shawls carrying cardboard luggage ringed with rope, dusty workmen in overalls and a woman balancing a watermelon on her hip. We were headed for Track 2, where luxury and romance beckoned. We had splurged and booked a private couchette on the Orient Express and within the hour we'd be rolling westward to Budapest in splendid isolation.

Our three weeks in Romania that summer of 1990 had been an ordeal. We went from orphanage to orphanage in Bucharest and the countryside, searching for a child to adopt. The gray, bullet-riddled buildings of downtown, endless skyline of construction cranes frozen in place after the execution of dictator Nicolai Ceausescu, long lines for markets with wilted produce, stores with nothing in their display cases, the continual "We have no adoptable children here" from orphanage staff who desperately wanted to maintain their jobs, all of that had gotten to us.

We had failed, and we wanted to get back home.

Our final day took a dramatic turn. As we packed our bags, our Romanian hosts knocked on the bedroom door and told us that they had found an adoptable girl. Though skeptical, we dropped everything, grabbed the camcorder and hopped into their car. We were introduced to a roguish-faced toddler,

59

fell in love and began the Romanian part of international adoption procedures—all by mid-afternoon. (Nothing else was quick. The adoption would involve two more trips to Romania, a two-year battle with U.S. and Romanian bureaucrats, mysterious Gypsies and lawyers who boldly strolled the Bucharest Hall of Justice with bulging briefcases of cash. But that's another story.)

We had booked the Orient Express (or thought we had) a week earlier. It was intended to be a measure of comfort to console us after our failed mission. The train loomed into view, on time, and chugged to a stop. We negotiated the hot, narrow corridors until we found our compartment and slid the glass door open, prepared for red velvet seats and brass fittings. We had been assured and re-assured by the travel agent in downtown Bucharest when we booked passage that we were getting two first-class seats aboard the Orient Express. So you can imagine our surprise when instead we were greeted by two benches made of rusted metal and cracked brown Naugahyde, separated by the door on one side and a window on the other, with minimal legroom in between. Dust had thickened along the windowsill, which Burt managed to shove open after great effort. The breezeless air outside did nothing to alleviate the heat. The Orient Express? No air conditioning? Netting to hold our luggage? Where was all the glamour we had read about?

Our puzzlement was interrupted by a pale, slender young man with large brown eyes who entered the compartment and casually tossed his backpack into the overhead net. He said in respectable English, "You are American, yes? My name is Catalin." Catalin was 16 and bound for Paris, his first destination beyond Romania's borders. Delighted that he spoke English, we explained that we held first class tickets and must have been sent mistakenly to the wrong car. Could he help us find the proper couchette?

"I don't think there's a first class on this train," responded Catalin.

"Isn't this the Orient Express? That's what we booked."

"No Orient Express on Wednesdays, I think," said Catalin with a strain of logic we had grown unhappily familiar with in Romania. He added that the conductor or "Chief" of the train was a friend of his father, and all our questions would be answered.

While Catalin was gone, three men in white shirts with buttons bursting over beer-bellies squeezed themselves through the doorway, carrying ramshackle valises and bulging paper bags. As they eyed where to sit, I blurted in broken Romanian, *"Nu, nu, rezervatie!"* ("No, no, reserved!") The men smirked and plopped their huge bodies on the bench across from us. They threw their luggage up top and looked ready to settle in for a long stay. They reeked of sweat and garlic, and their bulky presence seemed to suck up all the air in our small space. Just then Catalin returned with the conductor, and we convened in the corridor.

The conductor inspected both sides of our tickets and muttered something to Catalin who looked at us apologetically, "The Chief is most sorry, but this is Wednesday, and on Wednesdays, there is definitely no Orient Express. Also, I'm afraid the Wednesday train has no first class." Still hopeful, we pointed out that our tickets indicated a reserved compartment. Another exchange between Catalin and the "Chief" ended with a pained Catalin translating, "He says these men have a right to stay here." He added in a terse whisper, "We must be very careful. They are Gypsies and can make trouble. They are probably part of the ring that has been throwing passengers' luggage out the train windows to accomplices on the station platforms." Catalin looked really scared.

"Is there no other place to sit on this train?" I whimpered.

"No, the train is full. They frighten me," he continued, "but we must not show our fear. This is important."

Great. A 13-hour ride lay ahead.

We re-entered the compartment with neutral expressions. Burt and Catalin piled all of our luggage on the side of the netting that was farthest from the window. If the three Gypsies understood what we were doing, they gave no indication. They guffawed and drank beer from unlabeled brown bottles. We stepped over their giant legs gingerly, then settled ourselves along the seats.

The train picked up speed. People, signs and buildings became colored streamers, and we were on our way. Burt buried his nose in a book, with one eye on the men. I conversed with Catalin, wondering if he was overreacting. Sadly, even educated Romanians scorned and hated Gypsies. Maybe these men were harmless, even if they looked rough. Suddenly the scariest of the three men reached into his brown bag and pulled out a large knife! Sunlight glinted off the silver. Our hearts raced, and we froze. Neither of us dared look at Catalin. How could this be happening?

We would be cut down just when we had found a daughter to love!

Now the second Gypsy reached into his bag. Oh God, maybe this will be a gun. With a flourish he pulled out—a roasted chicken. Chuckling, he yanked off one drumstick, then the other. The Knife Man used his weapon to cut off a wing and yelled at us. Catalin reached over and patted my white-knuckled hand. "It's okay. They are offering us some food." We politely declined the invitation.

Our arrival at the next station jolted us into alertness. We had decided to leave the window open because of the heat. Now we had to guard the luggage without appearing to. Knife Man stood up and leaned out the window, calling a greeting to someone. Uh, oh. We watched that luggage like lionesses protecting their young, and there was no incident. And so it went, station after station, hour after hour.

We took turns being sentries in order to grab some sleep. Burt and Catalin managed to nod off, and I tried to concentrate on a paperback. The Gypsies had stripped to their undershirts, revealing massive amounts of upper arm flesh. They were quiet, slumped against each other like a mountain range.

My novel drew me in, offering me a respite from tension. As I was silently thanking the universe for good writers like Tom Wolfe, the lights went out. Complete blackness. I realized the Gypsy nearest the door had flicked off the light switch.

What was the trio planning now?

I let Burt sleep and frantically shook my young friend awake.

"Catalin, tell them I cannot sleep and must read. Tell them I am afraid of the dark. I cannot have darkness!"

Catalin did as commanded, and the man reluctantly switched on the light, hissing something that sounded like a warning.

"He says he turned out the light because it's time to sleep, but darkness or not, his pal (Knife Man) will start snoring. He says you better brace yourself because it will sound like he's dying."

Sure enough, not 10 minutes had passed before rasping snores filled the compartment. A crescendo of wheezes followed, then blaring trumpet snores. Then moans, slurps and gasps for air, desperate sounds, louder and louder. Burt woke up with a wild look in his eye. "Is that man dying?" Even in my miserable state, I couldn't suppress a laugh. "It's Knife Man. He's snoring, and he trumps even you!"

I yanked the Walkman from one of our stowed bags despite the fact that it might suggest other electronic gear available for stealing. I could find only one cassette, Jean Pierre Rampal on flute. I turned the volume all the way up, and the Frenchman trumped Knife Man's nightmare sounds. As the wheels of our Orient Distress turned in the night towards Budapest, the tiny wheels of my Walkman did their job, transporting me from a state of hyper-vigilance to a trance of indifference.

Dawn broke around 5 A.M., and the train slowed. Three undershirts heaved, and the men woke up, stretching and coughing. Catalin and Burt were awake, too. "We're approaching the Romanian-Hungarian border," Catalin informed us. Though exhausted, we were jubilant. We would shower at our Budapest hotel, drink wine, eat goulash and sleep serenely on feather beds. Soon the Orient Distress would be nothing more than an amusing story to tell at parties.

The train stopped. We looked out the window and saw a flat horizon. No real train station, just a low building on the other side of the tracks. Catalin told us we were near a town called Arad, but it looked like Death Valley. Uniformed Hungarian border guards, with guns holstered at their hips, boarded the train and all of us—Gypsies, students and tourists—had our passports at the ready. One guard took the passports, flipped through every page, studied our photos and stared at our live faces. He barked something guttural. As usual we turned to Catalin, who shrugged his shoulders. He didn't speak Hungarian. The official thwacked our passports with his bony finger. More strange sounds. Then, "Visa. Visa." He wasn't referring to a credit card.

Catalin looked edgy. "I think he's asking where your visas are for Hungary."

"We were told in Bucharest that no visa is necessary for U.S. citizens traveling to Hungary," Burt said slowly and loudly as if that would make the border guard understand us. The official remained unconvinced. Ever-helpful Catalin volunteered to find someone on the train who spoke Romanian and Hungarian. After several long minutes, during which our Gypsies were given clearance, Catalin returned with a blonde woman in a red blouse.

"Please tell her to tell the border guard it is not necessary for U.S. citizens to have tourist visas for Hungary."

Catalin translated our English into Romanian. The lady in red translated Romanian into Hungarian. The Hungarian official looked furious and spoke to the lady in red who spoke to Catalin in Romanian who passed it on to us in English.

"He doesn't care what they told you in Romania. You must have a visa to enter Hungary, and without it you must get off the train immediately."

We prayed this was a distorted message like in the game "Telephone," but the guy was serious.

"Tell her to tell him we were given wrong information, and we will get a visa as soon as we arrive in Budapest." The round of translations was repeated. The border guard was not swayed.

"You cannot enter Hungary without a visa, therefore you will have to get off this train. You can wait for another train back to Bucharest."

We had been on the train nearly 12 hours. It was unthinkable to return to Bucharest.

"Please," I begged, eyes moist. "You must not put us off the train."

Desperation inspired me. I turned to Catalin.

"Tell her to tell him I am pregnant! It would be a disaster for the baby and me to leave this train. We must get to Budapest."

Burt looked startled at the news. The guard simply fingered his gun and stood taller. The message back, "It does not matter. Without a visa you must get off this train."

A crowd had gathered around us. The three Gypsies were closest and strained to hear the trilingual conversation. We were informed that all passengers' documents were in order, except ours, and we were responsible for delaying the train's arrival in Budapest. We must get off NOW!

Burt sprang into action. His voice filled the car, and every face was turned towards him.

"You must show compassion," he bellowed. "You are a human being. We are human beings. Borders are unnatural dividing lines created by governments. We bear you no harm. We have been looking forward to visiting your country and meeting your people. My wife is exhausted. We will go directly to the American consulate in Budapest and get proper papers. We will follow the laws of your country."

He brushed a lock of silver hair out of his eyes. "So I am pleading with you, as one man to another, one brother to another, one human to another, please show your humanity and your generosity. Please allow us to stay on the train. Surely you can see this is the right thing to do."

Catalin translated Burt's impassioned outburst into Romanian for the crowd, and the lady in red translated to the official. The crowd murmured its sympathy. The Hungarian was unmoved and tightened his grip on our passports.

"Remove your baggage now. If you do not wish to return to Bucharest, you can take an hour's taxi ride to another point on the border, near Gyula. There you can obtain visas."

We protested that we were out of Romanian cash for taxi fare or train tickets, but of course the Hungarian didn't care. The conflict was over, and we had lost.

The sun was fully risen now, but there wasn't a soul to be seen outside the train. It was incomprehensible that we were being ejected. But there were Burt and Catalin, pulling our bags out of their nest. The lady in red, ashamed of her compatriots' behavior, took some coins from her purse and offered them to us. Several others in the gathered crowd did the same. Knife Man reached into his pocket and pulled out a bunch of crumpled Romanian *lei* notes worth more than all the coins. He shrugged his shoulders apologetically and handed us the money. We were stunned and felt guilty for our bad feelings toward him and his buddies. We were ashamed to accept his gift, but he insisted with an earnestness that was impossible to deny.

So the "bad" guys turned out to be the good guys—at least for us.

We exchanged addresses with Catalin, shook hands goodbye and dragged our luggage to the end of the car. The border guard followed us outside but continued to hold our passports. We pointed to them and asked for their return. We knew he understood, but he was enjoying his show of power. We were in the middle of nowhere without our passports, and I was seriously scared.

"He's got to return them," muttered Burt. Finally, the border guard shoved the passports at us and turned on his heel to board the train. Hands waved to us from the windows. Then the Orient Distress lurched forward, got smaller and disappeared.

The only thing grimmer than being on the train was being off.

We lugged our bags across the tracks, heading for the building. What did the guy mean, take a taxi? This wasn't Grand Central Station. The only vehicle in sight was a black sedan parked at the far end of the gravel. The building's door was locked. We were tired, hungry and frightened; we both needed to go to the bathroom and hadn't a clue what to do.

Suddenly the sedan pulled forward, and its white-haired driver nodded in our direction. What could he want? At first we ignored him but he kept at it, so we walked over. "Taxi," he smiled. We looked at the passenger side front door, which was badly dented and tied closed by a seat belt substituting for rope. "Taxi?" we repeated incredulously. The driver nodded. He spoke a little English, and we were able to communicate our need to get to the next border checkpoint an hour away. Yes, he could drive us. Well, what would he charge? Fifteen dollars. This was a miracle because fifteen bucks was about what we had collected on the train. We looked at each other, hesitant to get into the rattletrap car, but our options were obviously limited. We stuffed our possessions into the trunk and clambered into the back seat. We were now at the mercy of this stranger, who began driving at break-neck speed past cottages and herds of sheep, heading, we hoped, for a kinder welcome on the Romanian-Hungarian border.

Wrong again.

Only minutes had passed when our driver suddenly pulled off the main road. Instantly my head filled with fantasies of rape and double murder. My fears were heightened when a second man came running toward us and jumped into the car. It turned out he was the driver's son, who explained in labored English that his father realized his old car wouldn't make it to the border. We were making a detour to borrow a better automobile from a neighbor.

Safely inside the sturdier vehicle (with functional seat belts at that) we continued on our way and made it to Gyula in one piece, only to be told by the border official there that my Bank of America traveler's checks to pay for the Hungarian visas were not acceptable! Finally, after my shrieks of despair he called a supervisor who gave him permission to take the checks.

We weren't home free yet. We got the visas and drove across the Hungarian border to the railway station in Bekescsaba. Ready to pay the taxi driver the fifteen dollars he had quoted, we were now informed that the charge was *fifty*. More arguments, more negotiations, and a compromise was reached. Cash in hand, the father and son wished us safe journey and sped away. Soon we were on board a clean and uncrowded train headed for Hungary's capital.

Surely, few travelers have been so ecstatic to arrive in the city of Budapest.

It Was a Lovely View

by Larry Parker

I WASN'T GOING TO let the lice upset me. It was a dramatically beautiful day in the Columbia Gorge. A holiday weekend lay ahead and we had reservations at a bed and breakfast where, we were told, there was a Cordon Bleu chef, gracious staff and a lovely setting. This was not going to be like the place where the owner greeted us, cigarette in hand, while her husband watched basketball in the common room. We were not going to be served creamed chipped beef on blueberry muffins; this was going to be the elegant B&B experience of a *Gourmet* article. So, when my mother-in-law found lice on my 7-year-old son's head, I just dealt with it by pulling into the first pharmacy I saw.

With a bottle of medicated shampoo we pulled back onto the highway. We found our address without trouble and turned off the road, over the railroad tracks and in toward that lovely, white cap speckled river—what a view! As the road curved away from the tracks and the rusted out semi trailer appeared I thought, "maybe I got the wrong address?" We continued, past the pile of wheel rims, abandoned washer and dryer and rubbish heap and finally arrived at the bed and breakfast, which sat on a point on the river with spectacular views up and down the gorge.

Scratching our heads and muttering, we climbed out of the car and knocked on the door. The owner greeted us like a terrier starved for affection. He wrung our hands and spent every moment we were with him touching each of us in some overly familiar manner while loudly explaining that things were not quite as nice as they ought to be because "the wife here has just been through cancer treatment." We then got a recital of her maladies and the various and creative ways that she had been treated for them. This was followed by a run-down of the owner's life and times in politics back in Seattle. At last, we disengaged from him and checked into our rooms.

The rooms were delightful and cozy. The room my wife and I and the 7-year-old twins were staying in had a huge jet-ted tub that we immediately used to wash the lice out of my son's hair. The room my wife's parents were staying in had a great view down the river to a dam. We were able to relax, regroup and even laugh about the drawers full of hardware in the antique vanity in our room. An easygoing lot, we decided to concentrate on the lovely view and our plans for the week-end and overlook our disappointment that the B&B was not what we expected. We went out to dinner, laughed about our situation and went home to bed.

The first train came down the gorge at 10. The floors shook and the windows rattled. It was a long freighter that took a good 10 minutes to pass. When it did I was glad to have that over with and went back to sleep.

The second train came through at 10:20. It was just as loud and long as the first one. Agitated, I was only drifting off when ...

The third train came through at 10:40. I was now wide awake and wondering how many more of these trains might be coming down the gorge.

The trains came every 20 minutes the rest of the night. Our nerves frayed a little bit more with each one. By 4:30 we were all sitting in my mother-in-law's room thinking that this night was never going to end when a very loud siren went off not more than half a mile away. My mother-in-law jumped up and cried, "The dam's burst!" Well it hadn't, it was just some siren going off at 4:30 in the morning to provide variety while we were waiting for the 4:40 train.

After we calmed down from the siren, my father-in-law looked out on the moonlit river and said, "Well, we sure have a nice view from here," to which my mother-in-law replied, "If anyone mentions that view one more time, I'm going to scream."

Exhausted, we all finally passed out for a couple of hours before it was time to go down to breakfast.

Breakfast was laid out on the kitchen counter, rows of doughnuts glistening with sugar and fat, canned coffee and orange juice—nothing else. While we were staring at our breakfast, the owner put his hand on my shoulder, grinned and asked how we had slept. We allowed as how the trains might have been a trifle loud. He acknowledged that the trains did in fact "bother some people." We retreated from the breakfast room to decide what to do.

With two hypoglycemics and four exhausted adults there was no way we could face either the doughnuts or another night at this establishment. My father-in-law was volunteered by my mother-in-law to deal with the situation. He told the owner that his son-in-law was "sensitive" and just couldn't deal with the trains, and we wouldn't be coming back even though we had already paid for two nights. My mother-in-law shot me a warning look to not say anything about the way her husband was handling this.

When we got back in the car I clenched my jaw and was very surprised to hear her berate him herself, "Dan!" she said, "How could you put the whole thing on Larry?"

"You ask me to fall on my sword," he said, "and then you criticize my technique?"

Back at home, my wife confronted her workmate on his B&B recommendation. "Well," he said, "it was that one or one with a name like that. Anyway, the one I meant was really nice ... "

We have been back to the gorge and had a great time ... camping. I have never been to another B&B since.

Road Warrior

by Brian Abrahams

For the most part, Europeans drive like maniacs. And the Belgians have the deadliest roads. In fact, there was a roundabout near my office that was the deadliest roundabout *on the entire continent.* As hazardous as this was, however, parking was even riskier for me.

One day I had to make a quick stop at a store and was circling the area trying to find a place to park. Finally I found one whole side of a block with only one car on it, so I parked behind it and went into the store. When I came out 25 minutes later, I vaguely noticed how much traffic there was. Then I saw that people were trying to maneuver a truck around a tram that wasn't moving. As I got closer I saw the tram was blocked. By my car.

Brussels has a surface tram system. I'd been afraid of it since we moved there; the trams are huge, can't swerve to avoid a collision, can't stop quickly and because of the design of the streets are constantly in and out of the lanes of cars. In some places the trams have their own tracks separate from the street and in many place the trams share the street with cars. And to top it off there are people (not me, I swear) who jump off and on the tram tracks with their cars to pass slower moving cars. When I parked the car, I didn't realize that I was on a set of tram tracks and in a very busy and narrow thoroughfare at that.

Behind the first blocked tram were cars, trucks and buses. Down the street I could see three or four more trams that couldn't move. The cross street was also blocked, with more trucks, buses and cars on it. Probably other cross streets were blocked as well, since the line of immobile vehicles stretched as far as I could see. In addition to all that, there were several dozen spectators standing on the sidewalk, three or four police cars with lights on, assorted policemen and an official from the Transit Service in a suit, all gathered around my car. In that time they got all those officials there and no tow truck. All I wanted to do was have the earth swallow me up.

I ran over, apologizing profusely in English. Between all of those on the trams, plus the other vehicles there had to be 500 to 1,000 people waiting for me to move my car, hating the driver for being so stupid.

"YOU are sorry?" the transit official barked at me. "No, WE are much sorrier! You were here for 25 minutes!" Many of the people on the sidewalk laughed. "And don't leave this place!" he shouted as I pulled the car away. Given the number of police cars, I wasn't going to argue. As soon as I parked and got out a policeman asked me for my identity card. Thank God I had just renewed it.

My mouth was dry and I could feel that my face was bright red. Now they would find out I was a foreigner. I stood next to the police car and watched them untangle the traffic jam. One by one the various policemen came over to berate me in several languages. "You must look down when you park," one of them said, smirking. Totally humbled, I just nodded and didn't point out that there were no signs whatsoever on the block. I noticed that as each delayed tram came by the transit official asked the driver a question. And as each tram passed me, dozens of faces gave me dirty looks, or said things I couldn't hear through the glass. I stood there and took it as a kind of punishment but wondered what the official action would be.

Finally the transit official came over to me. Since no one had said anything, I asked him what was going to happen to me. In broken English, he told me that I was going to have to pay for the delay caused to each of the trams. That must have been what he was asking the drivers about. I took a deep breath.

"How much?" I asked him.

"I don't know. It's not my problem," he told me. "You are free to go now. We will send you a bill." He handed my identity card back to me. I couldn't look him in the eye.

Four or five trams, at least 20 minutes for one of them, less for the others. How did they calculate the fine? Could it run into thousands of dollars? As I drove home, I felt like every eye in Brussels was on me, knowing my shame. I have never felt such embarrassment in my entire life.

A few weeks later I was in the taxi of a man who had been a tram driver for 23 years. At first I tried the old trick of "I have a friend who once parked on the tram tracks and ... " but my French wasn't good enough and neither was his English. Finally I just admitted it was me since I could handle first person past tense in French. I had barely gotten through the story when he started saying "Oooh la la, Monsieur, oooh la la."

I hate when they do that "oooh la la" thing. Especially when my underwear is soaked in fear sweat. He conveyed to me that the fine could be enormous. According to him, and taxi driving former tram operators are a good source of info for me, the fine was the dollar equivalent of about $142 a minute per tram. Let's see, four to five trams, 25 minutes, that ran into an easy $20,000. When I told him the total number of trams involved and the time, he actually pulled over and stopped the taxi so he could turn around and look at me. I thought he was going to take a picture to show off at the Veteran Tram Drivers Convention.

"You'll never believe who I had in my taxi, oooh la la."

Then I pretended that I used the wrong French number for the time and it was really five to 10 minutes and one tram. Either he didn't believe me or just couldn't let go of his original amazement because the oooh la la's went all the way to my house. He actually missed an exit he was supposed to take. After the humiliation faded, and trust me, it was a few weeks, I called my company's European lawyer. He was Flemish, so he was much more practical, to the point and didn't pepper me with oooh la la's to emphasize what an idiot I was. Fortunately he happened to have a friend at the Transit Service. The friend took a week or two to check things out.

Finally word came back and the real situation was much worse than I imagined.

Apparently the Transit Service utilized the oil services company, Schlumberger, as an outside contractor to calculate the "damages" caused in these types of cases. Using computer modeling they plug in a variety of variables including time of day, data about the importance of the lines affected, the domino effect on other lines, the load factor of each tram, etc. (All this effort and precision for a parking ticket in a country where national government on down barely functions.) The final result was that they calculated a total of 150 minutes of damages. Then my lawyer tells me that under Belgian law they can charge the dollar equivalent of about $571 a minute, or in my case a total of over $85,000.

$85,000.

A few weeks before, a man was found guilty of driving on the highway and shooting a woman in another car in the head. He was fined $32,000. I was on the hook for more than double that, just for picking a lousy parking spot for less than half an hour. The worst thing is that the car could have only been worth maybe $8,000–$10,000 (and just $2,500 in the States). I would have been ahead of the game if they had blown up the car and the leasing company stuck me with the bill. The "good" news from the secret Transit Service source was that my taxi driver was accurate. In practice they charge less and the fine might be "only" $10,000 to $20,000. I thought about waking my son from his nap, abandoning the cats and just fleeing to the airport, but then the real good news came. In Belgium there is a bizarre loophole to the law (but Belgian authorities, please don't close it. Dumb Americans from cities with overhead trains need an out.) If someone makes an "offer" to the transit officials to pay a "suggested" amount (sort of like "suggested retail") before they've communicated the actual fine to you, then that offer can be accepted. Don't ask me why this is. The whole thing seems criminally fishy and there has to be some weird sneaky reason, like maybe most people offer too high. But in any case, we went way low, about $400 on the advice of my lawyer. The biggest parking ticket I've ever had but not even decent interest on $85,000.

The kicker for them was that my lawyer let them know I had counsel and would tie them up in appeals until their nose hairs went gray. In Belgium the legal system is so clogged that appeals aren't even heard for four years. They're no fools. They know their country is a judicial morass and I would be long gone to America before I saw the inside of a Belgian courtroom. Sure $400 was a low bid. Personally I would have gone higher, but that's what the best legal talent is for. I almost broke into a run getting to the bank to make the transfer and seal the deal. (In true European/Belgian fashion I had to take the letter they sent me, go to the Post Office to get some kind of blank postal draft, then take that to my bank, which then made the actual transfer. But I'm not complaining, it was better than turning over my life's savings to the public transport bureaucracy of a country I didn't even want to live in.) The headquarters for the Transit Service was right near the movie theater we went to sometimes, and I would shudder just walking past their lair. I always looked up in the windows though to see if I could see them swigging wine, laughing and telling the story of the American they nearly fleeced out of all that he had in the world.

Prior to this experience, during a year in Belgium I had never set foot in public transportation. (Unless you count taxis, which I do since you can catch diseases of the scalp from the headrests.) But in a bizarre Patti Hearst/Stockholm Syndrome twist, I was so spooked by the whole train incident that I embraced the enemy and began to regularly take public transportation from that point on. You can't run up $85,000 parking tickets if you're riding on one of the things. (Early on I nearly found a way to get into trouble. In my first few days I saw people getting on the tram and not putting fare cards in the scanners. So I figured I wouldn't either. Then I found out that those people supposedly have monthly or yearly passes that don't have to go in the card scanner. If you're caught without a ticket by the transit officials in frequent spot-checks, they make a real public scene and haul you off to show everyone not to mess with them. Luckily I dodged that bullet and starting paying like a good citizen.) In fact, I became such a veteran of the tram that I would curse cars that got in the way. I even started saying "oooh la la" when a car was slowing the tram.

Parking wasn't my only problem in Europe.

I should have known better than to be in a jaunty mood when I landed in Shannon, Ireland, one day to try and snag some business from the PC manufacturers there. One of the salespeople from our office picked me up at the airport and before I was even buckled into my seat he said, "I hear you're quite a driver. The police came looking for you today at your office in Brussels." I was instantly sick to my stomach. I do drive fast. ("But your honor, everyone in Belgium drives too fast!") In Europe they usually don't pull people over for speeding. They take a picture or video of the car, along with a printout on speed and mail a ticket to the registered owner of the car rather than worrying about who was driving it.

I had been pulled over and ticketed for speeding on the Autobahn in Germany and had been pulled over once in Belgium although not ticketed. I avoided the ticket by playing the dumb American bit to the hilt. However, part of my excuse was that I was so used to miles per hour that I was confused by kilometers per hour. The alert policeman pointed out that if I were going miles per hour on my speedometer then it would actually be *slower* than the same number in kilometers per hour. Luckily it was early and cold and he didn't want to bother ticketing me. My wife had received two ticket notices on her car that were almost certainly for when I was driving. And just the prior week I was told that the company leasing the car I drive had received notices for four tickets. Three means potential loss of driving privileges.

Wait. The churning in my stomach slowed. The Irish love to play practical jokes and tease, and LunaTek's Irish staff even more so.

"Patrick, you're messing with me." He looked at me dead serious.

"No, I'm not. The Belgian police came looking for you at your office this morning." My office? Where I go every day and have pictures of my family on the desk? There were police? I pressed him to just admit the joke. It was very probably the handiwork of Declan Ryan, the director of our management company. We had become friends and a few practical jokes had passed between us. Declan also knew about the tickets. "Patrick, if you're messing with me, it's funny but it's time to stop. If you don't stop and this is a joke I'm going to pay you back tenfold." Patrick and I weren't that close for me to be threatening him like that.

"I'm not joking," he insisted without so much as a blink.

"So how did you know about this?" I asked. He told me that Anna in the Belgian office had told everyone in the Shannon office.

I called Anna from my portable and asked for messages. She casually let me know that I had none. Then as an afterthought, she added, "Oh, and the police came looking for you this morning." I felt a cold, hard lump in my gut. If she said it, then it was no joke. The police must have really come to my office.

"What do you mean? Why?"

"Something about speeding tickets. I told them you were out of town but would be back in the office on Thursday."

"Gee Anna," I said through gritted teeth, "thanks for helping." Now they knew exactly where and when to find me.

"Did they say what they wanted from me?"

"No. But that's how it goes in Belgium. Have a nice day."

I felt sick. I was a foreigner whose work permit was about to expire and needed to be renewed. To add to any possible indictment, I had never gotten a Belgian driver's license as foreign residents are supposed to. When you get a Belgian license they take your native driver's license and I didn't want to give that up.

Curse the leasing company! Three of the tickets on the car had been in the same exact spot on a long stretch of road. They didn't tell me about the tickets until I raced through the same speed trap three times.

How could I have been so stupid? I pictured myself ushered onto a U.S.-bound plane by a fat Belgian cop and told to never come back into the country if I knew what was good for me. The police came to my office! That doesn't happen in America unless you are in seriously deep stuff. I pictured the scene in *Wall Street* when Charlie Sheen is handcuffed in his office and led away in front of all his coworkers.

Patrick started telling me about our appointments at AST and Dell, but I couldn't concentrate on what he was saying. All I could think about were the words of a Canadian I met who has lived in Belgium for 20 years. "They don't enforce things very much over here, but when they do go after you they do it with a vengeance." The only tiny comfort I had was that in wearing a dark suit, if I did pee on myself it wouldn't be so noticeable.

Frantically dialing my cell phone, I called my trusty Belgian lawyer. He told me I was worrying too much. He didn't know exactly why they would have wanted to meet with me for speeding tickets but reminded me that it's much more common for police in Belgium to come to someone's home or office on relatively routine matters. His extended explanation of the complicated steps needed for the arrest process, probably intended to make me feel better, did just the opposite.

The next two days in Ireland, which I had been looking forward to, passed slowly. I thought about marking the passage of days on the wall of my hotel room with hash marks.

Finally I was back in my office on Thursday. All I could think about was having to go to the police station. I decided to wait until after lunch. No reason not to get a final meal. Before I left, I realized I was tidying up my office, probably in case I wasn't going to be back soon.

Waterloo isn't a big place and the drive to the police station was short. I pulled very slowly into the parking lot. The policeman on duty in the lobby spoke no English. Fortunately, Evelyne, my French tutor, had just taught me how to do past tense. I was able to describe how policemen *came* to my office, *spoke* to a person there, *asked* for me, etc. Present tense never would have worked. I was frightened but proud.

He knew nothing about it and told me to sit down. I could smell the red tape piling up already and settled back with the patience their bureaucracy requires. There were three magazines in the entire lobby, all three the same French women's magazine. How and why did a police station (where I saw only men) wind up with French women's magazines in the lobby? I bided my time reading gossip about the various royal families in Europe.

A second policeman came out and asked me what I wanted. He knew a little more English and I told him that *they* wanted *me* and not the other way around. He wrote my name on a piece of paper, went in back and then came out again a few minutes later. He told me the chief wanted to see me. Only in French chief is pronounced "chef." The last final scrap of dignity was stripped from me. Here I was, standing alone in the lobby of a Belgian police station, clutching a French women's magazine and crying plaintively: "The chef wants to see me? Why does the chef want to see me?" He couldn't tell me much and wandered away.

Finally the policeman at the reception told me to go into the offices. I walked in tentatively. Why did I wear jeans? The Belgians are so formal. I should have worn a tie. In a room full of desks and police a man motioned me over. He was younger than I expected and actually nice. He spoke more English than the last two, but not a lot. He showed me a single speeding ticket (if this was what they did for one ticket what would happen when they caught on to all three?) It was eight months old—the Belgian government is a slow-moving beast. The ticket indicated I had been doing 100 kph in a 60-kph zone, (60 mph in a 36-mph zone.) I drive the road every day and know the limit is 70 kph and not 60. Possibly enough to make some kind of difference, but I didn't want to argue with him. I pointed out that the car I drive is shared by a group of people. (Absolute truth. In fact someone else had already claimed one of the four tickets on the car. The remainder I knew to be mine.) I asked him why I was called in. I could be wrong, but I thought he looked a little sheepish. He told me that the number of kilometers over was serious and police in the town where I was caught were having trouble figuring out who was responsible for the car. And I'm sure it wasn't easy. I drove it, and my company LunaTek pays our distribution partners for the use. They in turn sub-lease it from another company, which in turn leases it from a leasing company. Someone in that chain had ratted on me and told them to seek me out.

The chief wanted me to acknowledge that I was driving the car. I told him I couldn't be sure it was me, which is a kissing cousin to the truth. He said that the Waterloo police had to find the responsible party, so if I was the one then I had to acknowledge it. I was deep inside his police station and surrounded by his officers. Oh what the hell.

"Okay, even though I'm not sure it was me driving, I guess I'm responsible for the car as the head of my company here. So, in that capacity I'll accept responsibility for what may have happened with the car." I'm certain he caught all the subtle nuances of my English.

"Good," he said. He asked me for my home address. I told him that the office address was better for mail but he insisted on my home. Then he proceeded to write down a paragraph longhand in French. "Now just sign this." He put the paper and a pen in front of me. I stared at it. My grasp of French was shaky enough without trying to interpret his handwriting. I didn't understand a word. I told him that I didn't really know what tickets were mine, but I was willing to pay the fines since I was running the company in Belgium. He wasn't distracted. "You have to sign the paper. We must have the signature of the responsible person."

I was in a foreign country and being asked to sign a hand-written statement of some kind of guilt in a language I didn't understand. The nightmare of every American traveling abroad. He smiled at me genially but didn't blink. Now, I know what you're thinking. And it's easy to criticize from the comfort of America and with 20/20 hindsight. It's a lot harder to look the chef in the eye and tell him to piss off in his own station when I know I'm nailed dead to rights for speeding repeatedly like a crazed Formula One driver on methamphetamine. To get to work I had to go into Waterloo every day. If I was on the police watch list I was out of business.

I signed the paper.

"Great." He took it back briskly and folded it up. "That's it. You can go now." I knew I shouldn't have signed but I was intensely relieved to get out of there. I drove very carefully back to my office and still felt uneasy. Why did they only pursue me on one ticket when there were four on the car? Why did they want my home address? What in God's name did I sign?

Another thing nagging at me was that this whole speeding thing could draw attention to other legal issues in our household. For instance, one day a few months prior my wife had come home and found one of our Filipino house cleaners hiding behind the couch. Pressed for an explanation, he said that he saw police in the neighborhood and admitted that he and his aunt, who also cleaned our house, weren't in the country legally. Asking around, we found out that there was a $40,000 fine for hiring illegal immigrants. Two weeks prior to my signing the "confession," the nephew had been arrested at a Metro stop and sent back to the Philippines. Although the Belgian police could usually be counted on for not being pro-active, what if they found their way to the aunt and from her to us? Or what if in checking *me* out they uncovered the housekeeper? We sure couldn't afford to pay a $40,000 fine.

The next day was Friday and I was home around 6:30 P.M. It was quiet because my son's nap was going very late. Suddenly the doorbell sounded. We never got unscheduled visitors in Belgium because we knew so few people and the Belgians themselves would never dare do such a thing as show up unannounced. I asked at the intercom who it was. The answer came back: "Police." The word is the same in English and French. My head started to swim and I thought I was going to be sick. It wasn't enough to draw trouble into my office— I had brought this ruin into my home as well. As I came down the stairs, through the glass on the side of the door I saw a gun on the officer's hip. Evelyne, the goddess of Berlitz, had told me there are two kinds of police in Belgium. There are the local police who generally are nice and do not carry weapons and there are the Belgian National Police who receive military training, are mean and arrogant and carry guns. She had told me to avoid the latter at all costs. But what do you do when they are ringing your doorbell? And WHY?

What if I had signed a confession to some terrible unsolved crime? What if the chef was buying a boat with his bonus for identifying the "Mad Killer of Antwerp"? What if this had something to do with the housekeeper or her nephew? I paused before opening the door. If I was the Richard Speck of Belgium then the house had to be surrounded. And if this was just more speeding ticket formalities then I didn't want to act like a criminal.

I opened the door to face eyes hooded by aviator-style Ray Bans. Not a common look on the east side of The Pond. He spoke only French and indicated he wanted to come in and speak with me. In silence, my mind racing, I walked him into the dining room and offered him a chair. Now a policeman with a gun was sitting at the same table in the same spot where my son ate his yogurt. What hath I wrought? I called for my wife, whose French is way better than mine. The three of us made a cozy little trio in the dining room. He began asking questions, which Jenny was answering in French. I strained to pick out words. How did you say "maid" or "arrest" in French? Why was that damn dictionary never handy? What were they talking about?

Finally I couldn't take the suspense anymore and I interrupted and told Jenny to find out why he was here. She shushed me and said she was trying to hear him. When you could be sent up the river for a long time on a phony murder rap, the last thing you want is your wife shushing you. But she had the French and therefore all the power so I just ground my teeth.

Finally my wife paused to turn and talk to me, probably catching me seconds before the cardiac incident. Apparently, in an amazing coincidence that was nearly fatal to me, this was a routine check connected to our renewing our work and residence permits. He "just wanted to ask some questions," although her French isn't so good that she understood exactly what it was all about. I immediately put on a calm face. Maybe even cocky. I leaned back in my chair with satisfaction. The poor fool. He didn't know he was sitting in the home of one of the most wanted criminals in Waterloo. Someone that had just gone one on one with the chief of police, brazenly signed a confession without so much as a glance and then blew out of the police station parking lot in one of the fastest 1.4 liter diesel stick shift station wagons in all of Brussels. He had no clue he was also sitting at a table cleaned by an illegal Filipino. Dumb sap. I cleaned my nails while he finished asking Jenny questions. Then I walked him to the door and thanked him for his time. I thought about adding an invitation to come back sometime for coffee but I decided not to taunt. My signed "confession" was floating out there somewhere in the Belgian bureaucracy.

I was still a little shaken to have had a policeman first at my office and then at my home. I felt like I had a taste of what it was like to live in a police state, which in a sense Belgium was, albeit one with incompetent and corrupt police. As police states seek to do, my spirit was broken. They put fear into me, and after that my obedience to the laws increased greatly. I didn't know when the next police visit to my home or office would come, so like an old man, I sat in the right-hand lane and went one kph under the speed limit. Every time I saw a police car in my rear view mirror I assumed it was following me. They didn't pursue the guy who torched our warehouse, but they were going to come after me.

Although I would spend the rest of my time in Belgium waiting for the other shoe to drop, for some reason it never did. The police were so slow moving they are probably only now issuing a warrant for my arrest. In other words, if you are going there for a short vacation, you have license to commit a wide variety of crimes, because by the time they figure it out, you'll be at home boring your neighbors with slides of the Manneken Pis.

Ship Wrecked

by Carole Dickerson

It seemed so right when my husband talked of a boating vacation on Puget Sound.

"We'll rent a boat from a Seattle marina, load up the family and cruise off for the San Juan Islands," Mike said. I thought *perfect.*

The family: Geoff, 7; Gayle, 6; and baby Gavin, 18 months. The children loved the adventurous idea of being on the water for a family vacation. The baby didn't have a vote, or much of a voice, but he liked anything his older sibs did. Summer on Puget Sound cannot be matched anywhere in the world. A clear sky, warm daytime temperatures and cool nights to watch the stars. After a typical Northwest rain-drenched, leaden-sky winter, you can bet sun-loving Carole was ready.

We insisted on a seaworthy craft. The boat we rented met our cost requirement and space needs if not our dream. We selected an inboard cruiser that looked substantial and up-to-date although a three-masted sailing ship would have more fitted my husband's dream. The boat had a kitchen—to be called "galley" from there on so as not to mistake us for sea novices—and a toilet—strangely called "head" by seasoned boaters. This was to be our home on the water for a weeklong vacation. Oh joy.

Leaving Seattle on a boat is an adventure itself. Ours was moored on Lake Union. Some engineer figured out years ago how to let boats move between salt and fresh water and designed the Locks. Really called the Ballard Locks, they're well known in the Puget Sound area by natives and tourists alike and are practically a shrine. To spend time in Seattle and not visit the Locks is like missing the Space Needle. The Locks transport boats from freshwater Lake Union into Elliott Bay's salt water and then back again. Watching boats come and go via the Locks is a thrill no matter how many times you visit. Thinking back, we should have ended the vacation there.

But once through the Locks, our adventure began in earnest. The children were the most excited, probably because they sensed, as children will, that we were together which was good, but also heading into the unknown vastness of the sea, which was a little scary.

"Yep. We could go to China from here," Mike said proudly. The weather was definitely on our side. The eternal rains were not here for our vacation — it was blue skies from now on, just like in the song.

Mike at the helm certainly looked the Captain while I got the important-sounding title of First Mate. Mike had learned boating from Power Squadron classes and had taught other would-be sailors boating techniques including how to read charts specific to the traveled waters. Like everything else in life, Mike took this all very seriously.

As he made himself familiar with the workings and special effects of the boat such as the motor, battery, lights, emergency siren and life preservers, he said that the boat, (which, alas, didn't have a name) was fitted so tight that "the bilge was nearly dusty." Comforting words.

We chugged easily out of Elliott Bay past islands familiar to us from land, heading toward the Straits of Juan de Fuca. The last crossing of the straits on a ferry from Port Townsend was fresh in memory because I got seasick from the huge swells that tipped the ferry like a ping-pong ball. Mike assured me that crossing the straits from Port Townsend was much rougher since boats had to forge against very heavy winds.

We settled into our new environment and began learning the intricacies of the boat toilet and galley stove. In addition to such necessary family items as diapers, special foods, toys and clothes for both cold and warm temperatures, Mike had brought along plastic buckets so he could look for and capture unusual marine life found in the islands for the salt water aquarium that he'd built into our family room.

After a lunch of sandwiches, carrot sticks and milk, all was well as we looked forward to our first stop at Friday Harbor on San Juan Island, the busiest and largest of the San Juans. The baby, lulled by the drone of the inboard motor, slept while the rest of the family enjoyed the passing landscape.

"Daddy, can I steer?" Geoff asked. Mike agreed and placed a small box below the wheel for Geoff to stand on so he could see over the bow and told him to "head straight for that point."

With my face toward the sky I did not notice the logs in the bay from logged trees discarded from near-by saw mills.

K-rumph! The sound was terrifying. We'd hit something very hard, but even more frightening the boat began shimmying something fierce. I was sure we were all soon going to be in 50-degree saltwater with death near. Mike and I were the only ones who could swim; would the life preservers that Geoff and Gayle wore be able to keep them alive and afloat until help could come? I rushed to grab Gavin while scanning the boat hull to see where the water was coming in. I'd read somewhere that if you quickly stuff something, anything, at the break— or is it breach?—you can hold off the water.

My mind seemed to be working although my body was frozen in fear. But it was Geoff, I'm sure, who experienced the worst dread since he felt responsible. He must have yelled for his dad, who appeared on the spot assessing what the problem was and what to do about it.

We soon realized that there wasn't water coming aboard and that the only difficulty was the boat's shimmying. The closest marina turned out to be a snazzy facility where the workers wore crisp blue and white uniforms with their names sewn on in script. I was impressed. If anyone could fix this boat, these were the fellows. Since our lives had been spared maybe our vacation could yet be salvaged.

To fix the problem, the boat needed to be lifted out of the water with all of us aboard. It wasn't terra firma but being 10 feet in the air over a dry marina dock felt good and safe. No complaints from any of us!

They found the problem. The boat's propeller on the end of the drive shaft had been bent from hitting the log. The propeller could not be bent back into shape, it had to be replaced, and now the situation gets more tricky because the propeller had a "left handed screw" so the marina would have to order a new something that would take "a couple of days at the most."

Mike must have pleaded (threatened is nearer Mike's style) our case to the marina because lo and behold the replacement screw arrived the next day. We were back in the water by late afternoon headed for Friday Harbor.

Friday Harbor looks like something out of a picture book or what I'd always imagined Cape Cod must look like. From the water inlet you look up the main street, where cars neatly line up in season to catch the ferry off the island. Both sides of the street have cozy little shops selling everything from marine supplies to ice cream for the tourists. But we had our own boat so we would moor away from the tourist crowds. However, we needed to stop at the marina to buy gas and ice.

Approaching a marine dock is somewhat tricky. Your speed

has to be just so, you have to be careful not to bump your boat on docks or other boats, there is limited space in which to maneuver and above all, you need to know what you're doing! Show me where it says in any of the boating manuals that someone needs to hang on to one end of the rope when the guy on the dock says, "throw me the line"? Nowhere! It was the strange look on the guy's face that gave me my only clue that I must have done something wrong. Mike was NOT amused. Well, if he'd expected this trip to be perfect he should have gone alone.

Our next stop at one of the lesser islands looked like a nice place to stop. In positioning ourselves, Mike put the boat throttle into reverse—but nothing happened. When he tried to go forward, same thing. No control. The stupid boat just floated around as if it didn't have a propeller, but that couldn't be. We SAW the propeller on the shaft after the guys at the marina put it on, right? So what happened?

Mike got to a pay phone to call the marina where the boat had been repaired just two days before. A man from the marina came by and said something about a missing cotter pin and then added, "It sounds like the motor's missing."

"Missing?" I said hysterically. "The motor's missing???" Now I was ready for murder.

From the tone of my voice, everyone in hearing distance—and there were now about 50 people gathered around the scene—figured I was on the brink of something or other and they didn't want to miss it. The marina man quickly quieted me by saying it was only an expression, not that the motor was actually gone. "Sure," I thought. Nothing at this point could really surprise me.

The trip ended quietly enough. We loaded all our stuff, including the buckets full of saltwater with Mike's live treasures, onto a Greyhound bus to Seattle. Our last view of the boat was it being towed back to somewhere where someone cared about what happened to it. If you don't think we looked like something out of John Steinbeck's *Tobacco Road* you haven't got the true picture.

Some vacation.

The Mean Streets of Cairo

by Brooke Comer

CAIRO IS A SAFE CITY. I tell people this, and they don't always believe me. Some people who have never been to Egypt fall prey to the stereotype of men in turbans abducting blonde women into white slavery, or terrorists lurking in the alleys, guns folded in the sleeves of their gallabeas.

I have never been a victim of street crime in Cairo. I have, however, been a victim of the street.

It happened one night during Ramadan, when all the stores were open late and the streets filled with people shopping and eating. I followed a group of friends to L'Aubergine, a restaurant known for its upstairs bar on one of the narrow, tree-lined streets of Zamalek, an upscale neighborhood on the Nile Island of Gezirah and the current favorite hangout among upscale locals, expats and the Marines who guard the American Embassy.

After midnight, the crowd moved to a less atmospheric bar down the street that began selling drinks for half price. I'd been feeling mildly ill after ingesting a dubious falafel for lunch, so I was drinking Baraka mineral water. Later, I wished I'd been swilling Stella beer as heartily as my friends had. It would have numbed the pain.

As we headed along Sayed Bakri Street toward the half-price bar, someone produced a ball, tossed it to someone else and a spirited game of touch football began. Cairo has few streetlights, so we were running and jumping in the dark. I jumped to block a pass but fell on a sharp stone embedded in the street and cut my knee open.

Jack, a video editor known locally as The Ugly American because of the way his otherwise benign face contorted into rage when drunk, said he had a bandage at his place. Because of my injury, I really wasn't in a position to refuse his offer, even though we happened to be at the entrance of his apartment building, into which he'd already spent most of the night unsuccessfully trying to lure me and every other woman in our party.

I followed Jack upstairs into a dark, rank apartment.

"Damn!" he shouted. "They turned my lights off again!" He took off a shoe and threw it hard. There was a splash. I felt along the wall until I found a switch, and turned on the light. A stained beige carpet was strewn with socks, empty Stella bottles and a scattered collection of things that looked like they belonged in a bathroom cabinet—bottles of mouthwash, aspirin, deodorant, toothpaste and several rolls of toilet paper. Jack's shoe had landed in a large aquarium that sat on a shelf against the far wall. It contained murky water and, I hoped, no fish.

"Damn," Jack moaned again and staggered off (yes, he was very drunk) to retrieve his shoe. I found a Swiss Army knife in my purse and used the tiny scissors to cut off my left jeans leg at the knee. As soon as I got a good look at the wound, I knew I'd need stitches. The gash was a good five inches across and deep. My leg was soaked with blood, but I found I could control the bleeding if I kept the knee upright and still. Jack dropped on the sofa next to me, looking at my knee and breathing hard. "You're really fucked up." I could have said the same thing to him but instead just answered, "I need a hospital." I had been to Cairo many times and thought I knew the city. But you never really know a city until you have been to one of its hospitals.

Jack snorted. "Hospital! I was a medic in the fucking army. I saw some action in the jungle. I sewed my buddy's leg back on. Give me a needle!"

As if.

Jack was under 40, too young for a jungle war. The only action he'd seen overseas probably consisted of brawls in the jungle of expat bars, and if he'd sewn his buddy's leg back on, it was probably because he'd been the one, accidentally or otherwise, to have sliced it off.

I reached for the phone and called my friend Raymond, but he was not at home. Raymond was an American scholar whose fluent Arabic would ensure that I found a doctor, but he had an active social life and no cell phone.

Shawki was the only person whose cell phone I knew by heart (I did not have my address book in my purse) because, strangely enough, it was the same as mine. Shawki is a prominent Egyptian businessman and a notorious womanizer. Most of the responsible people I knew in Cairo would be in bed at 2 A.M. and Shawki would be too, but at least he wouldn't be asleep. He wasn't, but he also wasn't pleased to be disturbed.

"Kasr Al-Aini," he told me quickly. I imagined that I heard the flutter of sheets, a feminine sigh, in the background. "It's the best hospital in Cairo. It was built by the French. Look for a big, new, pink building. It's excellent; it's where they always took my brother for his heart trouble."

Shawki's brother was dead. While Jack got up and began weaving around the room, I wrapped toilet paper around my knee to control the bleeding on the journey to the hospital. Then I stood up.

"Where the hell do you think you're going?" Jack bellowed.

It was hard to walk downstairs without bending my leg, and I refused to let Jack carry me, which would no doubt result in a more serious injury. I have never had a problem finding a taxi in Cairo but could not find one that night. Jack stood in the street roaring and caught the attention of two guards from a nearby embassy. They came closer, saw my blood-soaked bandage and fired off questions in rapid Arabic that exceeded my limited vocabulary. Apparently they had as much trouble understanding me; the words "hospital" and "taxi" did not inspire them to run to the corner and summon a cab. They did, however, look concerned, point at my leg and nod at one another. I finally had to walk to the corner myself, and when Jack finally figured out I was gone jogged after me.

The cab driver, amazingly, spoke English and knew exactly where Kasr Al-Aini hospital was. It was not far, it was not pink, and it was certainly not new. It looked Gothic. It looked like an insane asylum in a 1940s horror film.

While Jack argued with the cab driver, who wanted three pounds (about 90 cents), that he was being overcharged, I walked into a dusty lobby. Two veiled women shrieked and threw themselves against the flyspecked wall. A man in blue cotton pajamas lay on the floor, his head bleeding even more profusely than my knee. A pregnant Muslim woman, her head and body wrapped in black, sat at his feet. The one bench was occupied by a man in a western suit who appeared to be in perfect health. Four men in black gallabeas sat cross-legged on the floor. I took a seat on the bench. Flies buzzed. Women wailed.

Jack lurched in, followed by the bewildered driver.

"He won't pay," the driver told me.

Jack, distracted by the other patients' ailments, wandered off in their direction while I pulled 20 pounds out of my wallet and told the driver he could have it all if he produced a doctor. He disappeared immediately and quickly returned with a bucktoothed young man who wore a loose-fitting white jumpsuit. I'd thought English was the international language of medicine, but I was wrong. Or perhaps this was not the doctor after all. The driver only made it clear that there was a doctor, that the doctor did not speak English, and that it would be four to six hours before I would be seen, but that I was welcome to wait and make myself comfortable.

"Tell him I need stitches." I pointed to my knee, wrapped in blood-soaked tissue. "You can't wait more than three hours for stitches. Something happens, it coagulates. Besides, it needs to be cleaned."

The driver said something to the bucktoothed man, who shrugged and mumbled something. "He says you can come back tomorrow if you don't want to wait."

I pulled the driver away. "Take me to another hospital."

A piercing scream stopped us in our tracks. Jack was sitting on the floor, his hands on the knees of the pregnant woman, pulling them apart.

"She's going into goddamned labor," he shouted. "Get me a knife! If somebody doesn't help her, I'm going to deliver this baby myself. I was a goddamned medic in the war."

The bucktoothed man walked uncertainly toward Jack, then stopped. He looked at the driver and spoke in Arabic. "It is her husband," the driver translated. "Her husband is sick. There is no baby. She is just fat."

The cab driver asked where he should take us next. "To a bar," Jack shouted. "We need a drink."

I was about to suggest that he go by himself when it occurred to me that a bar, full of international journalists, one of whom had to have sustained an injury serious enough to require emergency treatment, might be just the place to find out where such treatment was available. I directed the driver to Pub 28 and waited in the cab not really expecting Jack to come back, let alone with information, but he did. He also had two bottles of Stella that were actually cold, one of which I gratefully accepted.

Dr. Rashad's 24-hour clinic was right around the corner. Someone named Georges, a music video client of Jack's, happened to be at the bar, and he swore that Dr. Rashad saved Sasha's life, whoever Sasha was. Maybe, I thought, Jack had some redeeming qualities after all.

Sasha must have been a cat, because it turned out to be a veterinary clinic.

Until yesterday, I had been staying in the Marriott Palace Hotel, a guest of the Cairo Television and Radio Festival. The hotel no doubt had a doctor on call for emergencies like this. But the festival had ended last night and I had checked into the very charming but humble Longchamps Hotel. It occupied two floors of a building that also contained law offices, another hotel, and the Sara International Hospital. I cursed myself for failing to remember this hospital until now.

The Sara International Hospital had a majestic door decorated in red and gold. Velvet flowers in an intricate cut-glass bowl sat outside. There was a sign, in English, indicating a button to press for 24-hour emergencies. But there were no lights visible inside, the button did not appear to make any noise, and after no one responded to loud knocks and shouts, we turned away.

"I could break the door down," Jack mused. "I could get enough morphine so you wouldn't feel a thing. In the jungle, when my buddy lost his leg ... "

What jungle? "I thought you sewed his leg back on."

"Hell, that was another buddy."

I told Jack I appreciated all his help but that he could go

home now. It was close to 4 A.M. and I wanted to go to bed.

"Do you have a roommate," he asked, "or should we go to my place?"

I explained again. I wanted to go to bed. Alone.

Jack clutched his bottle of Stella and stared at me as the truth dawned on him. "Stupid bitch," he snarled. "I saved your life. My buddies in the jungle lost their legs! And you know what they did for me?"

I did not want to know. I hobbled as quickly as I could to the tiny elevator, capacity two. The door took a maddeningly long time to close and when it finally did, I could still hear Jack screaming as I moved slowly up to my hotel. He was calling me a communist.

The night clerk who manned Longchamps Hotel's tiny lobby carried me upstairs to my room and I slept until 10 the next morning. Then I called the American Embassy, and the embassy nurse gave me directions to the Shalaan Surgical Center. I asked if Kasr Al-Aini was really Cairo's premier hospital and the nurse assured me that it was, and also that it was the newest.

"But it's ancient," I told her, describing the scene in the emergency room last night. "That's the old Kasr Al-Aini," she explained. "It's a teaching hospital for the very poor. The new Kasr Al-Aini is wonderful."

Raymond went to the Shalaan Surgical Center with me. His fluent Arabic came in handy because the Shalaan Surgical Center in Mohandiseen, across the Nile from Zamalek, is not easy to find; streets there circle and knot up and untangle in unexpected directions, and street numbers defy chronology.

The Shalaan Surgical Center was quiet and immaculate. The marble floors and gold leaf suggested an upscale bordello, as did the only person in sight, a tall, sleek woman in a leather pantsuit that creaked when she walked and who paced the floor speaking in hushed, French-accented English on a cell phone. This small, private hospital for the rich was founded by Dr. Karim Shalaan, an Egyptian doctor who'd gone to medical school in Ann Arbor, Mich., where coincidentally, Raymond had done his graduate work. Raymond congratulated him, in Arabic, on choosing such a fine school.

Dr. Shalaan reciprocated; "How is it you speak such beautiful Arabic?" he asked Raymond. There was no mention of my leg. The conversation then moved to golf, which was Dr. Shalaan's passion. My extensive time spent in Egypt taught me that people there like to make friendly conversation before getting down to business and that it's considered rude to cut to the chase, but I had been chasing doctors for too long and I refused to wait any longer.

"Look at my knee," I told him and hoisted it onto his desk.

Dr. Shalaan glanced at it. "Uh-huh," he nodded. Then he turned to Raymond, not me. "Have you ever been to Dreamland?" Dreamland was Cairo's most luxurious and perhaps only golf course.

I was given a private room and a glass of water. Two nurses were provided to help me change into a surgical gown, and one of them offered to hold my hand while I received seven stitches, in case I was afraid. Everyone spoke perfect English.

I received a bill for 270 U.S. dollars, which my insurance would cover. The bill included the surgeon's fee, plus $3 for the glass of water I'd accepted. The x-rays, taken to see if there was any danger to the bone, cost extra. Dr. Shalaan would call me if they revealed anything serious.

Raymond took me back to my hotel in a taxi. "Dr. Shalaan is a charming man," he said. "I'd like to get to know him better."

I returned to my bed and fell asleep. The ringing phone, which was not by the bed as in most hotels but was across the room, woke me. It took a long, painful time to hop over to answer it. It was Dr. Shalaan.

"Is something wrong?" I asked anxiously. "Did you get the x-rays back?"

"No, no, no," said Dr. Shalaan. "I really enjoyed meeting your friend Raymond. He's very charming. Do you have his number? I'd like to have coffee with him sometime."

When I could walk comfortably, I went back to the scene of the accident on Sayed Bakri Street and looked for the rock that had cut my knee so badly. I remembered where it had happened, in front of Jack's building. I remembered it, gray and sharp as a knife. But I found nothing jutting out of the smooth surface. The two guards who'd been on duty the night of my injury were still on duty. They recognized me, waved and smiled, cheering my recovery. I waved back.

At a party later that week, Jack avoided me, surrounding himself with Marines, young men in their late teens, who wore crew cuts and khakis and tight T-shirts and who largely ignored him when he slung an arm around their shoulders and shouted that they were his good buddies.

"Watch your legs," I shouted at them. "It's a jungle out there!"

Raymond loved telling the story of my accident and told it as if he'd been there all along. Raymond loves drama. "It was as if," he told people, "Brooke was a victim of the street."

Thais That Bind

by Zona Sage

I DESPERATELY NEEDED a massage. Tatia and I had been in the jungle at Khao Yai for days, and our four-hour bus ride out had turned into something twice as long, with a full, harrowing series of near head-on, high-speed collisions. The bus released us late at night in hot and muggy Phitsanulok ("where the hell is that?" we asked each other), too late for the last bus to Sukkothai. And I had a ferocious headache.

Thanks to the perseverance of our tuk-tuk driver (a tuk-tuk is public transportation, something like a tricycle bred with a lawnmower) and despite our protestations, we ended up at the most expensive hotel in town — color television with two channels in English, room service, air conditioning, laundry and a massage service. Perhaps the driver knew that our last bed had been a mattress two inches thick, laid over open coil springs, in a tiny cinderblock room with a single naked 40-watt bulb dangling from the ceiling. The pit toilet had been in a separate building across the mud.

Hot water streamed deliciously from the Western-style shower over my dusty and tense body, a definite improvement over the ladles of icy water that had rinsed us in the jungle. Fortified further with some clean clothes, I got on the telephone and called the hotel massage service. "Please send two massage ladies to room 66 for two hours, for two female clients." I promised Tatia I would treat her, as payment for having dragged her out of her cafes and into the jungle.

Before we met, Tatia had traveled only to genteel destinations

—Paris, southern Spain, Mexico City. I was more adventurous. I had swum in piranha-infested waters up the Amazon, walked around with naked cannibals in the highlands of Irian Jaya, searched for tigers in remote reaches of Java and trekked in the Himalayas of Nepal. Modestly, I could say I was worldly-wise. Three months after we began dating I started testing her travel limits, and we went to the jungles in Costa Rica. It was an introductory course to adventure travel, and I was glad to be able to show her the ropes, to get her feet wet.

She had survived Costa Rica, and a year later we were in Thailand. This would be the true test of her mettle. I would introduce her to a non-Western civilization, a different cultural reality. I enjoyed the mentor role.

The masseuses arrived at our room, both wearing black pants and white shirts. They doffed their thongs at the door. One woman was older and quiet, somewhat tall for a Thai, her black hair falling straight to just below her chin. The other was chirpier, a younger and bouncier woman, whose medium-length black hair was in little curls. They instructed us to take off our sarongs and lie on the gigantic bed, actually two double beds made up as one.

They wanted to watch Thai soap operas on television while they did their massages, but we demurred, saying I couldn't take the noise because of my headache. Our initial conversations with them were brief, since they spoke only a little English, and Tatia and I weren't that proficient with our self-taught Thai.

It was my first Thai massage, and the older woman tending my head gave me the best work-over I'd ever had in my life. There is a long and honored tradition of Thai massage and a highly esteemed massage school at Wat Po, one of the most venerable temples in Bangkok. The techniques employed are different than those in Western-style massage and include massaging with the feet and applying heavy pressure on the blood vessels. At one point during our treatments my masseuse pressed her hand hard into my groin, stopping the blood flow of the femoral artery. After a bit she pulled her hand away quickly and the surge of the blood back into my leg was invigorating. Tatia, a trained nurse, was skeptical of this approach.

The massage ladies were talking to each other in Thai as they massaged us with strong but languid moves. Tatia's younger masseuse in particular was quite chatty. After a while she seemed bored with her friend, bored without the soap operas and she started trying to talk to us. "Shampoo," she giggled. Her friend giggled along with her.

"Shampoo?" we asked. Then she started pointing to things, like her black pants and the bedspread, and telling us words we recognized as the Thai words for the colors. She compared her medium brown skin with the milk-white skin on Tatia's body. Then she pointed to Tatia's deep pink nipples and said, "shampoo" and really giggled. And so we learned the word for pink. Once she started talking about Tatia's "shampoos," the younger masseuse went on to point out other points of interest on Tatia's body, such as her trim waist and full breasts. We didn't understand it all, but the tone was approving. She caressed Tatia's long, wavy, white-blond hair and called it "sexy," using the English word. That we understood.

Tatia was lying on her back, completely naked, her head in the lap of her masseuse. As the massage ended, her masseuse cupped both of Tatia's breasts in her hands, squeezing them a little, and she and the other lady laughed heartily.

After they had gone, Tatia told me she'd felt a little uncomfortable with all the attention on her body. Even with my headache I was able to muster a superior attitude, as I tried to dismiss Tatia's concerns.

"Oh, it's just an East-West thing," I assured her. "When I was in Bali, they always massaged your breasts, even on the beach with people all around, and they just acted so blasé, like they were touching your arm. It means nothing to them."

"Well, it meant something to me. I was embarrassed. After all, she grabbed my breasts, not yours."

The next day, despite the bliss of the previous night's two-hour massage, I remained quite sick with a migraine. Tatia was out exploring the little non-touristy town we now called Pitstop, and I was alone in the room, keeping it dark and quiet. I called down to the massage service again.

The masseuse arrived. In the darkness and in my pained state I didn't pay much attention to her. I explained that I had a headache, and wanted a massage for only that.

After about an hour of massage she began talking to me. She could take me on her motor scooter for a treatment for my headache to a nearby wat (a Buddhist temple) later that afternoon. I was unsure of her, what exactly she meant, and she quickly made the unclear situation murkier.

"I have no husband," she said, "and I have no madam like you do." At this she put her index fingers together, parallel to each other. Although I had never encountered the gesture before, something of its meaning was conveyed to me in the way her eyes lingered on me through her dark eyelashes. A small "uh-oh" sounded in my brain.

"Men are no good," she continued.

"Did you have a husband?" I asked her. She nodded yes, looking glum.

"What happened to your husband?" I asked.

She ran her finger across her throat, making a ripping sound. Oh, great, I thought. She slit his throat, and now she wants me to go away with her on her motor scooter.

I tried to convey to her that I could not agree to go to the wat with her, that I would have to talk to my friend.

OK, she would come back at 4:30 to take me to the wat for treatments.

To my relief, she left. A little while later Tatia returned, bearing gifts from the world of Pitstop—beautifully fragrant tiny blessing leis of white flowers and purple ribbons, which I hung on the bedpost beside my head, along with medicines from the local pharmacy. The cool moist perfume of the flowers reminded me of gardenias and I felt blessed.

I told Tatia of my encounter with the masseuse while she was gone and how she wanted to take me to a wat for further treatments. Suddenly, my feminine Tatia turned into Barbara Stanwyck. "You ain't goin' nowhere, honey," she said in her Jewish-Western accent, "especially not with no madam-hunting little Thai masseuse." Tatia in chaps and fringe and serious boots flashed before my eyes, and I heard the crack of her whip.

"She's going to be here at 4:30," I said.

"And so will I."

"Maybe this is one of those cultural misunderstanding things," I said, not sure who I was trying to convince.

"Show me again how she put her fingers when she said that thing about you having a madam."

I complied.

"Nope, no misunderstanding, my little madam. I'm staying right here."

At 4:30 sharp there was a knock on the door. I cowered in bed, and Tatia let the masseuse in. Basic words of Thai and English went back and forth. Tatia conveyed to her that I was too sick to go get well at the wat, and the masseuse left.

"That was Ms. Shampoo, my masseuse from last night! I

told you something was going on with her," Tatia remonstrated.

"God, I was so sick I didn't notice it was your masseuse."

The next day I continued to languish in the room, and Tatia brought me steamed jasmine rice and custard from the outside world. I held the bowl of rice and the warm aroma of jasmine caressed my face. The silky blandness of the custard slithered down my throat. Thus strengthened, I called the massage service again and this time quite carefully clarified that I wanted the same woman as I'd had the first night. I was relieved when she showed up.

Through the entire massage, Tatia sat beside the bed, reading her novel, saying nothing, acting as if she weren't paying the least bit of attention.

My masseuse gave another excellent massage.

After she left I said to Tatia, "You know, I never thought I'd need a bodyguard to get a massage."

Tatia looked at me over her glasses, and a slow smile grew on her face. She chuckled, a chuckle I would hear again when we returned home, whenever someone asked if we'd had any trouble with the men in Thailand.

What a Kick

by Cameron M. Burns

THE SUMMER OF 1998 was a strange one, at least in terms of weather. Meteorologists said that the continental United States was suffering from a post-El Niño weather phenomenon known as La Niña and predicted several weather patterns as a result. In Colorado it manifested itself in long periods of extremely hot, dry weather, punctuated by multiday periods of monsoon-like downpours.

In early July, my wife and I, along with two friends, undertook a four-day trek through the Hunter-Fryingpan Wilderness, a remote, little-known area of high mountains and swampy river valleys just west of the Continental Divide. It rained on us every day, and by the time we reached the trailhead at the upper end of the Fryingpan Valley, we were ready for home. I was determined not to venture out again.

But a few days later, a friend and neighbor, Bob Ward, called and asked if I was interested in another four-day trek, this time through the wilderness area directly south of my Basalt home.

Bob had long wanted to traverse the flagship wilderness area in Colorado, the Maroon Bell-Snowmass Wilderness Area. Even though I had just returned from a soggy wilderness trek, I was eager to go. As is so often the case with many of us who live in and around ski resorts, we never seem to bother with exploring our own backyards.

As we prepared for our trek, I got a wild idea. I had recently been rejected from entering Tahiti by the French government because of my Australian citizenship and was nursing a sort of personal anti-France grudge. For the most part, this campaign was manifested in my switching to California wines (which are better anyway), and not eating truffles (which I didn't do anyway, although the statement of boycott sounded good). When the French won the 1998 World Cup soccer tournament over the highly favored Brazilian team, I was incensed.

So, I asked myself, what could I do to out-soccer the French, to show French soccer stars like Emmanuel Petit, Laurent Blanc and Zinadine Zidane that they weren't the most creative players on Earth? The idea of dribbling a soccer ball across 15 miles of rugged mountains in Central Colorado was a sure, albeit demented, bet.

So, when Bob and his wife, Elizabeth, picked me up for the ride to the trailhead, I explained my pointless plan: to dribble a size four soccer ball from the southern trailhead in Lead King Basin, near the tiny town of Marble, Colorado, through to the Snowmass Creek trailhead, on the northern side of the wilderness area, near the town of Basalt. Over high mountain passes, across streams and rivers, over snowfields and across scree slopes, all without ever touching the ball with my hands.

Neither Bob nor Elizabeth could believe the plan. It was too wacky, even for these creative, uninhibited people. But, as they always did, they just let me do my thing and laughed out loud when I produced a tartan cap with tufts of fake red hair attached to it: "It ain't a soccer match without a few soccer hooligans along!" I said, explaining that the rowdiest hooligans were the Scots.

After we had dumped our packs on the roadside, Bob rode back along the rough four-wheel-drive road for several miles with Elizabeth to make sure she would be able to get the truck over some particularly nasty sections of road.

I picked up my pack, slung it over my shoulder, then wound

my foot back and let fly with a loud "whump." The ball flew up into the air, then bounced across some grass and came to rest in some weeds, 10 yards away. I hiked over to it and kicked again. Another whump, and another 10 yards. I continued up a small hill where the road petered out as it came to the trailhead, at the very edge of the wilderness. Since Bob was still with Elizabeth, I decided to descend to our drop off point and ferry his pack up to the wilderness edge. I then waited around for 15 minutes, hoping that Bob would return and photograph the ball's first "touch" on this epic and historic journey. Half an hour later, when Bob still hadn't turned up, I booted the ball up the trail and the game ("ding-ding") was underway.

I dribbled the ball while ferrying the packs for about a half-mile up the gently sloping trail. For the most part, it was easy work. The sides of the rail were lined with three-foot tall weeds, so the ball had a sort of gutter to roll along inside. Every 30 feet or so, I'd take a nice swing and punt it with my toe; the ball would rise, then drop, usually inside the grass gutter, then roll along a few more feet before coming to rest on an incongruity in the trail. Piece of cake, I thought.

However, 20 minutes later when Bob finally caught up with me, laughing hysterically at my antics, the vegetation along the trail was beginning to thin. We were probably around 10,000 feet in elevation, and the trail's edges were becoming rockier and rockier. Every time the ball hit a rock, it bounced wildly in all directions. To add to the challenge, the trail was contouring across a slope. There was a steep slope to our right (Meadow Mountain), and a creek-filled gully to our left (the Silver Creek Drainage). Once every half dozen or so kicks the rambunctious ball would bounce off a rock and go flying down into the gully, which meant I had to take my pack off and go dribble it out of the gully and back to the trail with my feet.

Regardless, we made good progress. By noon we were beginning the steep climb up towards a high pass between the Crystal River drainage to the south and the Avalanche Creek drainage to the north. The higher we crept up the pass, the more rugged the terrain. I was keeping the ball close to my feet, trying to prevent it from taking a long roll back down the pass. The technique worked, although had it been a real game, my teammates would've beaten me senseless and thrown my body in front of a speeding Metro for hogging the ball. After dribbling uphill for half a mile or so, Bob and I finally reached the crest of the divide. Only 100 feet or so separated me from our first major obstacle. But that 100 feet was taken up by a steep snowfield, sitting square in the middle of the pass. I took my pack off and placed it on a granite outcrop. Then, I began climbing a deep cleft between the outcrop and the snowfield, a sort of narrow gash that allowed me to exercise some kind of control over the ball. Near the top of the snowfield, however, disaster struck. I stumbled momentarily, fell forward onto my hands, and the evil ball slipped out between my feet. It then rolled down across the snow, bounced off a rock, and plunged some 500 feet down the pass.

I sat down for a moment and nearly cried. All that work for naught. Bob, who had been gazing at the vista on the north side of the pass, wandered over and asked where the ball was. I pointed down the side we had just climbed.

"Wow," he said, "that sucks!"

"Och! Wait here," I said, dumping my pack on the ground next to Bob. "I'll be beck, laddie!"

I scrambled down the south side of the pass and found the defiant leather orb in the middle of a flat, slushy snowfield. I heartily booted it into a gully running alongside the snowfield. It bounced around a few times, then came to rest behind a cluster of rocks. I worked the thing free with my feet and carefully started up the steepest section of the pass for a second time. As the hill steepened, it became increasingly difficult to control. At times I found myself on all fours, my palms planted in the gravel while my feet rolled the miscreant sphere, inch-by-inch, up the hill. After 20 minutes of tricky maneuvering, I had crested the divide.

"Woohoo!" I yelled, ecstatic. "One down, two to go."

Bob pointed at the terrain in front of us, which made me realize just how idiotic the task I'd created for myself really was. An enormous sweeping valley, the upper Avalanche Creek drainage, dropped off below us and swept across roughly five miles of moraines, creeks and snowfields. The terrain was a jumble of steep rises and dramatic drop-offs, all interlaced with drainages lying at impossible angles. I gazed at the landscape, taking it in on a step-by-step, kick-by-kick basis. The gray sky began to leak a light rain.

"Och laddy!" I said to myself. "What's wrong with my genes? They didn't get filtered properly from one generation to the next! I duu the damndest things sometimes."

Still, I let fly with a massive wallop and booted the ball into the air. It traced a long arc, then rolled several hundred feet down a snowfield. Bob and I loaded up our packs, and we were off.

This particular downhill run, about a mile and a half, was fairly straightforward. Our line of descent followed the fall line, and keeping the ball going was pretty easy. But when we reached the bottom of the valley and began traversing, things quickly became tedious. The ball had a physicist's sense of gravity, and with each kick—no matter how big or small— would fly straight for 10 yards, then hit something (a rock, a patch of dirt, Bob's head) and take off down the valley to the northwest like a frightened dove.

It became a murderous task. Constant retrieval was followed by constant loss. My legs were doing about four times the amount of travel they would have done had I simply hiked through the wilderness. The incessant rain made the scree loose and the grass slick. But I was determined to show Zinadine Zidane (France's top goal scorer in 1998) a thing or two. (Too bad he wasn't watching.)

Of course, Bob is a sensible fellow and had pretty much ignored my bizarre, neurotic soccer game from the outset. Although he had booted the ball several times in our first three miles, by the time we hit the first pass, he was content to watch, and laugh. And, he beat a fast time toward our next camp, in the Avalanche Lake area. As the afternoon progressed, I began to lag considerably behind Bob. By 3 P.M. he was at least a mile ahead of me. I picked up the pace of my dribbling to catch up.

Halfway across the upper Avalanche Creek drainage, the trail went through a swamp as it traversed the southeastern end of the valley. Although I had to walk in shin-deep, freezing water, the spastic sphere was much easier to control. With each kick, it splashed down in the tangled weeds and remained perfectly in place, until I could come along and boot it again. The bog, despite my mud-encased boots and frozen feet, was the best part of my vast dribble. The terrain remained relatively flat for a couple of miles, and the No. 4 Mitre ball (is Mitre a French company? I had to wonder) behaved like a little angel. I even caught up with Bob, who had stopped to study a few points on the map.

"Where to next?" I asked confidently as I arrived at Bob's feet.

"It looks like the trail skirts that rocky hill, then drops into the next valley," he said, pointing north.

I studied the view grimly. The land not only became incredibly tilted (i.e. perfect for a deviant soccer ball to roll to Redstone, a town about 10 miles down the valley on the northwest side of the wilderness area) but the trail, though perfectly flat, worked its way through a chaotic jumble of boulder fields. In fact, the trail was bounded on either side by rocks. One over-indulgent touch of the ball along this section of track and it would bounce to kingdom come or maybe even Grand Junction.

"Aye-yay-yae!" I said, wiping my brow. So far, we had come roughly five miles. Well, five miles if one followed the trail. In my nomadic-soccer-ball-shepherding trek, I'd probably covered about 20.

We continued across the boggy flats and aimed for the chaotic jumble of boulder fields. Within a few boots of the ball, it had bounded down several hundred feet of cliff into the drainage below. I dropped my pack and descended after it. Then, using as much patience as I could muster, I dragged the thing by my feet back up to the trail. This process, which took the better part of 15 minutes, was followed by 100 feet of dribbling along the flat trail until another pointed boulder punched my ball down the drainage again. I dumped the pack and scrambled down the valley to retrieve it. By the time I got back, I could see Bob on the crest of the next pass, the one that would drop us down to Avalanche Lake. He stood watching me for a few minutes, then dropped out of sight.

I longed for camp. I dreamed of relaxing in the tent. I wanted to stop beating myself up on these mad scrambles to fetch the game ball, which filled my boots with rocks and mashed my shins to pulp.

I reached the trail sometime close to dark. My nerves were shot. It began raining again. I sat down next to my pack and eyed the trail ahead. More of the same. After a few minutes rest, I set to work anyway, doing everything humanly possible to keep the spastic projectile from launching again. In the end, my concentration was my undoing. Inching along the flat trail, I was so intent on studying the snowfield that lay ahead that I didn't notice when the ball slipped between my feet and began bouncing away. It bounced madly, like you've never seen a ball bounce. Bouncing the way pigs will, when they fly. Within a few high-speed seconds, my wilderness World Cup was over.

I sat down on my pack and almost wept. Everything I'd worked so hard for had resulted in this horrifying defeat.

And so it was. I hadn't the mental fortitude to flail down another quarter mile of scree slope, as I'd done a dozen times before, to go and locate my ball. I didn't have the wherewithal to keep going.

I caught up with Bob a half-hour later and we continued on for the next few days, camping in La Niña's bountiful rains and even climbing Capitol Peak en route to the trailhead, enjoying one of the finest wilderness treks I've ever experienced. We returned totally happy, safe, and really felt as though we'd experienced the area we live in the way it should be experienced, not just as a pretty view that the typical vacationer gets from his Aspen condo or from a bus window that down-valley workers get as they're transported upvalley to resort jobs.

As for the dribbling challenge, it remains to be met. The 15-odd miles of rugged terrain could easily be dribbled, but the successful party will have to show fortitude, cunning and even a bit of daring to get through the rock bands at the head of Avalanche Creek. It remains a challenge for future mountaineers, future World Cup players and future knuckleheads with a lot of time on their hands.

And when they come and seek my advice, I'll advise a lobotomy. It requires a big sharp point.

Real Pain in Vietnam

by Kent Foster

SEVEN BACKPACKERS, three solo travelers and two couples got together in Saigon at the Prince Hotel to rent a van. We had an eight-day itinerary that would bring us far up the coast to Hue.

In the provincial capital of Nha Trang we spent some extra money on a boat trip, so our guide, whose only activity seemed to be getting drunk, took us to an ugly island with an ugly beach where we ate some little fishes for lunch. Trying to make the most of it, we took one last swim before it was time to head back. We were frolicking in the cool water when Anniken, an athletic teenage Norwegian, tried to jump on my back. Normally I welcome athletic teenage Norwegians jumping on my back, but with her weight on me I was pushed down to the ocean floor and on to some sea urchins whose needles shot up into my feet.

I managed to dog paddle to shore and walrus myself on to the pebbly beach. While sandflies swirled around me, two of those on the trip, Mike and Marie, examined my foot. I was fortunate that one of these Brits was an anesthetist and the other a nurse. Although the initial pain had subsided, I had to get the needles removed for fear of infection. I had 10 in one foot and three in the other. Mike tried pulling at one with tweezers and I tried with my fingernails, but neither worked, so I resigned myself to a hospital visit. Mike and another member of the group, a Swedish guy named Ola, decided that they couldn't miss this spectacle, so they helped me along.

Everyone at the hospital was taken with the sight of a Westerner wearing a huge, pink, happy face T-shirt tripping along with his entourage. Our guide eventually appeared and wobbled to the back of the waiting room, hoping we'd forget about him. A Dr. Hoa entered and sat at a desk. I swallowed. He looked like a kid, tall and gangly, but totally expressionless as he said, "Please tell me what I should do for you." He followed this in language that our guide, unable to emerge from his brandy cloud, didn't bother to try and translate.

The doctor finally said from behind his desk and without looking at my feet—if he even knew my feet were the problem—"you need minor operation." And so we trudged down to the operating room, which like "guide" proved to be a misnomer. It was open with a cement floor and had a metal operating table with rusting legs. Next to it was a small table and a lamp. The bottom half of the walls were bright green, the top blue and all were peeling. To ensure optimum bleakness, the windows were painted over in green.

There was some animated discussion about what should be done as we struggled to understand Dr. Hoa's English, and soon the ordeal turned into a farce. Mike asked how he was going to take out the needles and the doctor seriously replied, "With medical instruments." Oh. While we were waiting for these "medical instruments" to be sterilized we had a chat with the doctor. I immediately stuck my foot in my mouth when I asked if Ola could take a photo of us because I'd never seen a doctor wear rubber sandals. He agreed but added that he wore sandals because he was poor. I felt nauseous; it was such a stupid thing for me to say. Somehow I got out of it as Mike distracted him with questions about Vietnamese medical training and he even got the doctor to smile.

Zero hour came and they laid me on my stomach on the cold table. An incredibly evil nurse, I'd soon learn, started putting alcohol on the wounds with a used yellow and red cotton ball. She then moved a light and it went out. We all turned to the outlet. Instead of a plug there were two open wires. Ola, an electrician, cringed as he took one of the wires and tried to push it through the outlet hole to make it stay. I thought it was funny at the time, but Ola later told me if he grabbed the hot wire, put it in the hole and touched me on the metal table, we could have both been in for a jolt.

Instead of Novocain they decided to use a fluid that numbs the wound and feels like ice. However, it wears off after a short while and they have to reapply it. The nurse was to do the work while the doctor supervised. The doctor came over to my end of the table so I could see him. He leaned over nearer to my head and again with this absolute poker face said slowly, the English trickling out, "Call me when you have pain."

The nurse put on some of this numbing fluid and began the incisions. I believe the idea was to cut a little around the dark spots, the embedded needles, to get at the tips and then pull them out. However, not much time would pass before the magic fluid wore off. "Pain!" I'd yell, and the doctor would dutifully pass on my message to the nurse. This worked for maybe two repetitions, but then the pair became oblivious and ignored me. I had to have Mike tell the doctor to tell the nurse to put on more fluid.

By this time they'd sent away our guide because he was being obnoxious and smelled like a distillery.

I was developing deep feelings of vindictiveness each time this nurse kept digging away in spite of my yelling. She was in her own world, impervious to any words from me. Several times I shrieked, "Pain!! Pain!!" and the nurse would continue knifing away like she was paid per cut. The doctor, engrossed in her work, eventually came around to me to say, "Ah, I know. You're calling me in pain," and then the nurse would begrudgingly apply more fluid. (At one point Mike asked if Vietnamese patients were as loud as I was. The doctor said that Vietnamese yell much louder. Emboldened by this—anything to try and get the nurse to respond—I raised it an octave.)

The nurse began to put the fluid on one spot and cut on another, sending me through the roof. I was writhing on the table, but my ranting "PAIN!! PAIN!!" went unheeded several times until Mike intervened and showed her where to put the fluid. Dr. Hoa came by. "You're calling me in pain," he confirmed. "YES!! I'm calling you in pain! Stop that witch!"

Another time the doctor came over, showed a smile and with raised eyebrows said in his even voice, "I think you are in terrible pain." I spared him some choice words. I couldn't help but laugh—until the butcher began again. She was unstoppable. Ultimately, we decided to forego the fluid and resort to Novocain injections for the remaining needles. As this was being prepared, we suddenly noticed four scruffy guys with ragged clothes, cyclo drivers, I'd thought, standing in a row, silently enjoying this free theater. Mike asked who they were and the doctor, eternally undisturbed, looked over and said, "They're patients." Was it a stupid question? Is observing agony a Vietnamese right? I couldn't handle it and they were ushered out, not that they were any less sterile than the room.

The Novocain had to be injected next to each place to be worked on. They did a practice jab on my arm to see if I had a bad reaction. Dr. Hoa said, "Now you have AIDS." Yeah, very funny, Doc.

The Novocain injections were the worst, resulting in unbridled screaming. It was quicker, though, and near the end the doctor came over one last time to this sweaty, palpitating mass I'd become, let out a little smile and said slowly, "I think . . . this is impressive experience for you."

Hold the Salad

by Julia Niebuhr Eulenberg

WE WERE IN LONDON, at the end of my first trip to England. Even though my husband had been here before, he had left much of the planning of this trip up to me. I had depended heavily on our local bookstore, and ultimately we had followed author Rick Steves' advice. He had eased our entry into England with the warning that we should leave Heathrow and travel west immediately, never even thinking about going into London first.

Try Bath, he suggested. It's good for the soul, perfect for recovering from jet lag and not a bad place to be in any case. So, at Heathrow, we found our luggage, picked up our rail passes and caught a bus to Reading. From there, we took the train to Bath. The city was perfect. We had a lovely hotel, and we trained for all the walking that would take place over the next three weeks by exploring many inches of Bath.

We hadn't followed Steves every step of the way but had decided to end the trip with another of his recommendations. Back in London, we would take lunch at the "palatial Criterion Restaurant ... a world away from the punk junk of Piccadilly Circus." Though I can no longer prove it, I also seemed to remember his having said that, though expensive, the restaurant was worth the cost and that even he sometimes splurged by eating a meal there.

The Criterion is one of several restaurants designed by a young Yorkshire native who, in his early days, wouldn't have been allowed in the homes of any of the rich and elegant who chose to dine in his establishments. We walked into a dimmed room, so dim in fact that I had to check twice to be sure I'd taken off my sunglasses. I had. We were probably already in trouble. My husband prefers to dine where he can see the food. As a result, we do not have a dimmer switch in our dining room.

Two young women clad in black elegance greeted us at the desk. "Two?" one of them asked, eyeing our less than elegant tourist clothing and bags.

"Yes," we concurred. "And might you have a nonsmoking section?"

"No," they murmured, "But if someone is smoking next to your table, we can move you."

With that, we were led past an occasional table of diners. These were women dressed in elegant suits and little black dresses and a few men in suits. We were seated at a table near the back of the restaurant, directly across from the kitchen doors. Few would need to pass our table and be astonished at our choice of luncheon clothing, unless they needed to go to the restroom.

The waiter suggested several options, all verging on a full meal, which neither of us really wanted. I ordered a Caesar salad, "without the bacon, please," I said firmly, looking up at the waiter. A few days earlier I had made the same request to a steward on the train, and he had recommended against it. "Without the bicon, it's pintless. There's only a few bits of lettuce otherwise." I forbore telling him—*or* the waiter at the Criterion—that no self-respecting "traditional" Caesar salad—which both menus proclaimed—would dream of containing bacon. In any case, the Criterion's waiter had no problem with my request, perhaps because there were also anchovies on the salad, thus eliminating the problem of only a few bits of lettuce.

By the time our order had been taken, a young lad had arrived with our silverware and glasses. He then went on to set several empty tables around us. The sounds of clinking glassware and silver suddenly made the restaurant sound fuller, as if a new luncheon crowd had just been seated, even though we were as few as ever.

As soon as we had placed our meal order and requested a bottle of sparkling water, the lad was back to remove the wine glasses. Meanwhile, a maiden was proffering bread from a large basket.

"Yes," I said. "I'd like a piece." But when I inquired about a bread plate, I was told there weren't bread plates and I should just put it on the tablecloth. Right! Wine glass, water glass, two forks, two knives, hovering waiters and other minions—and the bread goes on the table.

My husband ordered two starters, rather than a full meal—risotto with saffron and a Salade Nicoise. I ordered only the Caesar salad. I finished my salad and he his risotto, and then we waited for the large staff to clear these dishes away and bring his salad. During the long interim, we had a great deal to watch.

Tables were cleared, breadcrumbs were scraped with small metal scrapers into waiters' hands, bread was proffered and glasses were moved, added and removed. Silver was rearranged and patted in place. Napkins were folded and placed just so. Sometimes this action took place at our own table; sometimes the rearranging was done at nearby tables. It was, in short, a perfectly choreographed dance better suited to the Mad Hatter's Tea Party than to an efficiently run restaurant.

The ceiling was quite lovely, a point Steves had made. It was composed of mosaics of unknown design and some gilt ones so that the whole effect was one of sparkling highlights in a seeming effort to defeat the low-wattage lamps directed upward at them.

A young man whisked away our clean plates. Another poured one glass and then another from our water bottle, until finally it was empty. Someone else arrived to remove it. The bread basket girl attempted to remove my bread, which I had carelessly placed on the butter plate, unwilling to put it on the table, despite her gentle recommendation.

Still no salad. My husband was beginning to wonder what was happening, and we were starting to snicker. All this meaningless activity and no one was really *serving* us! And then, for a moment, we got our hopes up. A young man came up to our table, but it's no good, it can't be the salad because he's wearing the wrong color of coat. He's dressed only in white; the waiters have all worn black. Indeed, he had come merely to scrape unwanted breadcrumbs from our table.

I resisted looking at my husband until the white-coated minion had left, then commented, "I knew it; I *knew* that was next!"

In the midst of all this elegance and fine food, two mild odors hovered, like the waiters. Cigarette smoke wafted gently toward us from two tables away—a cigarette held discreetly so it would annoy no one at its own table, but aimed toward the rest of us. The other odor made us wonder even more about the state of mind of the management. I asked the way to the restroom. A young lady pointed the way and said, "I'm afraid you'll have to use the gents', they're painting the women's."

Left unsaid, but possibly revealed in the surprise on my face, was the thought "In the middle of the day? When the restaurant is open and serving meals?"

All I said was that I wouldn't mind if I didn't have to share.

But when I passed the door and saw a man entering, it was quite clear that I might have to. So I simply kept walking until I reached the ladies' room. Two men stood in front of it, one wearing a white waiter's coat, the other a polo shirt.

"Hello, 'Moddom', mind the paint. It's wet. Only the black paint, 'Moddom'!"

I minded the paint and managed not to get any on myself. Meantime, the painters had moved on to the gents'. One can only hope that this was quick-drying paint since the dinner hour was fast approaching and a more elegantly and expensively dressed clientele might not want to be expected to mind the paint. All this meant that eventually my husband had to use the ladies' room.

He returned to the table and commented, "This place is getting on my nerves."

Are you still waiting in suspense for him to receive his salad? I have kept nothing from you. We were still waiting too.

Suddenly a black-coated waiter appeared at our table, as the gentle moving of silver and glassware at empty tables continued in the background. "Would you like anything more?" he inquired.

In civilized tones, my husband said, "I'd like what I ordered, the Salade Nicoise."

The waiter reeled slightly, then recovered, apologized and with quick hand movements set the others in motion again. Out of nowhere appeared silverware. Someone asked, "Would you like more water, something else to drink, perhaps?"

The large green bottle of mineral water had long since been emptied and removed. "No, we wouldn't," we replied.

A butter plate reappeared, and then the basket girl bearing bread. My husband took one, I declined.

As yet another waiter hovered, my husband requested a

dessert menu and said, "She will be having dessert, and we'll want it served with my salad so she won't have to wait, watch me eat and then be served."

"Oh, yes, sir, sorry, sir." The black-coated waiter came over, reassured my husband it would be just a moment for the salad—"terribly sorry, sir"—and took my order for a lemon tart.

Truth to tell, the tart, like the rest of the food, was very good. Creamy and lemony, the way a true lemon pie should be. Real anchovies, fresh, white flesh, skin still on them and delicately flavored, not tinned or brined, had topped the Caesar salad, along with delicate slices of fine Parmesan cheese. A real piece of freshly cooked tuna sat atop the Salade Nicoise. Strands of real saffron had been arrayed on top of the risotto. The silver was heavy, yet comfortable to use. The salt and pepper shakers stood on four little feet. The napkins and cloths were white and nicely starched.

In other words, the cooking was first class, and the milieu was that of a fine restaurant. I'm sure the service was intended to fit this mode as well. The problem was that it was so overdone as to be preposterous, pompous and annoying. Maintaining our own good American manners, we waited until we were outside in the more raucous space of Piccadilly Circus to look at each other and snort derisively. It was certainly, since we were in a good frame of mind and not starving, worth the experience. But it was most definitely not the experience we had expected.

The Ryokan Experience

by Loretta Graziano Breuning

I HAD MY HEART set on spending a night in a traditional Japanese inn. I'd heard that ryokan are hard for foreigners to navigate, but as a professor of international business, I fancied myself a pro at inter-cultural wrangling. Though a veteran traveler, I was making my first trip as a trailing spouse. My husband was meeting with physicists at the University of Utsunomiya, and I had nothing to do but plan the perfect country retreat, with the assistance of a department secretary to boot.

First, I researched the perfect destination. A nearby town called Mashiko is the home of the Japanese rustic ceramics movement. The book said it was bursting with merry potters spinning the endless array of tiny dishes you see in Japanese restaurants. According to the book, you rent bicycles to wander from one treasure trove to the next. I asked the secretary for a ryokan in Mashiko. Each of us only spoke a few dozen words of the other's language, but I sensed that my project was being discouraged.

She thinks I don't understand the ryokan experience, I thought. I know the drill: You take off your shoes, you sleep on the floor, and you eat raw egg on rice. Maybe you use other people's bath water. Maybe you pay more for less. But you immerse completely in tradition. Whether her misgivings were real or just my imagination, the secretary made reservations and our ever-gracious Japanese hosts raised the problem of transportation. Perhaps the physicists' search for a cheap, limitless energy source should be interrupted to drive the American colleague and his pushy wife to Mashiko. Not necessary, I insisted. Japanese public transportation is part of the adventure.

That night, over a lavish traditional banquet in nearby Nikko, they gave us copious instructions for the journey ahead and deposited us in a historic hotel where Albert Einstein had been a guest. We stayed in the room President U.S. Grant slept in, though it had been retrofitted with a Japanese paperless, water-squirting toilet. The control panel on the toilet was essential, and I will never again go to the bathroom without my reading glasses.

The next morning we got a dose of Japanese financial realities. The hotel bill was $320. Then, the desk clerk said the train station could only be reached by taxi, so we spent $11 for what would have been a five-minute walk. Ahead lay a train back to Utsunomiya, a cross-town trip from the train station to the bus station and a bus ride to Mashiko. In Japan, connections are quick and the seats are comfortable. But Japanese trains are priced like planes, and buses charge like cabs. When you get on a bus, you take a ticket that identifies your zone; the fare for each zone rachets up every couple of minutes on a big meter in the front of the bus. We spent $80 to cover 40 miles.

When we got off the bus in Machiko, a shopkeeper pointed us the way. We didn't understand her directions, but in a small town like this, how could you miss what we believed would be an architectural gem of rough-hewn timber surrounded by sculpted gardens? Unfortunately, reality didn't meet expectation.

Seeing nothing that matched that description, we kept walking until suddenly the shopkeeper ran up behind us. She had seen us pass our destination and ran until she caught us, then led us back to an ordinary storefront that, as it turns out, was our ryokan.

We stepped inside and beheld its linoleum floors and fake-paneled walls. It seemed dark and cold, and in point of fact it was barely heated and barely lit. Energy conservation is central to the ryokan experience.

A ryokan stay traditionally begins with Japanese tea and sweets brought to the weary travelers' room. In this case, the sweets were Halloween-size Nestle's Crunch, served by a woman in a polyester jogging suit with an apron over it. Instead of lingering over tea, we rushed out to see the sights. But it was almost 5 P.M., and in a few minutes all the shops closed and the last rays of December sunlight vanished. We tried strolling on pitch-dark country roads, finally retreating to our room by 5:30.

I had envisioned the room in an idyllic setting, but you don't see the setting once you're inside, I told myself. The room had no uniquely Japanese features except the regulation straw-matted floor. There was an advertising poster where the traditional scroll would hang, and a television that had to be fed with 100-yen coins (about a buck) every 15 minutes. We decided against TV. The news was only in Japanese, anyway, and we had wearied of guessing the news from the facial expressions of Al Gore and George Bush. (Back home, the Supreme Court had just stopped the vote counting in Tallahassee.)

We saw a heater, and there were control knobs everywhere, but you'd have to be a physicist to figure it out. Fortunately, one of us was a physicist, and I patted myself on the back for marrying him. We put on the cotton yukata and woolen robes, and were ready to lay back and read. But where? Futons were in the closet, but it's taboo to take them out before dinner. The room was empty except for four very thin seat cushions around a low table. It was just enough for a cushion each under the head, and another between the spine and the tatami mat. Not the lap of luxury, but free time with a novel is precious.

My head was near the heater, and in a few minutes my eyes dried up. I reversed position, but now I was staring into a bare light bulb. The far side of the room was cold, and the middle was taken up with the table that my husband thought we shouldn't move. I tried laying on my side, but my tennis elbow hurt and I couldn't steady the book. Each time I changed position, the clothing came undone. This provoked another etiquette crisis.

According to the guidebook, you shock the Japanese if you tie the kimono the wrong way because only corpses in Japan are tied left-over-right, or was that right-over left?

My husband had his own problem keeping the long dangling kimono sleeves from obscuring the page he was holding.

Dinner arrived. I was glad to see tempura among the many small plates. It was cold—another ryokan experience. Cold grease goes with red wine, I thought, and rummaged through my suitcase for that half-empty airline bottle of Burgundy. Or was it half full?

After dinner, I got up to use the rest room. When I opened our door, an artic blast rushed under my robes. The unisex bathroom was so dimly lit that I could not have seen any man at the urinal until I was upon him. I started worrying about middle-of-the-night urgencies and regretted all the tea I'd drunk with dinner. Managing all those layers of loose robes in a Japanese-style toilet did not come naturally, either.

Then it was bath time. We were led past a utility sink full of dinner dishes. I knew the Japanese routine of sitting on a stool to wash and rinse before entering the tub, but I hadn't imagined my feet on an icy cold floor in a dark room. It was no time for deferred maintenance on hairy legs. The bath was nice, but because I get dizzy in hot tubs, I got less therapeutic relaxation than the guidebook advised. All too soon, I was bolting through frigid corridors back to our cell. En route, I noticed one empty dinner tray and a beer can outside the door next to the rest room.

Apparently, the only other guest in the place was a single drinking man situated between the toilet and me.

The futons had been laid out in our room, and the bath lulled us into unconsciousness. In the morning, trays of seaweed and pickles and other dishes were brought to the door. While we slurped down clams in broth, we scraped together the cash to pay the hotel bill—credit cards are not accepted, and there was no internationally linked ATM in town. Then we walked off in search of art and craft—no bicycles in sight in the wintry cold. The town of Mashiko looked much like every place else, which is what you expect in a country that rebuilt itself in the span of a decade. Most of the pottery had a standardized '70s look, with millennial prices. The crafts museum was closed for the day.

Soon, we agreed that we'd had enough of the ryokan experience, and it was time to move on. I had my heart set on spending a night in one of Japan's famous "love hotels."

One Step Ahead of Trouble

by Neal Sanders

IN APRIL 1986, my wife and I set off for an 18-day trip to Europe. I was attending a conference in Monaco and we planned to use that as a jumping off point for stays in Paris and Vienna.

My conference went smoothly until the third day, when we turned on the TV hoping to catch the Celtics score from the night before. Instead, we saw a newscaster with a worried look on his face. Behind him was a map of the Mediterranean. "We've just received word that the last plane has landed safely," he said. My wife and I looked at each another: What's this all about?

The U.S. had just bombed Libya.

The conference never re-convened that morning. Instead, armed guards appeared in the hallways. In hours, the hotel was deserted. We took off ourselves. Avignon provided a pleasant respite, but in Paris bombs were going off as factions protested either the bombing or France's involvement, non-involvement or perceived complicity. When our sleep was shattered by an explosion less than a block away, we knew it was time to get out of town.

We drove up to Chantilly, enjoyed the royal stables and had lunch at a fine restaurant. Love those Brittany oysters. That night, my wife said she wasn't feeling well. At 3 in the morning, she was violently ill. The oysters! She was gallant for a day, claiming she was feeling better. She wasn't. The next day, we hailed a taxi and asked to be taken to the American Hospital.

Outside the hospital, French soldiers were running mirrors under every car and searching all occupants. Two hours later, we saw a doctor, who gave her the necessary medicine and shots.

Two days later, she was well enough to travel, and we set off by train for Vienna. That morning, I was feeling queasy. Somewhere near Munich, I was afraid I was going to die. Sixteen hours later, our oft-delayed train pulled into Vienna. I felt so sick I was afraid I wasn't going to die. For the next three days, I stayed in bed, whimpering.

Finally, I felt well enough to go out and enjoy Vienna in late April. We enjoyed three fine days. A Viennese gentleman explained that we were the beneficiaries of a "foehn"; instead of the cold wind blowing down from the north, we were getting a warmer, drier breeze from out of the east, from ... Chernobyl! Yes, three days earlier, Chernobyl had blown up, sending clouds of radiation across the Ukraine, Czechoslovakia, Hungary and Austria. The morning we flew home, the *International Herald-Tribune* featured a map showing who was getting the most fallout. Eastern Austria was right up there with Kiev. We were subjected to radiation checks in Zurich where we changed planes, and the Geiger Counter clicked away as we filed off the airplane.

We were never so happy to get home from a vacation. The remarkable thing, though, was that with the passage of time, it now ranks as one of our most memorable trips anywhere in the world.

Now, did I tell you the one about the time we got caught up in the anti-American riots in Venezuela?

Where Sins Are Forgiven

by Matthew A. Fike

"Woman is a vessel. Good luck to all who sail in her."
Lucy Irvine, *Castaway*

HIGH IN THE MOUNTAINS of southwestern Bulgaria stands the
Rila Monastery. Renowned for fine wines and medieval frescoes depicting the Bulgarians' torture by the Turks, the
monastery is the final resting place of *Sveti Ivan Rilski,* St. Ivan
of Rila. Visitors to the front of the church where his casket
rests can kiss an oval window over his withered hands. Above
the monastery, an hour's walk up a vast, wooded river valley
lies a cave with two openings—one in the rocky hillside,
another on the grassy hilltop. Legend has it that St. Ivan dwelled
there to atone for the sins of humanity. Those who climb
through the cave over rocks and up ladders are said to be forgiven for their sins.

Thirty miles away is the American University in Bulgaria
(AUBG), the first American university in Eastern Europe. It
occupies the former Communist Party building in the city of
Blagoevgrad, "an experiment in higher education," according
to its current president, and offers a Western liberal arts education emphasizing democratic principles and free speech, or
so it claims.

Sometimes, said a preacher, you are in a place to prepare
to be somewhere else. And sometimes, to adapt his phrase,
you fail in one place so that you will have no choice but to go
where you are needed. There is no better way to describe the
experience that preceded my arrival at AUBG. For two years

I taught at Cornucopia College of the Evangelical Lutheran Church of Christ in the Wilderness of This World in a nondescript Midwestern City (all names have been changed). Being unhappy at Cornucopia, I probably would not have weathered a tenure review had I managed to survive that long, for in the final analysis it is the *kind* of person you are, not the substance of what you have accomplished, that determines your fate, or so they told me. If your EQ is more important than your IQ, then your personality is your destiny.

My demise was hastened by a six-week relationship with one of our students, though I hasten to add that she was never my own student, hence there was no conflict of interest. She looked as if she had sprung from the collective male unconscious, or at least from an L.L. Bean sweater ad or one of Father Greeley's romance novels (Lutheran, though). This sassy redhead was breathtakingly beautiful and radiantly alive. I was blighted by graduate study and damnably foolish. Less than two weeks after declaring her long-term intentions for our relationship, she broke off all contact. Later I learned that her father had accused her of being "too big for her britches" and had threatened to stop paying for her education if she continued to see me. Thus was I saved from marriage in the deep Midwest.

It appeared that the young woman's learning curve was more of a flat line or maybe a parabola, for she ended up wedding and six months later divorcing an Italian movie producer years older than her own father. Extreme mental cruelty.

I would assume that her controlling father, who had shelled out thousands for the reception, was amply chastened by the whole situation. Surely, I often imagine him saying, the young professor really loved my little girl and would have treated her better than this foreigner did. My own take is a few degrees frostier: If you treat your daughter like a clothes prop, don't be surprised when she acts like one.

For me the relationship was the ejector button on my first and probably my last full-time college teaching job in the U.S. Fortunately, I learned what has oft been thought but never so well expressed as in this chestnut: "Screw me once, shame on you. Screw me twice, shame on *me*." My girlfriend made the same mistake twice. I got the picture and have not repeated my error, though, as irony rules the universe; I ended up in Eastern Europe where faculty-student fraternization is a commonplace occurrence.

Immoral goings on are not only allowed but seemingly condoned at schools in Eastern Europe, even at my own university, which purports to be a model of Western enlightenment and even has an American feminist president. The situation in this region is not as simple to analyze as contrasting a pseudo-religious environment like Cornucopia with the godless, post-communist East sans ethical barriers, or even noting the deep-seated sexism of Balkan males. It is more a matter of students doing what it takes to succeed in spite of deficiencies, and faculty seeking in sexual adventuring both an exercise in control and a false compensation for the lousy hand the economy deals people. If you are a full professor trying to support a family on $150 a month, you might not feel much guilt about a little immorality on the fringes of your lifestyle.

Students' response to their own deficiency was the theme of two stories I have heard over the years about state universities in Eastern Europe. At a Serbian university, a very attractive woman defended her M.A. thesis in the middle of winter. Knowing that her work was inadequate, she sought to compensate by dressing provocatively. Though it was a bitterly cold day, her attire left little to the imagination of her all-male committee. After they had informed her that she would have to come back in the summer with a revision, an inspired soul on the committee quipped, "If she dresses that scantily in the dead of winter, imagine the show six months from now!"

In another tale, a female student at a Bulgarian university gave a middleman $120 to give to her professor so that he would give her a high mark on her final examination despite her lack of familiarity with the course material. Exams of this sort are oral; each student is examined in the presence of the class, and the grades range from a high of six to a low of two. When this student's turn came and she responded inadequately to her professor's questions, he informed her that she would receive a two for the course. "A *two!*" she exclaimed. "I really think my answers deserve more than a *two!*" "Well," replied the gray-beard smoothly, "they don't, and a two is what you've got. Let me suggest that you learn the material next time." "You son of a bitch!" shrieked the student. "I gave you $120, and all you can give me is a *two?*" The professor's countenance slowly clouded over with wrath. "You *bitch,*" he spat, "you only gave me $20!" Where's an honest crook when you need one?

Students in Eastern Europe try to manipulate the system, but it is equally true that professors try to manipulate their students. At final examinations, each student leaves the class-room after being examined. The last student in the room is often the woman from whom the professor wants a sexual favor. One of my friends found herself in exactly this situa-tion at a Bulgarian university. For refusing to perform the requested intimate act on her professor she failed his course. The next year she was again the last student left in the same professor's classroom and he failed her a second time for refus-ing to pleasure him. Finally, the third year, his attention focused on another woman, and my friend was allowed to pass the course. The possibility of doing something about such sexual harassment doesn't even register on many women in Eastern Europe.

Someone who received repeated propositions from an East European professor actually thinks that he is a wonderful gentleman because he shrugs and accepts her decision every time she says no.

Equally amazing is the transformation Eastern Europe effects on Americans.

Heart of Darkness provides an apt analogy: Kurtz, the ambassador of civilization and light, a man to whose making "All Europe contributed," outdoes even the cannibals for butchery. Marlow wonders "how can you imagine what particular region of the first ages a man's untrammeled feet may take him into by the way of solitude—utter solitude without a policeman—by the way of silence—utter silence, where no warning voice of a kind neighbour can be heard whispering of public opinion? These things make all the great difference." So it is when Americans go abroad (and why many end up in foreign prisons). Finding that familiar societal restraints are absent, an American may think nothing of sleeping or living with one of his own students. Neither does the Eastern European student. Remarkably, neither may an American administration, an ocean away from our own litigious society, when it discovers absolute power and succumbs to the resulting corruption. A faculty member attacked a female colleague and threatened to kill her if she told anyone? Just ignore her complaints. We want to get rid of her anyway. And my personal favorite: "If you think you got fired unjustly, there are always the courts."

Like me in the Midwest, however, many of my colleagues have had genuine feelings for our Eastern European students.

There have been numerous affairs and relationships, and more than several marriages. Sometimes the girl—a word you can actually use in Eastern Europe—is a hunter, actively pursuing an American professor, even contributing to a marital rift. More likely, she is Nausikaa, offering a middle-aged professor a chance to start life over again with someone young and exotic who wants an assertive man rather than an equal partner. For her, it's not about screwing daddy; it's about genuine differences in gender roles, which is one of the reasons why marriage agencies featuring Eastern European women are such a booming business in the United States today. As an English professor, I am suspicious of generalizations, but there is truth to the statement that Eastern European women are less assertive and more soft-spoken than women in the United States (they may also be more subtly manipulative, but that's another story). Regardless of the approach, though, most of the relationships that I have seen between American professors and Eastern European students are based on genuine affection and mutual respect, as well as the eternal cliché, "Men want youth and beauty, women want security."

Properly inoculated by my horrendous experience in the Midwest, I arrived in Bulgaria in 1991, a happy exile from the kind of customer-driven education peddled by the likes of Cornucopia. ("We want you to teach to the average student," my chairperson told me after a disastrous first year of dealing with students who expected me to lower my standards to meet their expectations and then punished me on course evaluations when I didn't.) One might say that circumstances had exiled the fox to the hen house, but I was by this time a reformed and very chastened fox. I want to believe that a faculty-student relationship can potentially be a very moral and beautiful thing, but while my new environs proved aesthetically interesting (slim women in mini-skirts smoking cigarettes), I was determined not to touch any females of the student variety. I quickly found a Bulgarian girlfriend from the local community and the following year, as irony rules the universe, went out with an American feminist who believed that the cardinal sin was to date a student, though she herself had been married to one of her own former students. In eight years of teaching at AUBG, while I have had the inevitable crushes along the way, I have not succumbed to the charms of students who have stared at me with love in their eyes or offered me relationships. I avoid the student bars and socialize with female students outside the building only on special occasions like birthday parties. Rather than taking any risks, I have sat back and watched and listened as other men got away with far more serious behavior than what had lofted me to Eastern Europe. Most of the time resisting has been easy.

One student was not so easy to resist. In retrospect, I believe that the words of Montaigne apply: "A strong imagination creates what it imagines." Or in the words of The Phantom Menace, "Your focus determines your reality." I had been wanting someone like her, and the universe called my bluff. *Be careful what you wish for . . .*

Late one afternoon I was working in my office when I heard a knock on the door. In slunk a woman I had seen walking with her head down on the main stairway, a first-year student named after an ancient king. Katerina, as I'll call her, looked like a supermodel, had modeled at a high level in her native Albania and in order to attend AUBG had turned down an opportunity to model in Paris, or so she claimed. She had decided to study at AUBG partly because of a dream in which she had seen an enormous "A" in the sky, which she took to mean that she was meant to come to the American University. To that end, she had begun studying English a year before and had supposedly managed to score high enough on the SAT and TOEFL to receive a large scholarship from George Soros's Open Society Foundation.

Shortly after arriving, she had seen a male student from the back while he was studying in the library and had known that he would be an important person for her. Much to her disappointment, he didn't look as beautiful from the front. Nonetheless, she made him her first boyfriend, which to the mind of this Muslim female meant not only the loss of her family and her religion but also the certainty of marriage, though she was having second thoughts about the latter. Her attitude was not unlike fundamentalist Christianity in the United States—all or nothing, be chaste or be damned. She was in great emotional turmoil, lacked the proficiency in English to excel in her classes and was having trouble concentrating on her assignments. It was in such a state that she walked through my doorway that afternoon in 1995.

Katya asked me to be her academic coach. She said that she wanted me to teach her how to be a good student and that she wanted to make herself responsible to me. She wanted to map out goals and wanted me to make sure that she accomplished them. The main problem precipitating her request was the difficulty she was having in her writing course with my colleague, Professor Martin. If I agreed to her proposal, I would become her writing tutor. Why me? "Because you are the best," she replied.

The request was unusual but did not sound unreasonable, so I agreed to meet with her twice a week. I explained the virtues of noting all her assignments and test dates on a calendar and began helping her with paper assignments. The arrangement seemed straightforward to me, but hidden obsession was driving her action. Katya made her initial request because she thought that my diligence and academic success would pass to her by easy association. In literary theory, and perhaps as well in composition teaching, those who have the power control the discourse, but in an ESL setting it is equally true that those who control the discourse have the power. Katya desperately wanted the power of fluency and saw her tutorial with me as a shortcut around hard work on a daily basis. This was perilously close to the savior complex that many Eastern European women have in regard to Western men, and I failed to see problems lurking in the shadows.

In a similar manner, although I informed Professor Martin of the tutorial, it wasn't until much later that I understood the dynamics of his own interaction with Katya. He was a tall, slim and extremely worldly middle-aged man, a novelist and prize-winning author of erotic fiction who was married to a lovely American woman in her late 20s (his third wife). They had one of those ideal marriages in which each partner thinks the other is a terrific catch. Since Mrs. Martin had straight black hair, Katya mistook her for a "stupid Bulgarian woman" who wasn't good enough for him and from that premise developed full-blown sexual jealousy. Katya somehow communicated her interest to Professor Martin, who no doubt kindly explained the impossibility of any sort of involvement given his marriage and the fact that she was his student. Katya struck back by writing an allegorical essay in which a mean English professor and his wife torture a bunny rabbit.

It was only a short hop from Katya's rejection by her married professor to a fantasy about her single tutor. One afternoon, about three weeks after we began working together, she sent me a message stating, "Hello, Matt, may I come in your office?" I said that she could, but the preposition should have forewarned me. When she arrived at my office she shut the door and said, "Can I say you something?" Trouble was afoot. She sat down in a chair separated from me by my big bunker desk, which I had placed as a barrier for just such an occasion. "Will you be my boyfriend?" she asked.

The offer was on the table: I could have the most beautiful, feminine student at the school. I knew, however, that 19-year-olds, whether they know it or not, only want to try on an older man like a coat in a department store and lack all understanding of the professional risks for the professor. A wrong choice had sent me into exile; I had no desire to start an American university in Siberia.

"I appreciate the offer," I said, "and I do find you very attractive, but I'm afraid that I must decline. You sought my help as your tutor, and that means that anything more is a conflict of interest for me. That conflict will only continue because you say you plan to major in English. In any case, the university frowns on faculty-student dating, and I could lose my job if I dated a student. You obviously care about me, and I'm sure that you wouldn't want me to do anything that could harm me professionally. If you're still interested after you graduate, we can talk at that time about the issues involved. But right now the answer has to be no. I hope you understand."

She said she did and left. As a means of documenting my proper behavior I sent a long e-mail to myself. Then I realized that if I told someone about Katya's proposition, I would not then be able to change my mind. To shore up my resolve, I immediately told my female colleague Professor Cox about the situation. It is important when working overseas to have one person with whom you can vent your frustrations in total confidence. Cox and I had that kind of relationship. She listened and then advised.

"The student," she said, "might react negatively, and there is the very real potential that she will try to harm you by spreading rumors." *Hell hath no fury,* I thought. "You're right to send yourself e-mail documenting everything. Even keep a copy on disk and take a hard copy home. But remember that students can alter e-mail messages, so be extremely careful about what you send her." I found out two days later when Katya returned whether she would take no for an answer.

"You don't like problems, or you don't like *me?*" she demanded.

"I don't like problems; I like you just fine," I replied. Then I spent 10 minutes explaining that I didn't want to be an object of student gossip, faculty derision and administrative sanction.

"But I need to be with you in your bed," she countered.

"Look, Katya, you need to fix your problems. Only then can you have a right relationship with a man. Otherwise, you'll just be using a relationship to paper over issues. Sometimes 'no' is the kindest, most considerate response, and that's what I'm saying."

Two days later Katya came by for help on her history paper and advice on her next semester's schedule. Then she thanked me for "everything" and stated that she had said some "stupid things." Her manner was confident, and her face was clear and relaxed instead of clouded with excess emotion. In general, she affirmed her happiness that she was at AUBG and stated that she was now able to pray to God for the first time in months.

Three days later she visited me again and just wouldn't let up. "There are only two things I want in this life," she said mysteriously. "To go to Saudi Arabia to study theology," she paused for effect, her eyes widening, "and to be in your home."

"I really don't think that would be a good idea. And besides,

I can't have you over because you plan to major in English."

"I won't major in it, then. Oh," she shifted gears; "I am so tired. The dorm is so loud, and I can't sleep at night. I want to sleep at your apartment—no sex, just sleep."

"Forget it."

"Then I will find out where you live, I will come to your apartment at midnight, I will knock on your door, and *you will let me in!*" After she left, I wisely filed a verbal report with the Director of Student Services; an American woman who agreed that what I had described was sexual harassment. At my suggestion, she got Katya into counseling, and all seemed to fall into place until she decided to take my writing course the next semester. It was to be quite a class. By this time, Katya had hit on both my student assistant and me, and there were other luminaries on the roster: another former model who wrote a paper called "The Princess of Pain" about her struggle with being addicted to the pleasure of pain, and a hooker from Sofia who would come to class in her working rig—black stiletto heels, black fishnet stockings, shiny black leather miniskirt, black see-through blouse with a black bra underneath—and who was having an affair with my student assistant. I had, of course, advised Katya to take someone else's section, but I was stuck with her because after registration no one else had free seats. Her problems started almost immediately. She missed over one-third of the class meetings and had trouble with deadlines. At one point, she presented me with a medical excuse from the university's doctor.

"I know that missing the paper deadline has nothing to do with illness," I said.

"I just wanted you to know that I can lie," she replied defiantly.

I received messages from her like this one: "I am sorry that my paper will not be in time, because I do hope you will acept [sic] it during this week. Tomorrow, I am not going to come in class and in our appointment at 4:00. Please do not be angry at me. PLEASE." And like this: "I don't like you to misunderstand me. I know that you are my professor, but I also know that you are the second person that I respect in this world, after my father." When I finally got assignments from her, they would say things like this: "The pleasure I receive from everything I possess will be the main issue I will present in this paper. What I do possess are my touchable body and my mind. What were the circumstances in which I realized that I was exploring the pleasure that I give to myself, enjoying it? In what circumstances did I realize that I don't try to, but I do? Without knowing how the others define pleasure, rolled up in my blond hair, my brain, my blue eyes, my body, my blood, and my nails, I, occasionally, have found the pleasure, giving in this way, the chance to myself to listen to that voice: 'here you are again.' In that moment I felt like being in front of myself, but still in something; I felt I was inside the pleasure."

"So," said Professor Martin, "Katya wants to write a paper about masturbation. Praise Allah!"

Meanwhile, the tide of Katya's problems was coming in: trouble with her parents, critical messages from her siblings, inability to finish incompletes from the previous semester, frustrated artistic impulses, repeated break-ups and reconciliations with her boyfriend and a "see-food" approach to eating, men and smoking. If something or someone presented itself to her, she would consume it or become obsessed with it. "If I talk to a man, I must *kees* him, and if I *kees* him, I must make sex with him." I told her to eat something and to see a psychologist. She replied that she knew who she was and what she thought and just needed someone like me to talk to. I countered that she obviously had emotional issues to deal with and that a psychologist could help her figure out what to do about them. She took my point, or so she said.

The next fall a blessed thing happened. One afternoon Professor and Mrs. Martin came to my office to speak about Katya. Earlier that day Katya had visited Mrs. Martin. Still interested in the good professor, Katya had tried a new angle, saying that she had fantasies about both of them and that she saw them and me as a "family." She added (incorrectly) that the D she had received in my course was punishment for the fact that her on-again-off-again boyfriend had virtually written her papers for her. Mrs. Martin then broke confidentiality by telling Katya that I had spoken to them about her.

Fed up with Katya, I said, "If she is critical of my telling you guys about her, I'll just say, 'If you don't like it, don't talk to me.'"

Mrs. Martin then justified her decision by remarking that either her husband or I could have gotten into legal trouble because of this student, especially given the new sexual harassment policy. This policy took up 25% of our new faculty handbook and stated that even in the absence of a conflict of interest a disgruntled student could still claim sexual harassment. (That's another beautiful thing about working for Americans overseas—zeal to import the political correctness of American culture but indifference to equally important matters like academic freedom.)

Two months later, Katya came to see me.

"Can I shut the door?" she asked. *Here we go again,* I thought. This time she said that she wanted to go out with me and to study in bed with me. "I have my own apartment now, and it has a double bed. I know you're really lonely. I love you and want to make sex with you."

I said, "I can see in your face how conflicted you are. Part of you wants to be free and joyful and sensual, but another part won't let you."

A good example was her imagining me studying naked but then calling herself "perverse" for having the thought. Then she told me about guys she had slept with now that her boyfriend was in graduate school in the United States, but she hastily added that she wanted someone, like me was the implication, who could give her an orgasm. Round and round and round we went.

After thinking about the offer for a couple of days, I got angry. "This woman is John Malkovich," I complained to my journal. The allusion to *Dangerous Liaisons* would prove to be prophetic. "She wants to see if she can get me to trash my reputation, career or both. If I do anything, it's a conflict of interest, and I'm cooked anytime she wants me to be. All this secrecy is her way of isolating and controlling me. She can't resist the dictates of her own sex drive and then hates herself for what she does and how she feels. Her father wouldn't let her become a dancer, so now she wants to get back at him by fucking father figures."

Despite my anger, two days later when she came to my office at 7:30 P.M. I was taken by surprise. She came in wearing a long black skirt, black shoes and socks, and a brown leather jacket. She was carrying a book bag and a large bottle of mineral water.

"Do I stay at your place tonight?" she asked casually. Then she sat down sideways on a chair, leaned against the wall and placed the water bottle upright between her thighs like a giant liquid phallus.

I should have told her to leave immediately, but you have to understand the nature of the situation. I was alone in a foreign country, overworked and under-appreciated. Being in a room with Katya clouded the mind as if she had thrown magic powder on a fire. Like Howard Stern's audience, I just wanted to see what she'd say next (in a town with nothing to do, a wayward student's entertainment value should not be underestimated). And besides, we had a genuine friendship by this time. I didn't intend to succumb to her temptations, but I didn't want to be cruel to her or make her feel ashamed either. That evening we had a long talk, and when I told her the reason for my exile she finally understood that it was not sensible, or kind, to continue propositioning me.

But there were further conversations on other occasions. How she had passed up options to marry her way out of Eastern Europe. How her brothers had been allowed to wear bathing suits at the beach while growing up and she hadn't. How she loved me but at the same time hated me because I am an American. How she had prayed to God, "Please give me a man who loves me more than I love him, no matter what he looks like." How she figured she could do it with a girl. How she figured she could turn her emotions off enough to work as a prostitute. How she wanted to see what it felt like to shoot herself in the head, bullet in one side and out the other, her single regret being that she could savor the sensation only once. I told her how well she had acted in a student play adapted from a Bulgarian folk tale called *The Man, the Fox, and the Snake,* in which she, in all her sinuous glory, had played the snake. I also told her that when I had meditated on her most recent offer, I had received, among other images, a picture of a baby in a stroller. She replied by saying that she had always really wanted a little girl, "but without a husband."

A month later my student assistant shared his opinion of her. He and Katya had both been present at a viewing of *Dan-*

gerous Liaisons. It was her favorite movie, and she had clearly identified with John Malkovich's character, who manipulates a married woman (Michelle Pfeiffer) into a sexual relationship, then dumps her, though he genuinely loves her. Katya had been fascinated and wanted to learn how to manipulate men in the same way.

A further indication that it had been right to resist came in the form of a synchronicity. While traveling back to the United States for Christmas, I purchased a copy of *Maxim* magazine and found this quotation: "My advice to teachers, to anyone who works with young girls and might be tempted, is this: Remember they won't be any good in bed! After all, once you've got over the beauty of these girls there isn't very much more. It's a better idea to develop a friendship and wait a few years, because then something rather fine might result. You never know." (January 1997). The statement zeroed in on the saving paradox: Rejecting a female student's proposition can be a selfish rather than a self-denying act.

Spring 1997. Bulgaria's economy headed south, the dollar rose from 250 leva the previous fall to 3,000 in March, then fell to 1,600. There were protests, strikes and failed banks throughout the country. The Albanian students crowded around the TV in the cafeteria to watch CNN's coverage of their own country's descent into madness—AK-47s' staccato accompaniment to a full-bore economic collapse precipitated by a pyramid scheme. Meanwhile, I myself was under fire from three so-called full professors who wanted me out. Lies were written about me. My evaluation materials were tampered with. No one in the administration cared even after my Washington, D.C., attorney came out of hiding and started landing body blows. *No problem. We want to get rid of him anyway.* That terrible semester Katya made good on her wish to major in English and ended up in my Shakespeare class. Again her attendance was sporadic, and she never finished the course, or any other, because she married and left school without even doing the paperwork for a proper withdrawal. She came to my office to say goodbye and tell me that she would be moving to the United States with her Bulgarian husband, the young man she had picked out in the library. She visited one last time to accuse me of telling my friends about her. It was true—I had done so for my own protection. I would not let her isolate and control me. The most important thing, though, was the thing not said: She picked a fight to avoid having the memory of her love for me hanging over her marriage.

So it was that Katerina ran away from the liberal arts and the fiasco she had made of her first two years of college. I later heard that she had received another Soros scholarship for study in the United States. (It didn't surprise me to learn at the same time that her sister worked for the Open Society Foundation in Albania.) To this day we remain out of touch with each other.

In Eastern Europe, as my American colleagues have demonstrated, a male professor can get away with dating a student, or dating his own student, or dating two students at the same time, or making out with a student in public, or living with his own student, or even smoking pot in a student's dormitory room.

If you don't step on the bosses' toes, anything goes. Thus my little post-modern university in Bulgaria is truly a place where sins are forgiven, but the title phrase has a deeper meaning for me. My selfish decision to resist Katya's advances was also a genuinely other-regarding act that enlarged my capacity for empathy. On the one hand, the universe tested me with a higher order of temptation than I had experienced before.

On the other, it brought Katya together with someone capable of a compassionate response to her tortured overtures.

Even the most mature 19-year-old student is a woman-child struggling to grow up. Emotional problems and cultural differences present further perils. Those who dare may share her love, but the growth she experiences in a relationship with an older man may ironically prepare her to be with someone else. Nick Nolte's artist character in *New York Stories* gives "life lessons" to young women, and when they eventually outgrow him and move on, he takes in the next wannabe. Stuck in a cycle of mutual dependence with a series of Katyas, he gives them control of his emotional life and cannot embrace a more mature love in marriage. Nor have I made it to the altar. Katya was not meant to be my wife, my Héloïse, but thank goodness she was not my Lolita. With Katya I achieved instead the brass tacks of the forgiveness of sins: a synergy of compassion and self-esteem that enabled me to avoid making the same mistake twice.

Traveling by *The* Book

by Eva Mansell

It all boils down to a bed and bathroom at the end of a travel day, doesn't it?

Hong Kong, circa 1993. We were there to experience the British incarnation of the "Pearl of the Orient" before it reverted to its fully Chinese character. My husband and I had just spent two months being spoiled silly at three separate homestays in Fukuoka, Japan. Though we were seasoned travelers, this would be our first rented bed in an Asian country.

Studying our budget traveler's bible before touchdown, Derek assured me there would be no problem finding a room. We had one local contact in Hong Kong, parents of a girl who attended the boarding school in the U.S. from which we were on a year's sabbatical. The connection seemed far too tenuous to warrant more than a quick call at some point during our week's stay. Being catered to in Japan, where a guest is honored in a do-unto-others-as-you-would-have-them-do-unto-you-if-you-were-a-god, revealed its downside. Our hosts would look hurt if we expressed any spontaneous urge to veer off from their ever-organized activities. We were anxious to be on our own adventure again. With post-college backpacking through Europe behind us and years of flea-bitten Latin American travel under our belts, we were confident the next four months in Southeast Asia would renew the edgy feelings of youth and freedom that years of predictable vacation schedules had blunted.

I have never relished late-night arrivals, even in small U.S.

towns. One never knows if the odd Shriner's Convention might gobble up every available room in Jasper, Wyo. When young and foolish, I balanced my fears with the lack of currency in my money pouch. Calling a Hong Kong budget hostel from Fukuoka, for example, would have been a laughable idea in those days. In middle age, having accidentally become middle class, I had suggested that very idea to my husband. I still fancied myself the perennial vagabond. My husband continually challenged my aging hippie travel boundaries by eschewing reservations and refusing to hail taxis, even at 10:30 P.M., when setting foot on the Chinese mainland for the very first time.

Hong Kong's airport in those days teetered on the edge of the Kowloon peninsula, geographically a part of China itself. You looked across from this vantage point to the glittering hills of Hong Kong Island, where decades before the British had established their airy hill station. Even now, their address on Falcon Crest near "The Peak" told me that our student's parents still looked down from a protective perch on the riot of colorful neon backing Hong Kong harbor.

Qualms turned into twinges of panic as other backpackers jostled by us, first down the aisles of the plane, then in the line forming at the courtesy phones outside the customs hall. They all toted the same budget travel guides that my husband and I clutched, surely open to the same pages they too would consult in the rush to secure a room for the night. All camaraderie and even the genial pastime of travel oneupmanship tends to evaporate when you hit the street in a race for budget rooms.

I finally gained access to a courtesy phone. One set of backpackers after another scurried off, guidebooks flapping, presumably having booked their rooms from the airport as our guidebooks directed. During my ensuing conversations with several guesthouse owners, I realized Hong Kong had apparently never lost its essentially Chinese character.

"I didn't understand one word anyone said," I admitted sheepishly to my husband as I hung up.

We were both fluent in Spanish, as well as English and some French. I had been ill prepared for the humbling experience of not having the basic language skills to negotiate the essentials in a foreign land. Defeat crept into my voice as triumph flashed over Derek's face.

"I told you it would be just as easy, and quicker, to ride into the city and find a place."

"But most of the places I tried said they were already full. I think." When arguing with your own mate, at night, even before leaving a foreign airport, the lack of a room can quickly cause acute paranoia.

I followed my husband at a quick march toward the signs indicating "Ground Transportation." I envisioned grabbing a taxi. We needed to get a jump on the travelers who'd bypassed the phone option and were surely filling every available budget hotel as we spoke. Derek looked at me as if I'd suggested we find the airport Hilton and check in for the night.

"It says right here in the book (read, *The* Book, when referring to the dog-eared treasure the guide becomes to the budget traveler) that the public bus into the city will drop us right in the budget hotel district. And it only costs a dollar."

Who was I to remind Derek that, unlike the majority of our competitors on the backpacker trail, we had a steady paycheck being forwarded to us on a monthly basis? This was a point of honor with Derek as ingrained as the need to provide the guest with the best bed and finest food had been in our Japanese hosts. When Derek started taking taxis to Holiday Inns, he would have to admit that he was growing up, if not getting old.

The driver of the jam-packed public bus spoke the same kind of English that the hotel keepers had over the phone. We shared a few essential verbs and pronouns, like "You get off here!" But when it came to the fine points of conversation, shouted over other travelers pushing to get out, and locals shoving to get in, his English skills went out the window.

"Is this Nathan Street and Star?" I pleaded, as he silently jabbed his finger at the door and revved his engine. When the doors wheezed shut and the bus rumbled off in a cloud of exhaust, it was as if we were two yokels deposited at New York's 42nd Street and 3rd Avenue at midnight, before Mayor Giuliani made its streets safe for the disoriented stranger.

"Is *this* where the guy on the phone told you to wait for his uncle?"

Derek was pointedly leaving himself out of the equation. From the moment I pressed for the phone call rather than just following the guide's directions to a hotel, I'd been designated as the one calling the shots.

"I told you that I was not too clear on what the guy was telling me to do, but I thought he said wait on this corner and someone would meet us."

"Hmmm," Derek responded, avoiding eye contact with me. He'd sensed that my eyes were about to dispense the watery weakness that left him wondering if I was really the same travel partner with whom he'd happily bummed around half the Spanish-speaking world.

We had an unspoken pact regarding hotel hawkers that swarm around people exiting buses from the airport. We would never be browbeaten into following such touts to the "clean and cheap" accommodations they hustled. While a horde of high-pitched, in-your-face kind of salespeople corralled us, Derek stubbornly consulted his guidebook. I looked about me with the desperately expectant air of a girl on a grubby, dark street corner, awaiting a blind date. Minutes ticked away as an ever-changing cast of aggressive small people with loud voices screamed, "Mr., come this way!" "Mrs., follow me!" while attempting to cram worn business cards into our hands. I had read, in the guidebook, that Hong Kong was essentially a "safe" city, though of course, as in any city, pickpockets were not uncommon. I patted my money belt at regular intervals to assure myself it was still there. I opened our back-up guide-book and read to my horror that "a steady stream of business travelers gives Hong Kong hotels one of the world's highest occupancy rates." Furthermore, like New York City, due to the astronomical real estate prices and limited landmass, "there really are no 'bargain' places to stay. In fact, the traveler should expect to pay more than they might anywhere else in the world, to get less."

When I gave up all hope of a kindly uncle coming to fetch us off to our surprisingly fine accommodations, I breached the human fence of bed pushers and fled the chaotic corner. I swung through the revolving glass doors of a well lighted, nicely appointed hotel lobby. When a uniformed bellhop held another door for me on my exit, I had a crisp, embossed hotel card in my hand with room rates penned on the back.

Working my way through the huddle of room purveyors around Derek, I tried to sound chipper about the thrilling fact that there were double rooms available for "only $100 a night."

Derek got up, hefted his pack onto his back and without a reply took the reins in our room search at this point. Once again I was following behind, afraid I might otherwise be left to fend for myself on the seething street corner, or sleep alone in a plush bed with nothing but a pristine bathroom as my roommate.

"*This* is it?" My voice rose with the level of adrenaline encouraging me to flee.

Even Derek had hesitated at the threshold of the archway before us. It bore the address of the hotel listed in our guidebook, if not the expected appearance.

"This is Mirador Mansions?" I squeaked in a panic.

We were at the brink of a dark, empty, filthy commercial arcade. The shop windows looked like dusty wax museum dioramas of items sold in Hong Kong some decades before a neutron bomb hit. There were no street people lying in doorways. There were no people at all, just us, and mounds of garbage heaped in corners with either a cat or some creature off a Chinese place mat gnawing a particularly ripe piece of trash. This was clearly why uncles were sent to meet guests. No self-respecting tourist would believe a "guest house" existed at this address.

Derek stubbornly set forth. In search of an elevator, we walked through dim corridors with sticky concrete floors. The guidebook said that somewhere above this rundown commercial ghost town there were budget beds. We had followed these budget guides through many a suspect neighborhood from Belize to Lima. Derek would not be daunted. When the beat-up doors of an elevator creaked open, it was like something out of "Night of the Living Dead." Two pasty-faced people stood staring dumbly at us, even after we foolishly smiled in the idiotic way Americans tend to overuse the grinning response. They did not exit as we expected, and so we squeezed in for our ride to the fourth floor. The slow, silent ascent gave me time to wonder if these were the people I might spend the night with, stuck between floors in a Hong Kong tenement.

The doors miraculously opened and then closed behind us. Derek and I were in yet another dank concrete corridor, only this time there were not even ill-lighted, dilapidated shops ahead of us.

Something scurried by my feet and I yelped. "This can't be right. Let's get out of here," I whined unabashedly.

My husband, normally mild-mannered and accommodating, hardens into a steely zealot when a book provides directions. A quick flashlight referral to *The* Book told him that in these uninviting commercial mazes were separate lettered blocks, each with separate lifts. He reasoned that we had probably taken the wrong elevator. However, it appeared to him that we were in a lettered block that did in fact have a guesthouse, it was simply on another floor. He trudged toward the stairs. I swung my pack onto my sweaty back, regretting I had even put it down for a minute on the disgusting floor. I tiptoed after him, my peripheral vision acutely attuned to any floor movements. It was midnight in Hong Kong, but it felt like 3 in the morning on a forced march through a concrete jungle.

One floor up, dead silence reigned between the two travelers who had been toasting their good times with champagne and nuzzling affectionately just a few short hours earlier on a brightly lit plane. After another flight of stairs we reached a dead end. I groaned as my mate did an about face and passed me, a dutiful soldier in traveler's boot camp. Finally, we were making for a halo of yellow light from an open door, and a humming sound. When we reached the door and Derek attempted to get directions, the supervisor of the first real sweat shop I had ever seen did not respond to Derek but squealed some order at the hunched over figures who'd stopped sewing briefly to view us. At this point a wave of depression layered itself over the exhaustion that had somehow kept this surreal journey from coming into complete focus in my mind. If this was the "Pearl of the Orient," I wanted to do my jewelry shopping elsewhere. I could not imagine what traveling through Thailand, Indonesia and Malaysia with my husband for the next four months would be like. By the time Derek pointed with pride to the open door of Mr. Chen's GuestHouse a short way down the hall, I had dissolved into a puddle of tears.

Mr. Chen and the two other men in the stunted office space averted their eyes from the embarrassing sight of the crying woman. Derek forked over $35 for the shoebox in which we would spend the night. You bumped, literally, into the edge of the bed on entering the room and could barely find a space between the bed, chair and sink to let a backpack fall to rest.

When Derek raced out to reward my perseverance with drinks and snacks, my listless inspection of the sheets and the bathroom down the hall revealed moderately sanitary conditions. I could appreciate the whitewashed cubicles that had appeared like an oasis in the desert round an unexpected corner in this Hong Kong tenement. Ironically, just across the street was the backside of an Omni Hotel. It could not be such a "bad neighborhood" after all, I consoled myself. I could imagine those well-heeled travelers stepping onto a red carpet, hopping into a taxi hailed by the bellhop who held a shiny bronze handle of the sparkling door. The problem for me was that I'd had a peek beneath the lightly lacquered veneer of the tawdry Chinese box in which I would spend the night. The $35 we had just paid Mr. Chen was probably a week's pay for any one of the 20 people hunched over their sewing machines down the hall. I felt miserably middle-aged without the benefit of the recreational drugs and strong drink that had often colored my light-hearted romp through the budget travels of my youth.

When I called our Hong Kong contact the next morning, there was an audible intake of breath and an awkward pause when I mentioned where we were staying. "I'm going to give you our address and you should taxi over here at once. You can have accommodation with us." I accepted the offer without even consulting my travel companion.

Later in the week, as we rode the trolley up and down from our guestroom in a penthouse on Victoria Peak, I struggled with my feelings. I still held an imaginary thread of camaraderie with all the budget travelers, not to mention Hong Kong residents below in the Tsimshatsui district of the Kowloon peninsula. After we had all our clothes whisked away to be laundered by the maid on entry to our new "accommodations," our hostess had warned us where we must go and not go in her adopted city, and lectured us as to what we should do and not do there as well. I knew I had traded our freedom for a clean bed and bathroom in Hong Kong.

Hormones and Horses

by Stephanie L. Freid

IT WAS AUGUST 1990. Iraq had invaded Kuwait, the allied forces were beginning their Persian Gulf buildup and I was working in Tel Aviv's NBC News Bureau when my boss walked in and asked: "Want to go to Cairo for the weekend? We need someone to hand-carry tapes and your American passport will get you there without a visa."

Like I would say no. I was 25, eager to please and this was an opportunity to travel, make my mark and meet the exciting news staff. I was to deliver taped interviews to the bureau chief and then take in the city's sights until my return Saturday night.

I landed in Cairo's dusty, squalid airport the next afternoon and was greeted by Ahmed—an energetic local driver in his mid-20s who spoke broken English. He grabbed my overnight bag and proceeded to rush me outside to his waiting car with a "Press" placard taped to the windshield. Generally used as an aid in maneuvering through demonstrations or war zones, the Arabic/English signs also serve as a wonderful alibi for joy riding.

The drive through the dusty streets of downtown Cairo was anything but joyful as Ahmed alternately lurched forward, slammed on the brakes and hit the horn. Gridlocked vehicles moved haphazardly along the freeway, their drivers disregarding lane markers and traffic lights. Red meant *go*, green meant *go*, yellow meant *go* and the horn meant *go*. Had Cairo's 6.5 million residents simultaneously ventured out for an afternoon drive?

We arrived at the Hilton and left the grimy, hot confusion behind, entering a wonderfully air-conditioned lobby filled with Kuwaitis decked out in flowing white robes, black leather sandals and red kaffiyahs who had fled home at the first signs of Saddam.

We rode the elevator to a top floor, walked down a long corridor and entered the Cairo Bureau. Formerly a three-bedroom suite, all traces of splendor had been replaced by zigzagging cable taped crudely to the carpet, ringing telephones, computer terminals, office chairs, boardroom tables, edit machines, stacks of tapes and a dozen producers, assistant producers, stand-by drivers, editors, camera and soundmen.

"Stephanie!" greeted Victor, a former Tel Aviv boss, from across the room. "Welcome to our humble office. Want something to eat? We're ordering from room service." Tables were littered with food in various stages of decay. My stomach turned slightly, but adhering to Middle Eastern etiquette, I ordered a sandwich.

"Meet the crew!" he called out, wrapping an arm around my shoulders and guiding me around the room. I nodded hello to the Egyptian producers busy arranging press conference cover, snickered at the Italian cameraman engrossed in maneuvering paper airplanes off the balcony towards the Nile River, remained silent as I handed over the tapes to an agitated editor pushing BVU buttons and drew in a sharp breath when introduced to the correspondent.

Later coined "The Scud Stud" by American female audiences for his good looks and charm while reporting under missile fire from Saudi Arabia, Art Kent's presence sent blood rushing to my face. Next to him stood a tall, rugged man with long blond hair, wearing faded jeans and cowboy boots who introduced himself as Kyle. My heart palpitated wildly while I coolly shook hands with both.

The food arrived, I self-consciously ate my tasteless ham sandwich and fries and departed the suite with plans of enjoying a leisurely bath, dinner from room service and air-conditioned bliss until the morning. I stepped out on to the balcony of my room as the sun was setting and surveyed the winding Nile and snaking mass of gridlocked, honking cars blanketed in a hazy layer of pollution below. *So this is Egypt . . .*

My thoughts were interrupted by the ringing telephone. "Stephanie, it's Kyle. Listen, we're all going out horseback riding at the Pyramids tonight. Want to join?" *If "we all" means you and Art, are you kidding?* "Sure. Why not?" was my casual reply.

Two hours later I found myself squeezed into the back seat of yet another miniature, air-conditionless scrap pile on wheels between wondermen Kyle and Art. We chatted but I paid little attention to conversation, as this fantasy was too incredible for concentrated thought. En route we made a pit stop at a touristy Papyrus factory outlet where several of us purchased hieroglyphic wall hangings for loved ones in distant places and then set out again, reaching the stables by 10.

Hisham, an Egyptian producer and personal friend of the stable owners, negotiated riding details in Arabic while the six of us quietly stood by. "You know horse?" a stable hand asked, which I interpreted to be a survey of my riding talents. "Oh, sure," I boasted, recalling weekly childhood riding outings with my family. "Good," he answered and flashed a smile.

We mounted our steeds and trotted off in a line across the desert sands with Hisham leading the way. The Pyramids were miles away and impossible to see on that moonless, pitch-black night, but it didn't matter. Unable to contain my excitement, I slapped my mare on the backside for increased acceleration and she broke into a gallop.

I yelped aloud with the thrill of reckless abandon as we moved at full speed, savoring the sensation of arid wind coursing through my hair. The other horses followed her lead but were unable to keep up the pace. Ha!

The excitement dissipated and was replaced by a feeling of impending doom as I realized this filly was a far cry from the Springer Farm ponies I had ridden as a child in Ohio. In fact, she was wildly out of control. I attempted to reign her in while balancing myself in the saddle but she blindly sped forward toward a set of bright lights in the near distance. My heart lurched into my stomach and I prayed that she not stumble on one of the numerous rock piles we were passing at lightning speed.

The blinding lights 50 yards away, I saw the parked Mercedes nano-seconds before impact. "We're going to hit that," I said to myself before we proceeded to smash into the front hood at full speed. The horse rolled over the hood kicking a leg into the windshield along the way and I was tossed from her back through the air, landing shoulder first on the hard, cold desert floor.

"Are you alright?" asked a voice through the haze. I looked up to find Art kneeling at one side and Kyle at the other.

Oh God! It wasn't supposed to happen this way! "The horse ...?" I weakly queried. Kyle pointed to the mare standing beside the dented sedan with its shattered windshield and replied, "She's fine. And you?"

Not all that great, thanks. My shoulder and head throbbed, my humiliation threshold was at maximum and my powers of comprehension were grappling with this in the desert at night. But first things first. Off to Cairo Hospital for x-rays and diagnosis—dislocated shoulder—a stop at the pharmacy for painkillers and back to the hotel where I skulked into the bureau after midnight. Eyes averted to the carpet, I sheepishly muttered an apology to a scowling, waiting Victor, then vanished to the safety of my room.

I had made my mark alright. By the next morning, the tale had spread throughout the Cairo Bureau, ricocheted to Tel Aviv and arrived via satellite to NBC New York. A mere 25 and I would be remembered not for heroic efforts, outstanding news coverage or even for delivering essential tapes. I was the one who had smashed up an expensive German car while trying to impress two men on a company outing.

The next day I avoided everyone and ventured solo back to Giza's Pyramids and the Sphinx to view the magnificence I had missed the previous night. I visited the bustling open-air markets for some midday bargaining, headed to the museum for a look at Tutankhamen's treasure-filled tomb and arrived back at the hotel late in the day. I quickly packed, hailed a taxi to the airport and returned to Tel Aviv, preferring to avoid Kyle, Art and the wrath of Victor.

The incident caused a stir within NBC when the Mercedes owner wanted compensation, but eventually, praise Allah, all was forgotten. I took riding lessons to overcome a newfound fear of horses and pushed memories of that night and thoughts of Kyle and Art into the recesses of my mind.

Years later, when Kyle sauntered through the Jerusalem Bureau door, I nearly dove underneath the table. *What in the hell is he doing here?* I blushed furiously as he greeted me. "Hey Stephanie. How've you been?" he casually asked.

As we exchanged our three-year histories in four sentences, a notion dawned: *He's still rugged and handsome, but I don't have to prove anything.* This newfound courage allowed a dredging of long-ago demons. "Kyle, can I just ask you something?" I inquired before we parted ways. "What was that Mercedes doing parked in the desert, anyhow?" "Midnight picnic," he replied casually. Naturally. Why hadn't I guessed?

Urchins and Minks

by Ralph A. Bolton

I HAD NEVER BEEN to the Caribbean islands and had no idea what to expect as we flew south on our corporate jet. I was taking three top customers on a tour of the company's Puerto Rico operations and a weekend of golf.

The plan was to fly over the factory before landing so we could say we saw it and then play golf Friday afternoon and Saturday and Sunday mornings before returning on Sunday afternoon.

Chuck, our pilot, and I had become good friends from flying around the country together, and he was just as eager as I was to have the opportunity to have a few days in the sun.

We landed in Puerto Rico about noon on Friday and went immediately to our hotel, located on the ocean approximately 10 miles from the airport. By the time we had registered and unpacked it was almost 1:30 P.M. and too hot to play golf. We decided that we would tee off around 4 P.M., which would still give us plenty of time to play at least nine holes before it got too dark.

Since I had never been swimming in the warm waters of the Caribbean, I decided that this was the time to head for the beach. The sand was hot, so I ran as fast as I could across the 30 feet of beach. I probably had taken three full strides into the water when I felt the sting. It was as if someone was driving hot needles into the bottom of my right foot. I hobbled out of the water and tried to see what was causing so much pain. It looked as if I had stepped on a porcupine. Long nail-like spikes were sticking into the sole of my foot. The pain was excruciating. My ankle was already starting to swell.

By the time I got to the hotel lobby, I could barely walk. The desk clerk took one look and said "Señor, you have stepped on a sea urchin." He called the house doctor. It took the doctor about 30 minutes to dig the spines out of my foot. He gave me some pain pills and said, "You won't be able to walk for a few days. I suggest you sit by the pool and soak your foot in the water to help reduce the swelling."

Chuck agreed to fill in for me with the customers. He was a much better golfer than I was anyway.

The next morning, I got a large bucket of ice water and sat by the hotel pool soaking my foot. There weren't many people at the pool, but there were three women playing cards at a table nearby. I felt ridiculous sitting there with my foot in a bucket, and it wasn't too long before one of the women playing cards noticed me. She said, "You really put your foot in it this time." They all laughed. Another asked, "What happened to your foot?" When I explained that I stepped on a sea urchin, they all said, "Oh you never walk in the water at the beach without something on your feet. There are sea urchins everywhere. By the way, do you play bridge?"

I took my bucket and hobbled over to the table where they were playing cards and joined their game.

We played bridge all day and broke only for lunch. For the first couple of hours, we took our bridge game quite seriously. However, it wasn't long before they began to ask me questions. "Where do you live?" "What do you do for a living?" "Who are your friends?" "How long are you staying?" "Do you have one of the suites?"

I evaded most of their questions and gave only a few details about how long I expected to stay. On the other hand, they began to tell me all about their lives, their husbands, their homes, their kids and on and on.

"My husband gave me this new ring," said one. Another told about her husband buying a chain of bakeries in Brooklyn. He had given her a full-length mink coat for Christmas last year. The third gal let us know her husband was a famous Park Avenue doctor. They usually went to Hawaii on their vacations, but this year he was just so busy he couldn't take too much time off. On and on they went, all day until we quit playing cards about 5 in the afternoon.

That evening, the gang I was with told me how great the golf course was. Chuck was an even better player than I suspected. He let them win a few holes. "It's too bad you couldn't play with us," they said. "What did you do all day?"

I told them about the three gals, about playing bridge and how I had to listen to those women brag about themselves all day long.

Chuck said, "We'll give them something to talk about tomorrow morning."

The next morning (Sunday) we decided it would be best not to play golf. The game would take too long and we needed to be in the air by noon. My foot was still sore, but at least I could wear shoes again. As we arrived in the dining room, I saw my three bridge partners eating breakfast with their husbands. I introduced them to my friends and we sat down at a table to wait for Chuck to join us.

In he walked. I don't know where he got the uniform, but he was dressed in a white suit, with all sorts of ribbons and medals on his jacket. He carried a captain's hat with gold braid on the visor under his arm. Chuck walked smartly up to our table and saluted me.

"Sir," he said, "I've just been informed that the prince and princess have arrived at your villa. I've instructed the captain to have the yacht ready for departure at 0900 hours tomorrow. Your jet is fueled and ready for immediate departure and I have arranged for the helicopter to be on the pad in one hour. Do you have any other instructions?"

I responded, "Thank you, Charles. As usual, you have everything under control."

With that, Chuck turned on his heel and said to my bridge partners, "Ladies, if you will be on the beach at 11:30 this morning, we will fly by and say farewell."

You never saw so many open mouths at one time. The gals looked at Chuck, then at me and then at themselves. "Who is he?" they asked. "Don't you know?" responded Chuck as he walked out of the dining room.

The helicopter came, just as Chuck said it would. As we left the landing pad, there were my three card-playing gals standing off to one side, waving goodbye. We flew by the hotel at exactly 11:30 and there on the beach waving frantically were the three women and their husbands surrounded by a hundred or more other people.

I often wondered what they told their friends about the mystery man who stepped on a sea urchin in Puerto Rico.

Day Trip to Denver

by Docia Schulz Williams

IN 1981, I WORKED as a freelance contract tour director for several companies. On this particular tour, I was escorting a 10-day Western trip for a group of senior citizens from a small community in East Texas. We had flown to Boise, Idaho, and from there we had embarked on a pleasant, scenic motorcoach tour of the western portion of the United States.

We arrived in Salt Lake City where the itinerary called for the group to depart on an early-morning Amtrak over a lovely mountain route to Denver. We would stay there overnight, and then return to Texas.

I cautioned the group not to eat breakfast on the morning we were to depart Salt Lake City because I had been told we would hook up with a dining car in Ogden, just up the track a few miles, where a lavish gourmet breakfast had been planned for the group.

We arose early for our 6:30 train departure. The coach dropped us at the curb in front of the Amtrak station and the driver unloaded the bags, leaving them (there were 44 of them, I recall) alongside the curb, while I went into the station to arrange for a porter to come and pick them up. Well, there were no porters at the station, nor were there any luggage carts! Since the company for which I was working had long advertised "no baggage handling . . . we do it all!" the "we" became "me." I huffed and puffed as I dragged all those suitcases into the Amtrak station, while my passengers, many of whom were able-bodied men, just looked on. We barely made the train on time because I had to make over 20 trips to the counter, carrying two bags at a time, many of them weighing 40 or 50 pounds. I later had to be hospitalized with a shoulder separation as a result.

When we finally boarded the train and got settled in our private coach, a number of my hungry crew started asking, "When will we have breakfast?" I assured them that we would hook up with the dining car, and their breakfast had been pre-ordered in Ogden. About 45 minutes into the ride, the train came to a stop in the middle of nowhere! The conductor came into our car and announced that there had been a heavy rain several days before, causing some damage to the tracks. There would be a "short delay."

The short delay became an entire morning, and on into the afternoon. A few people in the group had put an apple or a candy bar in their carry-on luggage, but most had nothing, and there wasn't even a vending machine available on the train. Most of the people were angry with me because I had told them not to eat breakfast, per orders from the travel company.

We finally got going about 2:20 P.M. having missed the breakfast completely. We stopped at a small town where there was a little sandwich stand. The people were allowed to leave the train and go in and purchase a few stale sandwiches and some soft drinks. We had been scheduled to arrive in Denver in time to have a lovely "farewell" dinner at the hotel, but I knew that would be impossible since our train had been delayed. I called while the group was making sandwiches to tell the hotel that we would be late. Later, I learned that the person to whom I gave the message never relayed it to the catering department, and the meal was ready for the group that never showed. Of course, we were billed for it!

We finally arrived in Denver, not at 5 P.M. as scheduled, but at nearly midnight. An irate female Greyhound driver met us at the Amtrak depot and informed me that she had been waiting since 5 P.M. There was also no porter service at the Amtrak station. The driver and I had to load the luggage onto a huge wagon and push, shove and roll it out to where the motorcoach was parked. We then had to take the bags off the wagon and load the lower luggage bins on the bus. Not a soul offered to help us.

Once we arrived at the hotel, I ran in to the front desk to get the keys and asked the bellmen to come and unload the luggage. I asked the driver if she would assist the luggage handlers to speed up the operation and told the group to please stay on the coach until I returned with their room keys. The driver went around the off side of the bus and opened the luggage bins and started shoving the bags towards the bellmen on the curbside of the coach. As I returned to the coach with the keys, I suddenly heard a scream. The driver, I recall her name was Peggy, had been kneeling with one leg extended into the street pushing the luggage towards the hotel men when a car full of teen joy riders driving without any lights on came careening around the corner and ran over her leg.

I rushed into the hotel to call EMS, and then did what I could to comfort the injured woman, who was in intense pain. I gave out the room keys and tried to placate my hungry, irritable group, who had missed their breakfast and dinner and had very little to eat all day long. After the ambulance had taken the injured bus driver away, the hotel management asked me to please move the bus. Its still-running engine was noisy and disturbing the sleeping guests. I explained that I didn't drive buses but would call Greyhound and ask them to send somebody to move it.

I called the Greyhound number. And waited. And waited.

It was one of those "please do not hang up. The next available operator will be with you as soon as possible," while music I didn't care to hear played in the background. After what seemed like eons, I was able to get through to a human being and I told them they had a driver who had been rushed to a hospital (which one, I didn't have a clue), and I needed someone to come quickly and move the coach. It was over an hour before anyone came, and it was around 2 A.M. when I got to my room.

We had a nice buffet breakfast for the group before we departed for the airport. I recall the people devoured everything but the tablecloths that morning. After a good breakfast they were in a much better mood, and thank goodness, our airport check-in and our flight home were uneventful. I still have trouble with my shoulder after all those years.

Riding a Mule in Molokai

by Charles Nevi

CERTAINLY THERE IS VIRTUE in planning carefully for a trip, and just as certainly there is satisfaction in trips that go off as planned. But there can be beauty in imperfection, too.

Take my mule ride down a 1,600-foot cliff to a leper colony in Molokai, Hawaii. That may not sound like a good idea, but there was something about the way the trip sounded that made it seem appealing.

The first lesson I learned is that mules are not small and cute. They are big and horsey and part jackass, as I would find out.

In what was probably an attempt by the expedition's operators to ease some anxiety about the trip, the mules had names. Mine was named Holani, which meant A Mythical Place.

Climbing onto Holani was not easy, and once on top there was an uncomfortable stretching in my groin. I am used to sitting on smaller and flatter surfaces. I figured I could use the stirrups to relieve some of the pressure by occasionally standing up, though the standing was a bit shaky and required a tight hold on the saddle horn. Just as I was beginning to get comfortable and convince myself that I truly would rather be riding a mule in Molokai, a woman screaming "STOP THIS HORSE!" brought me back to reality.

The rider, I'll call her Ms. Stop This Horse, was frantic. The guides were rushing to her, I assume, to prevent the "horse" from bolting. After a few minutes of trying to calm her, Mr. Stop This Horse, in a firm quiet voice meant only for her but heard clearly by everyone else, told her, in effect, to shut up and calm down because we are going to do this no matter what you think.

After a brief discussion among the guides and Mr. and Ms. Stop This Horse, one of the leaders took the reins of her mule and the procession began. As her guide made soothing sounds and led her mule, I couldn't tell if he was trying to relax Ms. Stop This Horse, her mule or the other 15 of us making the ride.

I couldn't help but remember one of the few pieces of advice I'd ever received about animals: Don't ever let them know you're scared or they will immediately take control. But what the advice didn't include was how do you not let them know? My hands were shaking. I knew that if I tried to say anything to my new friend Holani my voice would also be shaking. So I hoped stoic silence would be interpreted as courage, by the mule as well as the other members of the expedition. I stood lightly in the stirrups and assumed my best John Wayne pose as the procession headed for the trailhead.

I tried not to think about what was ahead of us. But how can you not think about a 1,600-foot cliff, a narrow, rocky trail with 26 switchbacks and a traveling companion who at any second could resume her screaming and stampede the caravan? John Wayne never had to face problems of this magnitude.

As the mule began to tilt forward down the cliff, my attention was naturally drawn to negotiating the rocky trail. When I am required to walk down a steep, slippery, narrow, rocky trail, I look for a spot to put my foot, gently test the spot to be sure it's secure, and then carefully move my other foot to a similar spot. And I proceed slowly down the trail, using hands and arms for balance and support as needed. Now apply these common sense survival strategies to a mule, reputedly a surefooted animal. A mule's head extends well beyond his feet. His front feet, that is. And even if he could see his front feet, which he can't, there is no way he could see his back feet. So if he can't see his feet how in the hell can he be considered sure footed? I have no idea how he decided where to put any one of his four feet. There certainly was no looking for a spot, testing it gently and then searching for another secure spot. And obviously there was no balancing with hands and arms. The entire 1,600 feet and 26 switchbacks were all guesswork as far as I could tell. Each foot just plunked down wherever it happened to plunk down.

There were occasional odd breaks in the descent. On the rare level spots in the trail, some kind of herd instinct would take hold and Holani would run to catch up with the mule in front of him. Well, it wasn't actually running, certainly nothing like a gallop, but there was a sudden lurching as he closed the gap between him and the next mule, and my tilting downward was thrown into reverse as I suddenly tilted backward.

After about an hour and a half of tilting forward and back, mostly forward, with legs extending outward, we reached the level ground of the Kalaupapa Peninsula. Dismounting for the tour of Kalaupapa was more difficult than expected. Legs that are used to extending downward but that have been extending outward for 90 minutes simply will not work. At least not on the first few attempts. But eventually I was on the ground and discovered why cowboys walk the way they do.

The Kalaupapa settlement was founded over a century ago for people suffering from Hansen's disease, more commonly known as leprosy. This is a community where people were exiled to die and have chosen to remain to live. It is a story for another time, and a very different story from the mule ride to and from the peninsula.

The return trip up the cliff was a bit more comfortable. Legs could no longer feel pain. Tilting backward is easier than tilting forward because the saddle horn is easier to hold on to. So we were about an hour into a rather uneventful return trip when we were again confronted with something not in the plans. There was a flurry of movement ahead in the trail.

Holani kept moving forward until he was blocked by the mules ahead of us. Someone had fallen. On one of those level spots where the mule lurches forward, the rider had lost his grip and fallen backward and was apparently dragged a few feet before he could get his foot untangled from the stirrup. He was dirty, bloody and a pasty white. It was Mr. Stop This Horse. Fortunately, nothing was broken, no apparent permanent damage. But he was bruised, physically and I suspect emotionally.

Did his mule dump him on purpose? Is there some kind of justice system or sense of vengeance among mules? Should they be known for more than just being stubborn and surefooted? Was it something his wife said or did? Was she in cahoots with the mule? Apparently not harboring any such suspicions, Mr. Stop This Horse was soon back up on his mule and the journey continued.

Near the mule stables is another of the attractions on Molokai, the phallic rocks. Some believe that rubbing a particularly large and unmistakably phallic shaped rock can lead to conception. Others believe, at least I do, that it is a good idea to sit on this rock at the conclusion of the mule ride. It may or may not have any restorative powers, and restoration may or may not be needed, but after several hours of stretching and bumping on a mule, a few minutes sitting on a phallic rock seemed in order.

The morning after the ride I noticed a statue in front of a

nearby apartment. It seemed like an odd place for a statue. Then it seemed to move, ever so slowly. Then it moved again. It was not a statue. It was a moving object, though an object that moved very slowly. It was him, Mr. Stop This Horse. It appeared that every bone, muscle, joint, cartilage and tissue in his body were sore. He was trying to make it from the condo doorway to his car, probably to head for the airport and then home. I don't know if he ever made it to his car. It was too painful to watch.

But if he ever did make it home, what part of the trip do you suppose he talked about to his friends? The plane being on time, the luggage not being lost, the restaurant food? Or was his highlight, like mine, that he'd rather be riding a mule in Molokai?

The Road to Tunis

by Dorothy Thompson

"I'M ON THE WRONG CONTINENT," I said over the phone to the agent at my travel insurance office, "and, so far, my vacation has been like one of those *The Road to wherever* movies … only without Bing Crosby or Bob Hope."

The good news was I had my luggage. The bad news was that I was in Frankfurt, Germany, and the ship I was supposed to be on had left Istanbul, Turkey.

The trouble began days earlier when I was home in Wisconsin and over a foot of snow had fallen by the time a decision had to be made—stay or go. The cruise line said I should make every "reasonable" effort to get to the airport, and so I went.

At the gate, I learned that my flight to Milwaukee had been canceled because the airport there was closed due to snow. Over the next 12 hours, the folks at Madison's airport tried to re-route me through Chicago, Minneapolis and Detroit, but virtually every airport in the Midwest was closed.

Only a few taxis were operating and I was fortunate, after a mere two-hour wait, to get one to take me a few blocks to the home of a gracious relative who lives near the airport. Snowed in as well, she didn't seem to mind having company, though I wasn't good company as I spent most of the time unsuccessfully trying to phone the airline and the cruise line for assistance and advice.

The next day I taxied back to the airport, hopeful of a better day. The same gate agent was on duty. (Had he been there all night?) The only difference as I began Day Two was that the lines were longer and the people, many of whom had spent the night in the airport, were in very bad moods. After hours of delays, my flight was canceled and I realized that there was no possible way I could make Istanbul before the ship sailed. I would have to go home unceremoniously and miss a once-in-a-lifetime cruise tour of Africa ... or catch up to the ship at the first port of call, in La Goulette, Tunisia. The arrangements I'd made at work and at home in order to be gone this long would simply be impossible to re-do at a later date.

"I need a ticket to Tunis," I said to the gate agent.

"Where's that?" he asked.

"North Africa," I replied.

I don't suppose many tickets to Tunis are sold at the Dane County Airport. But he got on the computer and found a way to get me there via London, leaving the next morning. Over $700 in unanticipated expense, so far. But at least, after some more delays, fits and starts, I was on my way, heading to Tunis via a connecting flight in Frankfurt.

During the seven hours of my flight, I did what research I could, asking flight crew members if they'd ever been to Tunis. Only one had been there. He was not exactly reassuring, but later, realizing I was determined, tried to soften his initial advice (which was not to go there) and offered to assist me to my connection once we got to Frankfurt. All I needed to do was stay on the plane until everyone else got off.

I followed him, found my luggage and, as we approached customs, he asked for my passport. Though this concerned me a little, I handed it over. He held it up, smiled at some guys in uniforms, said something to them in German and I was through customs without stopping or even slowing down. We walked right around the lines.

"What did you say to them?" I asked.

"I told them you are my wife," he said.

I kept up with him as he led the way to the check-in gate for my connecting flight, then said thanks and away he went.

I checked at the gate. I could spend the night in Frankfurt and take a flight the next day.

At the airport hotel, the bellhop said that the bell captain was from Tunisia and might be able to assist. I found him fast. He told me that I was fortunate since La Goulette is only about three miles from the airport. He offered to phone ahead and have a car waiting but I politely declined. I went to my room and called the travel insurance agent to check on my ship.

The next morning I headed to the lobby for my continental breakfast and was chatted up by an official-looking man.

"May I ask where you're going?" he asked. He explained that he was the chief of security at the hotel and also an American. I said that I was going to Tunis, that the bell captain was going to assist me and that in spite of delay, everything was fine now. But he had other thoughts and was only too willing to share them. He referenced State Department bulletins, talked about recent kidnappings in the region and advised me about the dangers of women traveling alone.

At the gate, I noticed only a few women, some of them in traditional dress. I was wearing jeans. From what I could see on luggage tags, most of my fellow travelers were, if not from Tunisia, from places not so friendly toward the U.S.—like Libya and Algeria.

I felt very American. There were four Westerners aboard, including an older couple who had been stranded in the snowstorm in Minneapolis and were now trying, like me, to catch up with the ship.

The four of us stood out when food was served. Since it

was the holy Ramadan, we were practically the only ones eating. For a while I thought of how comforting it must be to be like the nice couple, having each other to depend on until they got into an argument and started shouting at each other, slamming trays and causing a scene—not once, but twice, during the flight.

Finally, the plane landed in Tunis. I waited by the carousel in the hot, stuffy terminal for over an hour as everyone's luggage but mine came around. Mine was the last bag off. I knew I had a couple of hours to find the ship and I knew it wasn't that far away. But I also knew I hadn't made it yet. I hopped into the first cab to pull up to the curb and said, "Take me to La Goulette." The driver said something back that I couldn't understand. He said a lot of things I couldn't understand over the course of our travels together. He didn't understand English, my only language. I think he was asking which of two La Goulettes, old or new? Left or right? What to do?

I started saying words that might indicate where I needed to go.

"Harbor."

"Dock."

"Ship."

I tried the name of my ship. No response.

"Port," I said.

"Ah! Port!" he replied and launched into a lengthy speech, none of which I understood.

"Do you take dollars?" I asked, realizing that I had no local currency.

My driver again launched into a long speech, which I didn't understand but I responded, and he didn't understand.

As we were leaving the city, he suddenly stopped the taxi in the middle of the street and got out. "Oh, no," I thought.

"Is this the thing I was warned about? Will I now be robbed or kidnapped or worse?" But I tried to look confident. He dashed to a corner and briefly spoke to a couple of men there and then was back in the cab and we continued on our way.

Outside the city, at a crossroads just past a farm field, the same thing happened again. Now that we were out of town, away from witnesses, was I in danger? After long minutes of silence, he started chatting again. As we neared what I could see to be the ocean, I was growing more confident that I might actually make it. Then, one last time he pulled over, leaving me and the cab in mid-road for one more uncertain moment, before he left my luggage and me on a corner outside the dock where a large group of rugged-looking longshoremen were taking a break.

"Ten dollars," he said. I gave it to him.

As best I could decipher from his conversation, it may have been his first day as a taxi driver. The stopping and chatting was to inquire about directions, exchange rates and the like. I was annoyed that he'd left me and my bags so far from where I needed to be, until I think I understood him to explain that he'd taken me as far as taxis were allowed to go.

I thought I was in the right place, though I couldn't read the signs or understand anything that was being said. I guessed that I needed to enter a terminal building about a block away from a ramp that led about three stories above the ground. I couldn't carry both bags that far at once and I didn't want to leave one while I carried the other one. The longshoremen were giving me looks as I checked my watch. Would I get to the ship in time?

I asked the men if one of them would help me with my bags and explained that I could pay. They didn't appear to understand. For a moment, I considered abandoning the baggage, which had cost me an hour at the airport and was now keeping me out of the terminal. Suddenly a very large man who spoke French and English got out of a shiny black car that I hadn't noticed parked behind me. He graciously translated and one of the men carried a bag, and I was able to manage the other. The others tagged along.

Yikes! After that tip I was down to $3 in cash. But from the top of the ramp I could see my ship, not so very far away but beyond shouting distance over some fences.

The uniformed man at the main doorway to the terminal said something, again that I didn't understand but which seemed to be on the order of "You can't come in here now. We are closed."

"You HAVE to let me in! I can see my ship from here," I said. He understood my message, if not my words, went to an office and made some phone calls. A few minutes later he motioned for me to come inside and to one of the longshoremen, apparently to help with my bags. But two men responded to his motion and then exchanged some hostile words until he waved them both through, one per bag. I followed.

We headed down a poorly lit and dingy stairway, and down, down, getting dimmer and dimmer. I'm so close now that nothing more can go wrong, right? At the bottom of the stairs, there was a commotion, apparently an assault in progress. For just a second I felt some panic, until I noticed that the two guys had hurried to position themselves between the fight and me. They said something. Again I didn't understand.

But soon I figured it out. Whew! They were taking me to the port authority police station to have my passport examined before I could enter. However, the police were busy at the moment breaking up a fight.

That settled and my passport stamped, we headed down the docks to my ship. I gave them each $1, leaving me exactly $1. The security officer checked my documents, and I was finally aboard.

The next few weeks of travel through sometimes rough seas, Third World ports, unpaved roads in and around Morocco, Senegal, Ivory Coast, Ghana, Togo, Benin, Namibia and South Africa would prove to be easy compared to getting there.

A Detour in Paradise

by Burt Dragin

THE TINY AIR MOOREA prop sputtered down the runway at Papeete Airport on the island of Tahiti enroute to Moorea, first stop on our two-island Ten Day Tahiti Paradise Package. My wife, Nadine, and I were both quickly captivated by the lush scene below—bold strokes of turquoise, aqua and purple, accented by the billowing white foam of the ocean.

Our first three days were sublime. The Moorea Lagoon Hotel rests on several acres of tree-lined hills and red hibiscus. Our thatched hut was smartly furnished and barely 50 feet from two red clay tennis courts. We swam. We strolled the beach at dusk. We dined on succulent lobster at our pool side restaurant. We sniffed the perfumed plumeria. After a morning of tennis we sailed to Cook's Bay, thrilled by the spiky volcanic mountains. Perfect!

"And we haven't even been to Bora Bora yet," Nadine said in happy anticipation. (That's when I felt a knot in my stomach. Nadine's comment reminded me of an old high school football cheer: "Hey, hey, look at the score / That's OK but we want more." It presaged disaster; our team inevitably fumbled and lost. But not here in paradise, I reasoned. I put it out of my mind.)

Our next flight was less luxurious. Rain pelted Bora Bora, and the pilot aborted a landing, pulled up and banked left. I banked right, instinctively reaching for a concealed airline-size bottle of gin. As we circled over grayish water, word trickled back that the pilot was waiting for the rain to abate for a safer landing. And if it didn't? Not a productive thought. I recalled another flight on Garuda Airlines from Bali to Jogjakarta. The young captain allowed passengers to duck into the cockpit for a pilot's-eye-view. While Nadine and I did so a piece of the ceiling cracked off and fell near my feet. Another real confidence builder.

But the rain stopped quickly, and the pilot set the plane down easily on an airstrip near the water. We tossed our luggage onto a white powerboat awaiting our arrival and were whisked around the gorgeous island to the Hotel Tuateora Club, the Bora Bora part of the Ten Day Tahiti Paradise Package. As we approached the pier, Nadine and I absorbed the stunning contrast between the Hotel Tuateora's slick brochure ("private beach," "spacious grounds," "charming decor") and the Hotel Tuateora itself.

"There doesn't seem to be any beach," Nadine lamented.

My eyes went past the wind-whipped flags of Italy, France, the U.S. and others on the pier's end toward two white structures across the road that were in fact Hotel Tuateora. They were about 100 yards from the boat and looked prison like, drab concrete rectangles radiating doom. We walked half the length of the pier and were greeted by a matronly French woman, hands extended, "Welcome to Tuateora," she beamed. "I'm Suzanne. Come have your complimentary Mai Tai!" Suzanne nimbly led the way while Nadine and I exchanged looks of dubious hope. The drinks were the first clue: sad, plain glasses with tasteless fruit juice. Each bore a tiny umbrella swizzle stick that looked like it was bought at a flea market.

We went into the restaurant, which had the ambiance of a reform school cafeteria. Three guests huddled at the only other occupied table. They munched on piles of strange fruit that looked like it had been harvested from a nearby planet. I sneaked glances at the lunch menu. The special appeared to be some exotic fish with wings.

I began to ponder a hunger strike.

Suzanne broke my reverie. "Drink up," she said. "Your room is almost ready."

"Where," inquired Nadine, "is the private beach?"

"Oh, we have our own atoll," Susanne replied proudly. "We'll take you there."

Our room was across a gravel road and was true to the decor of the main buildings: wooden exterior of chipped white paint, sliding glass doors divided by sickly green wooden slats and a cement lanai. We peeked inside. Bare walls framed a dingy gray carpet that supported post-industrial period furniture. We retreated to the lanai and pulled up two plastic chairs. "We'll only have to sleep here," we agreed. And now my mind drifted back to a similar shock on a visit to the Grand Bahamas. There was riotous green splendor on the heart of the island, but a visit to the West End revealed long-abandoned piers and sad shanties barely supporting life. This is where most vacationing Americans are skilled at averting their eyes. But Nadine and I had trekked on in search of a legendary fish eatery. Quickly lost, we asked a local man for directions. He and his ill-clad children sat on a huge abandoned steel cylinder. His response to our request for directions, though a non sequitur, has never left me. He shrugged: "We're the same as you," he said. We trekked on.

Once unpacked at our Bora Bora retreat, we were eager to visit the "private beach." The boat cut a swath of water as it hustled us to our own private atoll. We couldn't wait for sublime snorkeling to offset the Tuateora's "amenities." Masks in place, we slipped in hoping to spy some exotic species but instead were greeted by water that was roughly 80 percent mud. We finally discovered the only species to be seen: bottom-hugging sea slugs. Quickly we grew nostalgic; saying it seemed like only yesterday that we were in the pristine waters of Moorea. (Then we realized that actually it was.)

A few hours later as dusk enveloped the Tuateora, Nadine and I took out our novels, only to find that the lamps had no light bulbs. Then we heard the start of the night's acrobatics within the walls, where small creatures scurried ceaselessly.

"Only six more nights," I noted.

Two days later, having endured Tuateora's unique ambiance, Nadine and I were as downcast as a couple of hooked fish. We feigned excitement on a walk across the craggy beach where we plucked a perfectly formed cone-shaped shell. "Our memory of Tuateora," Nadine said.

Later that night, as we mulled an "Escape from Tuateora," Nadine bolted up and announced, "Our thing is moving!" Sure enough, our souvenir shell was moonwalking across the floor, leaving a thin trail of slime in its wake. Nadine scooped up our living momento, and we tiptoed past the main Tuateora building, hoping no one was standing guard. (I felt like James Cagney in *White Heat*, ready to have some filthy screw plug me in the back. But we cleared the yard; no searchlights blared.) Nadine lovingly placed the mobile mollusk in its watery home.

We returned to our room just as the tiny Flying Wallendas were warming up. Once more we contemplated escape from both the grounds and our prepaid contract. It was a daunting challenge. We needed the cunning of a Steve McQueen and a negotiator with the savvy of a Henry Kissinger. We had, unfortunately, pre-paid our entire stay. Our addled brains produced no plan of substance as we lapsed into deep sleep. But the very next day our Ship of Gold sailed in! Suzanne, acutely aware of our long faces, could take it no more. "I don't want the other guests to see you so distressed," she admitted. (Where those "other guests" were staying was a mystery. Perhaps they were so enchanted with the decor they remained in their rooms.)

"What if I agree to refund the remaining four nights lodging? Perhaps you'd like to find another hotel for the rest of your stay." Perhaps? Perhaps we broke the record for the Bora Bora one-mile run! Two hours later, in the comfort of the Bora Bora Beach Club, we took our final glance at the Tuateora brochure and noticed one promise that had the unmistakable ring of truth: "Visitors shall not soon forget their Club Tuateora Hotel island experience."

The Great Train Robbery

by Dorothy Ciminelli Delmonte

I KNEW THE MOMENT the train came to a halt and the aisles filled with men carrying machine guns that this was not going to be a dream vacation.

"What the hell did you get us into?" my husband screeched. "You and your soft adventure. Where in the world are we anyway?"

"Shhh," I interrupted him. "Let's see what's going on."

We were in the vast state of Chihuahua, Mexico, riding the *primera clase* vista coach toward a tiny shantytown called Creel. There we were to be met by our guide Raphael, who was then taking us to our lodge. Our final destination was Barranca del Cobra, Mexico's Copper Canyon, a vast area in the Sierra Madre Occidental Mountains, which is seven times larger than the Grand Canyon and is home to the Tarahumara Indians. The Tarahumaras are the oldest pre-Columbian Indian civilization in North America. They live in the caves and canyon land and avoid contact with outsiders. Our goal was to reach and explore this area, then to continue south to Los Mochis, Mexico, and the ferry across the Sea of Cortez to Baja, California.

The men with the machine guns were on our side, there to protect us from dangers we were previously unaware of. They were a strange-looking lot, dressed in suits and ties with a spare round of ammunition draped against white shirts. I recognized one man as the same one who had greeted us as we boarded the train that morning. After welcoming us, he proceeded to seat all the *Norteamericanos* in one car. Then he went on to give us a short history of the Mexican territory we were about to traverse. He told us the story of Pancho Villa, a Mexican rebel who led revolts against President Venustiano Carranza in 1914 and who successfully hid for over 10 years in the rugged terrain we were crossing.

Looking out the windows, we could see men lurking and lurching along the railroad tracks.

"What's going on?" a passenger blurted in exasperation.

"*Bandidos*," mumbled one of the guards, shifting his stance to secure himself. It was obvious he was ready to fire his gun if anyone entered the train.

Meanwhile, the blue-black heads of the robbers weaved in between the railroad cars. A pair of grimy hands slapped at the train windows. They were a ragged crew, caked with dirt and plied with liquor. As they stumbled around the train looking for an entrance, I—who consider myself a nonviolent person—was suddenly glad that a man with a machine gun was standing in the aisle hovering over me.

"They're lying down in front of the train!" someone shouted. Apparently this was the tactic *bandidos* used to stop and rob trains in the countryside.

When I looked at my husband, I saw his face had turned the color of a cooked tortilla. Despite the fact that my own heart was beating wildly, I began to giggle. This was all so absurd. Here we were, a couple of nondescript people in the middle of a train robbery. There was an exciting element to all this.

"I don't know what you find so amusing," my husband snipped.

"Just think what a great story this will make for our future grandchildren," I gasped, smothering my chuckles.

"Yes," my counterpart muttered, "if we live to tell it."

Slowly the train began to pull forward, leaving our partners in adventure in the dust. Our armed guards stowed their guns and returned to the more mundane task of serving us a boxed lunch—green baloney sandwiches. Deciding that the sandwiches were more dangerous than the *bandidos,* we skipped the meal and spent the next five hours on the train wishing we had eaten breakfast or packed some food.

We learned a lot on that vacation.

Are We Done Yet?

by Ann L. Egan

"Good afternoon, folks. Welcome aboard your charter flight direct to Toronto's Pearson International Airport. I understand that most of you are pretty hungry. We will be airborne shortly and as soon as we reach cruising altitude the flight attendants will be serving your meal." That was when the cheering broke out. Never seen an entire plane full of people cheer the food? Neither had I until now.

Things had started out on a promising note. It was early January and my daughter and I were getting out of the cold and snowy north for our annual sojourn in the warm green lushness of the Caribbean. What could be better? (As it turned out, almost anything.) We had rented a condo outside of Puerto Plata in the Dominican Republic.

Our flight from Toronto landed around dinnertime and by the time we picked up our rental car and got on the road it was dusk. We had one of the usual "road maps" supplied with a rental car in the islands (the place mats at a Howard Johnson's go into more detail), along with some verbal instructions ("stay on the main road for eight to nine miles, watch for a road to the right—it's not marked well") from the rental agent and the comforting comment from a couple who were returning a car that even a fender bender would result in immediate jail. We missed the road to the condo complex several times in the dark and finally asked a group of young men hanging out on their motor bikes at the side of the road to direct us. As they led us down a single lane, unlit, unpaved, deeply rutted dirt road, I began to have visions of the hometown paper reporting that two local women had been robbed/raped/murdered (take your choice) while on vacation. Not so! They delivered us cheerfully and safely to the condo offices and waved us on our way.

Once we were checked in, the night manager drove with us another couple of miles into the complex and installed us in our second floor condo, commenting that the couple who owned the first floor unit had arrived earlier in the week and were "doing some work" on their place. Since it was dark and we were tired from traveling, we decided to unpack, have something to eat and go to bed. That was when my daughter discovered that she didn't have the keys for her luggage—they were home on her dresser. A minor annoyance. We had enough in our carry-on for immediate needs. Time enough in the morning to look for a locksmith.

As our motor bike escort took us along that dark rutted road to the condo office I had noticed a billboard advertising something about "Hilton." The next morning we decided to treat ourselves to breakfast at the "Hilton" and then go into town and find a locksmith. Something I hadn't noticed in the dark the night before was the dead donkey lying by the side of the road next to our turn-off (or the dead dog and assorted other dead creatures along the roads. These sad sights and others were still there when we left two weeks later). "Hilton," it turned out, had nothing to do with any hotel chain; it was a local tobacco product. Oh well, who needs breakfast! We found the locksmith without too much difficulty, but we had to wait outside while he worked on the suitcase. His tiny kiosk had no room for us to be inside at the same time he and the suitcase were in there. (It was drizzling but rumored to be clearing soon.) While neither one of us is fluent in Spanish, it didn't take a native speaker to get the meaning of "ayeee yiee yiee caramba," muttered with increasing frequency. An hour and a half later, we took the open suitcase and its broken locks back to the condo to unpack. Forget breakfast! Who cares about a damaged suitcase (it was getting pretty worn anyway)? Let's get changed and down to that beach.

Down the stairs, down the street, through a stand of pines and we were on the beach. At last, sun, sand, surf, this is what we came for. But wait, what is this black gooey stuff? Nothing to worry about we were told, just the results of a "minor" off-shore spill. "Wear something on your feet, though, that tarry stuff is pretty hard to get off. Oh yes, and don't take any good towels to the beach, you'll never get that stuff out of them." My daughter still has the shoes she wore there. Attempts to clean them have been, by and large, unsuccessful. At least one attempt resulted in some minor notoriety when, having failed to rinse out all the detergent, she wore them in the rain and they started foaming.

The travel guides we had read in planning our trip indicated that there was lots to do on this island besides playing on the beach, and so we modified our plans and set off. We visited the Fort of San Felipe and took the obligatory tourist pictures; it misted. We went to the beach resort of Sosua; it rained. No, it poured. So, we shopped in Sosua. When we got tired of shopping we stopped for lunch in a handsome open-air restaurant. Club sandwiches sounded good. "What," my daughter asked the waiter, "is on the club sandwiches?" (I told you we weren't novices. We once asked for rolls at dinner and ended up with a basket of hot dog buns.) "Oh," said the waiter, "pork chops, chicken livers, goose beaks ... " Goose beaks!! (Obviously something gone awry in communication or in the kitchen.)

We settled for French fries. The people at the next table were busy discussing the outbreak of meningitis in the town. The rain persisted and had a nasty chill to it.

That single unpaved, rutted lane to our condo complex was now soaked and the ruts had become pools. Back at the condo, damp and cold, we discovered that we were more likely to slosh than to slouch. The condos were constructed of poured concrete and the rains had been particularly heavy that entire year. We could see the line of dampness creeping down our walls. We really noticed it as they became thoroughly soaked and the rain began to drip and puddle on the bedside table. One evening it even put out our candles. The electricity turned out to be intermittent. The condo management attributed this variously to the rains or the revolutionaries, depending on which one you spoke to. We went to bed early—many nights.

We planned a trip to ride the cable car to the top of Mount Isabel de Torres, which we could see from our windows. Mount Isabel de Torres, the guidebooks say, has a pastoral park and spectacular views of land and water. It has a massive statue of Christ the Redeemer. We can only verify the massive statue from personal experience. The cable car wasn't running; the system was being rebuilt with reopening anticipated sometime the following year. We contented ourselves with looking at Christ the Redeemer from our windows when the rains let up enough to give us a peek at the peak.

We spent one overcast, wet (but not pouring) day driving inland to Santiago. The drive was fascinating; the road cuts through the mountains and past fields of coffee and tobacco. Everything looked green and fresh—we didn't have to wonder why. We shopped for amber in Puerto Plata and were harassed constantly by young boys who promised to "introduce" us to the merchants and get us "good" prices.

Staying at the condo turned out to be as much of a challenge as going out. The "doing some work" in the ground floor condo sounded like a major reconstruction job, apparently done by workers who suffered from serious hearing deficiencies judging from the volume at which they communicated with each other. We spent a lot of time looking for ice to put in our electric refrigerator and for candles so that we could at least play backgammon after dark.

Then we both got sick. I had an asthma attack and a recurrence of a problem with kidney infection. My daughter had an uncomfortable upper respiratory infection. We contacted a representative of the tour company, and they provided us with a local representative to get us some medical assistance. Bruno was a charming, personable and helpful young man. He took us to a clinic that, according to him, his grandfather had founded and where he attended "all the briefings."

We were both seen by a cardiologist (the only physician available who spoke any English). He was sympathetic, helpful and efficient. The facility was not for the faint of heart. The lavatory had no running water and the x-ray room was missing part of the outside wall. After a thorough examination and some obvious hesitation about the right term, he diagnosed my daughter as having the "grumpies." We never did find out exactly what "grumpies" are but take them to be something similar to grippe. The pharmacy was another surprise. Apparently it used to be the lunch counter for the clinic and so one of my prescriptions came out of the ice cream cooler.

At the condo offices my daughter asserted herself as only she can. Her assertiveness, compounded by the grumpies and aggravated by rainwater that had now seeped into the bed linens and the never ending reconstruction, got us moved to a new, single-story unit. The noise was replaced by thousands of tiny ants and a maid who kept wanting to take our temperatures. The tiny ants covered every surface. They were on the counter tops, on the dishes, in the pots and pans, on the stove burners, in the toaster and the coffee maker. It was necessary to brush them off the toaster both before and after making toast. We inadvertently incinerated many of their little bodies while trying to heat soup and make toast. We got desperate and decided to eat out. We went to a restaurant attached to a training school for students in the hospitality industry, but we couldn't cut the meat. We tried a pizza place, but when they didn't know what pepperoni was we decided to give it a pass. By this time we were really sick of pastries, something that has never happened before or since. Mother Nature took care of this for us by producing a REAL storm, which flooded some of the main roads in town, and cut us off from our supply of sweets.

We began to count not only the days but the hours until our vacation would end. Why not just fly home early, you ask. Why not, indeed! The charter we had flown on was a once a week arrival/departure and anything else would have required full fare on a regular flight. Sadly, not an option. So we spent our time brushing ants off everything, taking our prescriptions and going for rides to the clinic with Bruno.

That, my friends, is why *we* cheered when the captain of our flight announced that dinner would be served soon. I don't know why the rest of the passengers cheered. I was too tired and sick to ask any of them. No vacation is ever a total loss though. We have some lovely souvenirs (my granddaughter fit perfectly in her basket for the first few months of her life), some sharp-looking sandals that continue to get comments and some very interesting pictures. How many times can you come back from vacation and say to your physician, "I brought you my vacation pictures" and hand him a set of x-rays?

Side Trip to the Hospital

by Jan DeGrass

OUR PROBLEM STARTED in Zagreb, Yugoslavia, after we ate rich, sweet cakes and Viennese coffee with whipped cream. Dan complained of indigestion.

It worsened at Lake Ohrid in Macedonia. We spent the day seeking traces of early Christian frescoes on the walls of tiny, dark, mean churches. The early saints were depicted as gaunt, almost savage men with blackened bellies and moss growing over their teeth, enough to turn anyone's stomach. That evening, Dan pushed a piece of fish around the plate at an outdoor restaurant. "Light meals from now on," he said. "I've had enough 'svinski kotlet.'" Pork chops had been standard fare on the Yugoslavian menu.

We were travelers who had arranged our own tour in 1979 during a more peaceful, gentle time for that country. The next day we had booked a flight from Ohrid airport to Beograd, the capital. The Yugoslavs treated this domestic flight with the same grim determination with which they boarded a bus.

The incoming plane had no sooner touched down on the runway before the 50 passengers were massed, sweaty and panting, at the boarding gate blocking the disembarking passengers with all the efficiency of an American football team.

The plane was stuffy and crowded, but we had already paid for a top-notch hotel in which to unwind. We reached the hotel at noon and by 1 P.M. Dan was in bed. The brochure promised modernity, private bathroom and air conditioning. The bathroom proved exceptionally modern and similar to the one in the brochure photo, a delight as we both had had our fill of squatting over holes in the ground. The air conditioning was another story. On each window a sign had been neatly taped. Roughly translated, it explained that because of such a modern technological marvel as this clunking, smelly box permanently affixed to the window, guests were requested never to open the windows again, under penalty of eviction.

I asked Dan if I could get him anything. "How about yogurt?" he suggested. I consulted the dictionary for the appropriate Serb-Croatian word and armed with this knowledge and a dwindling budget of dinars, I set forth.

By the following morning Dan had consumed two containers of yogurt and some weak tea. He was nauseous and had decided to sit in a lukewarm bath.

As the groaning box struggled to change the air, I booked another night at the top-notch hotel. The desk attendant seemed weary.

"My friend is sick," I said. "How do we find a doctor?" He managed a fabricated smile of hospitality. He would arrange everything. A doctor would come to the room. No problem. We waited. Dan, stripped to his underwear, was now groaning in unison with the air conditioning. Presently a small crowd arrived at the door— the doctor, a swarthy, tanned man in his 50s, his young assistant and a giggling desk clerk who said she would translate.

The two medical men took a glance around the room observing the air conditioning sign on the window, then asked the first question. "Do you smoke?" asked the doctor.

"No," we choroused.

The doctor shook his head sadly and brought forth a pack of Marlboros. He and his assistant lit up and resumed what sounded like a conversation about soccer scores. The desk clerk stepped closer to remind me that it was not permitted to open the window no matter how much cigarette smoke was in the air. In so doing, she caught sight of Dan's purple underwear, began to blush and giggle and then excused herself. We heard her laughing all the way down the hall.

Doctor and assistant continued to chat, then conducted a pidgin conversation with the patient. Finally they stood up, stubbed out their cigarettes on the tea saucer and pronounced the verdict. "It is only gastritis," the doctor said grandly and left a prescription. Already 300 dinars into next week's budget, I now had to stalk the streets in search of a pharmacy.

Night descended on the top-notch hotel. We lay in our twin beds, awake.

"I must be hallucinating now," Dan said. "I feel as if there are insects crawling up my arm."

Tenderly, I reached across from my bed to soothe his fevered skin and placed my palm squarely on the hard shell of a bug the size of a baseball. Snapping on the light, I smacked the bug with a magazine, marched eight flights down the modern highrise (the elevator was out of order) bearing the cockroach on a saucer and placed it before the same weary desk clerk.

"That is only small bug from kitchen," he soothed, mustering another approved hospitality grin.

The night wore on. The gastritis became more localized and painful. "I think I should go to the hospital," Dan said miserably at 1:15.

Our desk friend, who was dozing while propped up in his seat, swung into action. Dashing into the street he hailed a cab. Eventually, one pulled over and we climbed in. I gave my rehearsed speech in Serb-Croatian to the taxi driver.

"We must go to the hospital, quickly."

The car bumped to a halt, the driver turned in disbelief and repeated my words so strangely I thought perhaps I had said "to the slaughterhouse" by mistake. After some rapid muttering, he slowly enunciated, "The hospital is only three streets away."

"Good," I answered, not grasping the point.

He spoke again as if to a naughty child. "If the hospital is only three streets away, how can I make any money?"

Summoning my mastery of the language, and accompanied by appropriate groans from the invalid, I said melodramatically, "We must go to the hospital. This man is sick!"

"He's sick. I'm sick. We're all sick. I take you to a nice nightclub now." He cursed loudly and squealed his tires. I crossed my fingers.

The hospital waiting room looked like a scene from Dante's visit to hell. It was an unadorned concrete bunker lighted only by a single, glaring, naked bulb. Friends and family waited uncomfortably on benches stained by years of oozing fluids. A weeping grandmother railed at the staff while her black-eyed, bruised youth retched and moaned beside her. Another man conducted a feverish babble with an imaginary companion. After some explanation in a jumble of languages, Dan was shuffled through a tiny door guarded by a burly tough with a face like a pit bull.

I waited. One hour passed in which I contemplated my sins at this first circle of purgatory. Finally, I was summoned to the narrow door by the pit bull. "Go in," he urged. I passed the portals and stepped into the shiny glow of stainless steel and smiling, busy attendants in white uniforms.

"Good evening," a young, curly-haired, cherubic man greeted me in flawless English. "You may see your friend now. Please approach. He has appendicitis."

Before I could digest this information, the doctor leaned forward again. "Let me show you my stethoscope," he said, waving a bright red, vinyl instrument hanging around his neck.

"I got it in Texas," he said with a grin. "I studied there under a famous heart surgeon." We hurried down the hall. "You are lucky to find me here," he went on. "I told your husband that no American doctor had examined him like I am able."

Dan, who was sitting up on a table, looked happier as he clutched an ice pack.

The doctor continued breathlessly and garrulously, "I poke him here, like so," and he demonstrated once again on Dan's exposed stomach. "'Oooww!' he said to me, so I know right away." Dan echoed the doctor, "Oooww!"

"No other American doctor has examined him in this way."

"Wonderful," I said unenthusiastically. "Appendicitis."

"We shall operate in the morning," the grinning doctor continued. "Now, good night. You will please go home." Interview over, he abruptly left the room. We looked at one another.

"Uh, how do we get back to the hotel?" Dan asked.

"Good God, we'll have to get another taxi." But it was 2:30 A.M. and there were no taxis in sight.

"I'm feeling much better," Dan said. "Let's walk. After all, it's only three streets."

When we entered the lobby, the weary desk clerk jumped to attention as if he had seen a ghost.

"Appendicitis," we explained breezily. "The doctor told us to go home."

"To-go-home," he repeated slowly. "I think this doctor is very stupid man." Clearly, he had visions of the international visitor expiring at the top-notch hotel and souring its tourist reputation. "Please go back to hospital. Please!" he begged. "I am phoning the ambulance. Immediately."

In the end, it was the right thing to do. Dan's operation took place that morning and it was successful. I passed many happy hours walking the "only three streets" to visit him.

No Stiff Upper Lip

by Jennell Woulf

FLINCHING AT THE RAINDROPS pelting my face, I saw the sign above a set of heavy purple doors. "The King's Arms: Great Beer, Lousy Food." *At least I could dry off,* I thought.

"Excuse me," I mumbled, leaning across the linoleum counter.

The man behind the bar turned from the pint he was pouring to face me.

"What'll it be?"

"Actually, I need some help. I've lost my travel papers," I sighed. "My money is gone, the train passes, plane tickets and the traveler's checks too. Oh, shit," I gasped as I remembered there was more. "My passport and my friends' passports were in there, too. God, I'm screwed." I broke down and sobbed.

"Aww, come now," The bartender thumbed the weathered stool next to me. "Have a seat, love."

I slumped on the worn stool.

"Here," he said, planting a pint of heady black sludge in front of me. "Why don't you start with this?"

Reluctantly, I hoisted the weighty glass to my mouth and sipped the strange brew. Licking the froth from my upper lip, I remembered my plight. "I'm sorry, but I can't pay for this."

"No worries," the barman smiled, exposing a shiny gold incisor. "It's on the house."

"Oh, thank you. So much."

"You're welcome. Tell me, what is an American girl doing all alone without her passport and all that?"

I pulled a little more off that immense glass. It wasn't half as bad as it looked. Relaxing as I drank, I confessed my irresponsibility to that golden-toothed bartender, while my hair dripped little pools of London's sorrow on the counter.

"My friends, they're waiting for me at Victoria Station, downtown. We were supposed to be in Dublin tonight, but I, I left this notebook with our tickets and money and passports and everything at this campground where we stayed last night, but now it's gone." I sighed, flustered. "Basically, I'm lost and broke, and I'm 5,000 miles from home." I closed my eyes tightly, as if shutting my troubles out would return me to carefree afternoons of foreign delight.

My anxiety lessened with each inch I gained on my glass.

"Would'ya getta look at that," the barman cracked to an anonymous gray face a few stools down. Turning to me, he teased, "You like that Guinness, eh? Most you little girls can't stand the stuff."

I blushed. "It's not bad."

Back in the States, I wasn't old enough to drink, but I guess I was old enough for England. I felt oddly mature as I sipped that beer and licked my wounds. I unloaded my sob story on the Northern Hemisphere's kindest bartender before begging.

"I'm sorry to have to ask this," I began, more than slightly embarrassed, "But it would really help if I could borrow two-pounds-forty from someone so I could at least get back into the city. I promise to pay them ba … "

Before I could finish, the bartender reached into his pocket and slid a five-pound note across the liquor-stained counter. "Seems like it's for a good enough cause."

"Oh, thank you. Thank you *so* much. If I could just get your address or a business card or something so I could send you … "

"Cheers, luv." Winking, he dismissed my offer. "Now you go catch that train and keep yourself out of trouble, for God's sake!" He pointed me toward the underground station just around the corner. I thanked him profusely and dried my eyes before slipping off that stool and back into the gray haze outside.

Back in the city, I stepped off the subway at Victoria Station. Rising to the platform from one of the terrifyingly steep escalators that accompany London's underground, I scanned the surging crowd for two beloved faces.

"Jennell!" My name shot across the crowded station. I recognized the boys sitting on their packs in a corner, looking more than slightly bored. Spotting my dragging frame across the sea of hurried bodies, Chris jumped to greet me, his platinum dreadlocks animating his motion. He shouted, "We found the tickets!"

Found the tickets?! What? I rushed over to them, where Pat was hunched over his pack and what appeared to be our missing notebook, his face obscured by long, dark curls. Systematically, Pat produced all our vital documents: the train passes, plane tickets, traveler's checks, cash and all three passports. "Where did you get these?" I demanded, absolutely astounded. "Somebody took them from the campground!"

"No, no." Pat mumbled, obviously embarrassed. "They were in my pack the whole time. I, uh, I forgot I repacked everything in this back pocket, because remember the other day when my pack got all wet. I was letting everything dry and then forgot where I put them back, so here, I, I've had them all along." He smiled sheepishly in apology, uncomfortably tucking loose strands of hair behind an ear.

"You had them the *whole* time?" I scoffed.

In my angered relief, I wasn't sure whether to kiss him or

wring his neck, so I did what came easiest. "My God, Pat! I thought we were done for. You don't even know what I've been through today, OK?"

Watching the last shreds of contentment slip from Pat's face, I wanted to eat my words. Trying to change my tune, I offered, "I did get a free beer, though."

"Free beer?" the boys chimed, brightening at the prospect.

"Yeah, that dark stuff called Guinness. I met the nicest bartender and he even helped me out with my subway fare. I guess not *all* the people here are rude."

"Maybe not," Chris reluctantly agreed. "Dude, I'm just glad we won't be sleeping at, like, the embassy tonight. We're goin' to Dublin after all!"

Pat delegated himself to locating the next train bound for Dun Loighrea where we could catch a ferry to Dublin. I remained, guarding the packs while Chris made off in search of dinner, which would invariably be burgers in a bag.

Though I am ashamed to admit it, we dined almost exclusively on the American comforts of McDonald's and Burger King during our entire stay in London. However, I'm really quite sure we weren't missing anything in ignoring the local cuisine. The pot pies and roast beef we sampled early in the week left so much to be desired that even an 11th consecutive meal of a burger wrapped in paper and fries in cardboard became an especially tasty and welcome alternative.

I waited among the packs and let my mind drift. I couldn't believe Pat had caused us to waste a whole day but couldn't help feeling relieved it wasn't entirely my fault. From some distant corner of my memory, my father's words ricocheted around my brain. "You've got to be responsible, girl. If something happens when you're away, we can't just come pick you up. And we're not going to send you any money. Got it?" I probably rolled my eyes and said, "I know, Dad." But I guess I didn't know. Or, I didn't realize the capacity of trouble we could get ourselves into. I had only very recently begun to sense the vast possibilities.

Simultaneous with my last thought, a mottled brown brigade of Boy Scouts swirled into view. Carrying their luggage in a pair of neat single-file lines, they looked almost military in their precision. A pubescent American voice broadcast itself across the crowded terminal from one Scout to another. "Bobby, our platform is just ahead," the boy announced, pointing at a sign. "You guys hang out, I'll go check in."

These kids can't be more than 14, and not an adult among them. I watched in dismay as the boys assembled themselves and made off toward their platform. *What am I doing here? I thought. I can't even keep track of my own passport. Boy Scouts showing us up.* Returning across the station at a dead sprint, Pat breathlessly revealed that we had three minutes to catch the train, which would be departing from the far end of the station.

We're not gonna make it, I thought, heaving my pack onto my back and strapping Chris's to my front. Pat slung on his pack and we made a frantic search for our missing party member at all the fast food counters in the station. Once we located him, we made a hysteric dash to the platform. We arrived just in time to watch its little red taillights blinking out of the station and into the night.

"Looks like we're sleeping here tonight, because we're not going back to that campground." Chris told us. "I've had enough earwigs in my sleeping bag for one summer. Those vile little demons ... " he trailed off, squirming at the thought.

"Sure makes the embassy sound luxurious," someone mumbled.

It didn't matter who said it. We were out of luck and knew it. So we spread our sleeping bags on the gum-encrusted concrete floor. Way too soon, Chris's watch alarm blared in my ear, ending what couldn't have been any more than three hours of broken slumber. The night spent tossing and turning on the station's cold floor left our necks kinked and our moods less than pleasant.

We boarded the first train for eastern Wales and settled into a cozy table with what we hoped would be a decent view. Underway 15 minutes later, the conductor came around to collect tickets and stamp passports and whatnot.

"Reservations, please," An expressionless uniform demanded, palm out in anticipation.

"Reservations?" Chris asked, "We don't have reservations, but we've got these Eurail passes." We presented our tickets to the conductor. Again we were out of luck. We did not have reservations and the train was overcrowded. People were standing in the aisles a few cars ahead, he told us. Those without reservations were to ride in the cargo car at the back of the train.

Ejected from our comfy seats, we gathered our packs and grudgingly set off for the rear of the train. The rattling cargo car was packed tight with bicycles and the young bodies belonging to them. Pat slumped against the rattling wall, engrossed in a GameBoy, while Chris read. I chose to stare out the paneless, barred window at the fog-encased industrial wasteland unfolding before me.

England's indistinct gray forms mixed with my mood to concoct a disheartening cocktail. This trip had been one disaster after another. Yeah, sure, we'd seen all the sights: Westminster Abbey, the Tower of London and Big Ben, but they were just a whirlwind blur amid overspending, non-repellent raincoats, frequent fights and repeatedly winding up lost, all of which could be blamed on our poor planning. Or, more distinctly, our complete disregard of the plans I'd made before we left home.

I curled my reddening hands around the window's bars and rested my forehead between two cold, steel rails. The wind, strong enough alone but invigorated by our train's speed, whipped my long hair into a nest of damp tangles, whose loose wisps cracked upon my rosy cheeks. The human silence in the car, despite the ceaseless creaking of its wooden walls and the scrapings of that worrisome tower of bicycles, filled me with a feeling of contented solitude. Almost prison-like, that rickety wooden car became for me the symbolic cell of our journey. Held in by our preconceptions, poor planning and the frequent confusion travel seems to survive upon, I realized our minds were not entirely open, our perceptions had been tinted with worry and anger and were masked by our reluctance to relinquish the familiar in favor of the foreign.

Sighing I turned my back on the dismal scene and slumped against the reverberating box we rode in, settling between the boys.

In a faraway corner of my mind, I heard the musical sorrow of Tetris's inevitable end. Pat tossed the game aside and looked at me. "You're thinking about going home, aren't you?"

I stared off a bit, trying to ignore his question.

"We should be having fun," Pat continued. "I mean, here we are halfway across the world and we can do anything we want."

"I know, I know. It's just ... Everything is so difficult. I just didn't picture it this way." I couldn't formulate a decent sentence on the subject. "I guess this isn't the romantic adventure I envisioned."

"Yeah," Pat picked up where I lost my thought. "Figuring all this stuff out, all the trains and those stupid subways, trying to find a place to sleep, and carrying these five-ton backpacks, it's definitely a lot harder than I imagined. And just think, in a couple weeks, we'll be doing all this in a different language. Then it's going to be really tough. This will probably seem like nothing. But, I mean, look at where we are now." I was pretty sure he didn't mean the bicycle car.

Chris leaned in on my other side, his golden dreadlocks brushing my arm. "Pat's right. We've got it under control. We're on our way, you know? This whole, like, *lifestyle* just takes some getting used to. Right? By the time we have to go home, we'll be old pros at this."

I rolled my eyes, ruefully remembering the fiascoes of the day before. "Yeah, if we can manage not to lose our passports and everything else."

Pat assumed a serious tone. "Look, Jennell, I, I'm sorry about that. It was stupid of me, but if I hadn't moved them, everything really would be lost."

I couldn't hold it in any longer. A week's worth of travel anxiety and reactions to our poor group dynamics spilled out of my mouth, dripping with sarcasm.

"No, *Pat*, everything would still be in the same place, but we still wouldn't know where. I wouldn't have wasted the day chasing that notebook around the suburbs, I wouldn't have gotten soaked, *again*, and we wouldn't have had to sleep on the floor at the train station. We probably would've realized we needed reservations, *and* we wouldn't be sitting here in this baggage car, *AND* we wouldn't have wasted an entire day. *That*'s what would've happened."

Leaving the boys too angry to speak, I stood, wondering what was unfolding outside my chugging cell. In the few moments that had passed since my previous peek, both the light and the landscape had changed. England's heavy gray clouds had broken slightly, allowing the morning's lazy sun-beams to penetrate the downpour while isolating patches of the emerald expanse before me. I inhaled deeply, slowly, thank-ful for the only ray of sunlight I'd seen since we left home. In a seeming answer to my appreciation, the sky's flannel lining slowly dispersed, spreading golden light across the rolling plain still slick and twinkling with raindrops. We had been travel-ing a week by then, and I figured it was time for a reevalua-tion of our attitudes, my attitude specifically, toward our adventures abroad.

I scanned the horizon idly, suddenly stunned by the sight of a decrepit stone castle nestled at the wooded foot of a high green hill. Immense boulders littered the gentle knoll before the ruin. Imagining they broke free from their place in the cas-tle's ramparts, I pictured them rolling slowly to their current resting places. The castle faded quickly into the distance as I could barely make out a group of light-colored objects amid that rolling sea of kelly and lime greens: sheep! Flocks of them, possibly a few thousand blanketed that grassy knoll, grazing lazily. Straining to count the woolly figures from the train, we reached the edge of Welsh headlands, where the continent drops immediately into the sea. Foaming white atop undu-lous waves of a deep, dark blue waited less than a mile ahead, in Dun Loighrea, where we would board a ferry bound for Dublin. Had we been in any car except the cargo car, perhaps we would have heard an announcement to that effect.

Our train slowed, coming to a gentle stop where I had an unimpeded view of the writhing sea ahead. Without breaking our taciturn code of silence, the three of us exited the cargo car like the human parcels we had become, and were herded through a sterile building before boarding what appeared to be a ferry. In actuality, the boat was a small cruise ship, minus a pool and the cabins. Packed with casinos, an arcade, three different bars, a restaurant and gift shops galore, this boat was sure to set sail toward good times. In celebration, the boys made a beeline for the bar, but I remained on the aft deck, preferring to watch the small hump of green continent slip away as we lolled farther into the churning Irish Sea. I was quiet with wonder. Or, I was quiet with the fear of my steadily turning stomach. I was astonished at how suddenly my lunch leapt from my throat. As I heaved over the rails, a small crowd gathered nearby, then dispersed. Still deep in the clutches of my nausea; "Take me home!" I choked, bile rising in my throat until I gagged again, and began to cry what had become my daily expense of tears.

Draping myself over the rail, dangling above the sea, I marveled at my own words. How could I say such a thing? Yeah, we'd had a rough time of it so far. *Real* rough. *But,* I thought, *how could I say such horrible things to these guys who've been life-long friends?* Despite the fact that I was deeply ashamed of my attitude, I couldn't control my tongue when things got tough. Knowing I'd better buck up and be a trooper or get left behind, I realized I needed to relax and take everything in stride.

I tried to be positive. There was still so much more to see! I remembered Chris's description of Europe long before this trip's conception: the deep ochre of Italy's ruins, the clear cerulean waters of the Mediterranean as seen from the shores of the French Riviera. I pictured it all, the three of us arm-in-arm strolling cobble-stoned boulevards, lolling over espresso in Parisian cafes or tall pints in a Scottish pub. Whatever our journey would become, *adventurous* would certainly describe it. My heart swelled as I remembered the scenes of foreign delight Chris lured me in with so many months before. I cleaned myself up and headed toward apologies in the bar.

I ordered myself a Guinness and slid into the comfortable booth next to Chris. "Hi," I offered, taking a minute sip.

"Hi." Their monotone responses indicated that they were less than enthusiastic to see me. *How was I going to start?*

"I just puked. All over the deck of the boat, too." No one looked up.

"You OK?" Chris asked, staring deep into his half-full glass.

"Yeah, I'm better even. But I'm pretty sure I deserved it." Shaking my head at the memory of my bad attitude, I laid my hands out on the table and prepared myself. "Look, guys, I'm really, *really* sorry about the way I've been acting. All through our troubles, I've just complained and blamed everything on you guys. It's like I just realized I need to make the best of this, because I don't want to, like, *ruin* the trip." I was half joking, but I could see they saw no humor in it. Was it possible that I had already broken their spirits?

A few beers and a thousand apologies later, our ferry docked. Staggering once more beneath the weight of our packs, we planted our first footsteps on the Emerald Isle. Land of the Blarney Stone and the shamrock, we had arrived. Ahead on the pier, I could just make out the sound of someone singing a Patsy Cline classic.

"I fall to pieces ... Oooh, oooh, oooh." The aroma of spilled beer wafted through the host of drunken serenaders as they surrounded me. Pulled into the circle by arms animated with intoxication, the men's Irish-tinted voices boomed and swooned around me. For the first time since we'd been in Europe, I let myself go. No worries about this or that, just reveling in the moment, completely entranced by these silly Irishmen. Chris took my hands and we began a little jig of our own within the crowd.

Pat's furrowed face soon surfaced among the drunken chaos. He was digging through his bag. "Um, hey, guys? Who's got our bus passes into Dublin? Guys?"

Believe me, it wasn't the last time I heard that fearful phrase. Every time we thought we had things figured out, we continued to lose our tickets. We lost them in Copenhagen and Geneva. We lost them under benches, left them on a bus once and even forgot them in a camera shop. We lost them in Rome and actually accused a maid of taking them. We lost those tickets anywhere we could.

"Don't worry about it, Pat," I shouted from within the throng. "I wouldn't mind the walk."

Not Such a Grand Tour

by Christine A. Brady

It was dark when we arrived at the Grand Canyon, so we had to wait until morning for the spectacular views. Up early and raring to go, my husband Dave and I and our blended family of four kids were off.

There are three ways to experience the canyon: on foot, on mules or by air. We decided to walk along a lovely path named Bright Angel Trail. My husband talked to a park ranger in the lodge who assured him that hiking to the first water station on this south rim trail was no big deal. (I later suspected that this young lady was either masquerading as a park ranger that day or was so cute and perky that my husband became delusional.)

The six of us headed out. I was shocked at how narrow the trail was. I like more than 18 inches between instantaneous death and me. Not only was the path impossibly narrow but it was also littered with rocks, roots and piles from the apparently well-fed mules that preceded us.

It occurred to me that this sweet name, Bright Angel Trail, could be a tribute to all those naive tourists who fell to their death, mistakenly thinking that they were taking a 20-minute walk to see a pretty view. Molly and Laura, my 6- and 9-year-old daughters, were unnerved and frightened. Dave's kids, Brett, 19, and Bryonne, 16, risk-takers by nature, took off in a dead run.

I couldn't help but notice that other tourists on the trail were dressed differently from us. They looked like hikers, we looked like tourists. They had backpacks and water bottles, leather hiking boots and hats, we wore lightweight shorts, T-shirts and sneakers. No hats, no canteens filled with cool water, we were clearly underdressed and unprepared.

We walked and walked the downward spiral of the canyon. Unfortunately, the beauty of the surrounding cliffs was lost on us as we measured every step. That "dry" heat that Arizonans boast about ad nauseum was roasting us alive. There was no indication that we were nearing any water station and our teenagers were nowhere in sight.

Suddenly signs began to appear at every turn. We were assailed with vivid descriptions of all the dire consequences of heat stroke and dehydration. These symptoms began to sound a bit too familiar to me. Were we having fun yet? A resounding "no" was the answer. It was time to re-evaluate. Dave and I decided that he should go on ahead and find his kids. I would turn back with the girls. Now if going down into the canyon was not particularly thrilling, climbing back up was torture. I ended up carrying Molly on my back while Laura clung to my side. There was no shade, and my legs and back ached from the exertion. At one point one of the well-prepared hikers approached me. He offered my girls water. "Make like a baby bird," he encouraged as they turned up their flushed faces to catch the water as it dripped from his water bottle.

I felt like a totally incompetent mother and vowed to hunt down that perky little ranger if it was the last thing I did. Finally we reached the top. My jelly legs barely carried us to a shady rest area where we waited for the rest of the family. Reunited, tired but safe, we stopped for some lunch. We were ready for another view of the canyon, this time by air!

An airplane ride seemed like the perfect vehicle in which to view the Grand Canyon. After our grueling trek this should be a snap. For $200 we rented a small plane. The pilot, Joe, was handsome and funny. He began joking with the kids and instantly put us all at ease. Assigning us our seats, Joe put Laura in front, Brett and Dave in the second row and Bryonne and Molly in the last row. Then Joe explained that I would be seated in the tail, "To balance the weight of the plane!"

More than a little insulted with this job description, I dutifully wedged myself into the narrow tunnel of the plane's tail. Then we were off.

We called to each other excitedly as the small plane took off and circled around to make its first pass over the canyon. As the plane cruised over the rim of the canyon, the updrafts, huge gusts of wind, suddenly whooshed up and began tossing the plane around. The smiles on our faces vanished. Joe seemed oblivious to our distress as he enthusiastically pointed out the different rock formations, "There's the Snoopy rock, and over there is where a plane, just like this one, went down!" He laughed out loud as he banked the plane steeply, pretending to narrowly miss the canyon wall.

Helpless, I watched as Molly took on the color of skimmed milk. Bryonne, who is normally pale, assumed a pearlescent gray hue. Frantically, I called to the kids to grab their airsick bags. The pilot chatted on. Once again the view was lost amid the effort to simultaneously locate my own stomach and coach the kids. As our heads lolled around I could barely keep it together enough to croak, "STOP, TAKE US BACK!"

But we paid for 15 minutes of airtime and that's what we got. By the time the plane landed I had placed Joe on my hit list, right after that ranger. Once again on jelly legs, we weaved and wobbled out of the plane. I wanted to drop to the pavement and kiss the ground, but I was too dizzy. As we passed the line of the next unsuspecting victims, I had to fight the urge to scream, "Run for your lives! Save yourselves!" But I didn't have the strength. We surrendered. It was time to call it a day.

All were silent as we rode back to the lodge. We returned to our rooms, closed the drapes, cranked up the air and passed out.

There are three ways to view the Grand Canyon: on foot, on mules or by air. Personally, I don't recommend any of them. Get yourself a subscription to *National Geographic!*

The Out of Towners

by Janet Barton

MY HUSBAND AND I decided to fly to Miami, rent a car and drive to Key West where we would spend a week. We flew from Cleveland to Miami and arrived at about 2 on a Sunday afternoon. We rented a car not far from the airport, got behind the wheel and breathed a wonderful sigh knowing we had finally reached sunshine.

The rental car agency had given us a map of the area that was printed on a 4x4-inch piece of paper and nearly illegible. As we drove onto the highway, we began to look for signs only to find that they did not exist. After a while my husband determined that we had probably gone too far and needed to turn. We turned onto the first major thoroughfare we could find that was a four-lane highway. He pulled over into a bus lane so we could both look at the map.

As we sat there poring over this map our back car doors were opened on both sides. Two young men began removing our carry-on luggage. Then my passenger door came open and another young man reached for my purse. It fell outside onto the sidewalk and only when I reached for it, did I realize we were being robbed. The robber finally dragged me out of the seat onto the pavement while I was still buckled up. Ultimately he freed the purse and off he went. My husband set off to chase the men, but there turned out to be a fourth man in a getaway car.

A mailman came by within minutes in a vehicle and told us to get in the car and lock our doors. He would call the police.

Apparently robberies were common here. A policewoman soon arrived and got out of her car saying, "Don't tell me what happened, let me tell you." She then recited exactly what had happened to us. The only thing that saved our lives was that we could not get out of our seat belts. Otherwise, we would surely have been stabbed, our identification taken, and it would have taken weeks to determine who we were. She then told us to go to the Miami Police Station first thing Monday morning. That sounded easy enough.

Once the policewoman led us to our hotel, we found our room and flopped down on the bed. I was in tears and as my husband comforted me, we decided we had better call and cancel our credit cards. We called our daughter, asked her to go to our house and find the file where we keep our credit card numbers and make the cancellation phone calls for us. Since we were only going to be there one evening, we had a special restaurant picked out and my husband suggested we try to clear our minds for that evening, have a good dinner and get some rest. Easier said than done.

We found the restaurant and sat down, only to realize that we could not read the menu. Our reading glasses had been in the carry-on luggage stolen by the robbers. Our waiter helped us out; we ordered a glass of wine and sat back to await our dinners. After dinner, the waiter brought the bill and my husband presented his credit card, which, of course, had been cancelled. The money we had was going to have to pay for the hotel and stretch out for other necessities. The only thing to do was to ask the person at the register to speak with the owner, who accepted our explanation and promise to send a check when we returned home.

Monday morning we were up early, anxious to get to the police station to file our report. Once inside the main lobby of the station, we had to walk through about 25 young men playing basketball, none of whom were happy we had interrupted their game. We got to the counter and found two policemen leaning back in their chairs with their feet up on the counter, toothpicks in their mouths, staring at us. My husband explained the situation and one policeman told us it was not worth his time or ours to file this report. Robbing tourists had been going on for a long time, and we might as well just get on with our trip.

He finally let us fill out some paperwork and gave us a number we could call daily to see if my purse had been turned in.

We got in the car and headed for Key West. As we checked into the hotel there, the desk clerk said we had two messages, both from a woman telling us she had my purse. We had been told not to return any calls if we received messages, as the robbers knew they did not have my husband's wallet. They would set up a meeting place to return the purse and rob us again. We called the Miami Police. They had us on hold for about 20 minutes trying to locate the report and eventually told us we had called the wrong police department. Since the robbery had happened in another county other than the city department, they had nothing.

We called the other police department, left a message for them to call and you guessed it. No return call. We called the next day and they had found the report but no purse. We called each day thereafter only to find the same thing.

The next morning we called again. They had no clue as to what we were talking about even though we had the report number. However, they did reiterate that we should not call this woman back. The policeman said the police department would call and meet her and get my purse and make an arrest.

Two days later with still no call we gave up and decided to take our chances. What if the woman was honest and had my purse? My husband called her. She said she had been walking her dog in the park and came upon the purse. What stood out were the pictures of our children scattered all around. She picked it up and found us by the itinerary on our airline tickets. My husband asked her why she hadn't called the police and she said she had called them—several times. The police said they would come and pick up the purse but she had never heard back from them. She agreed to take my purse to the station for us.

On our last day of vacation we drove to the police station to pick up my purse. They would not give it to me without proper identification. Naturally that was in the purse. We argued with this officer for nearly 10 minutes trying to get him at least to go and get my purse, look up my license and verify that I looked like my picture. He finally did and presented me with a box filled with my possessions. Everything was still there except for the Visa card and the cash.

Later, when we had returned home, our credit card statement came in the mail. The robbers had charged $1,600 in just a few hours buying everything from pizza to televisions, washers and dryers to tires. The credit card company canceled the bills and card. A new card was mailed.

When we went to dinner a week later the waitress came back with the card and said it would not go through as it was listed as stolen. We paid with cash and the next day I called the credit card company who said they were very sorry. They would issue yet another card and cancel that one.

A few weeks later during Christmas shopping, my husband's purchases were rung up and the new credit card was presented. The clerk made a phone call, turned and cut my husband's card up in front of 10 people behind him and said, "Sorry, this is stolen."

Another phone call. We finally had to change banks to get a card that we could use.

From that point forward we had seven vacations in a row that were jinxed. I suffered food poisoning in Cancun in the spring of 1991, and Hurricane Bob threatened us while in Myrtle Beach during the summer of 1991. We were in Palm Springs in April 1992 for the Rodney King riots and spent a weekend in Fancy Gap with a broken-down car on our way to Myrtle Beach that summer.

In the spring of 1993 we went to Antigua and were congratulating ourselves for a lovely vacation. When we got home we discovered that our daughter had left her husband and was ready to move into our home with her three children. In the summer of 1993, a few hours before leaving for our Myrtle Beach oceanfront rental house, our second daughter was involved in a bad automobile accident.

In 1996 we made a trip to San Diego where I became ill for the entire trip. After a summer of medications for a sore throat, it was discovered I had contracted mononucleosis.

In 1997 we made a successful trip to Santa Fe and Albuquerque.

In 1997/98 we went to Florida for Christmas and New Year's without incident.

In 1998 we went to Las Vegas without incident and have made several other trips since. We are starting to believe our string of bad luck is over.

Not a Fish Story

by Ruby E. McCreight

SOME VACATIONS JUST aren't meant to be. No matter what you do, they just keep getting worse.

My husband and I usually spend summer vacations traveling with grandkids and friends as we make the rounds visiting our family. But this summer we had all to ourselves. The kids were grown, so I was looking forward to a nice relaxing trip.

We stopped at Quesnel in south central British Columbia and did a little fishing and sightseeing. I decided I'd have a shower and turn in early. There were community shower facilities with our accommodations. One of the shower doors was open so I naturally assumed it was empty.

I went to push the door open, and a fairly big lady slammed the door shut shouting, "It's occupied."

My hand was caught as she slammed it, breaking my finger and spraining my wrist. I didn't even stay to shower.

After getting my finger and hand seen to, we pulled out and headed for Castlegar to visit my husband's mother. She had just baked some fish in the oven and I said, "I'll get the fish while you lay the table."

I had summer shorts and top on. I thought I could balance the tray with one hand, but the fish slid across the tray right on my belly and the heat was terrific.

I ended up with blisters, a cut and a wrapped belly button.

My husband said, "You'll feel better when we get to Joyce's place."

Joyce, our daughter, lives in Salmon Arm to the southeast of Quesnal. We got there early, so Joyce took us fishing for an hour.

We caught four little fish and decided to go back and cook them for supper. I didn't like sitting around doing nothing so I asked Joyce if there was something I could do to help without affecting my hand or belly.

She gave me a little bucket of apples and said, "Here, take these and throw them over the fence to the pigs and their babies."

So I threw the apples over the fence to the pigs. A couple rolled under an old tub they had their water in. So I got a stick intending to try to push the apples out, but no one had told me *it was an electric fence.*

I hit the air—bounced on the ground, and then ran screaming into the house.

"That does it!" I shouted. "I'm going to rest for five minutes and then we're going home."

They tried to comfort me, but I was so hurt and upset I told them to leave me alone. After I calmed down, I apologized to Joyce and we headed home.

As we traveled back, I told my husband I felt a little bit better and would like to stay the night at a nice quiet little campsite in Enderby.

We pulled in, and I said, "Let's use the bathroom before we make supper and retire." The toilets were on a little mountain uphill. Everything went OK until I started down the hill. My husband was waiting down below. I must have hit a rock or something; anyway I tripped and tumbled down the hill.

I limped back to the trailer and decided I'd go to bed. My leg was painful, and my wrist and belly were acting up again.

The next morning I told my husband I wanted to go down

and sit with him while he fished, my leg in the water, hoping the cold water would ease the pain.

While I sat there I got him to throw a line in the water. A man came to me and asked, "Are you the lady who tumbled down the hill last night?" I nodded.

"That leg looks quite swollen. Can I look at it? I'm a doctor," he said. Just as I turned to answer him the line started pulling. I started, or I should say tried to get up but fell back down again and dropped the rod. The fish and the rod were gone by the time I stood up (with the man's help).

He said he was sorry I lost the fish but told me that I should be at the hospital. My leg was broken.

I went to the hospital. Then we headed home. No more stopping.

Sleep Tight

by Elena Nicoladis

WE WERE VISITING BRESSANONE, a small town in the Alps of
northern Italy, for an academic conference of my husband's.
Our first-born son, Nico, was 3 weeks old and not yet sleeping through the night.

The morning we were to return home, after a week, we had
allowed an extra half-hour to walk to the train station, which
was only about two miles away. We had also explained to the
proprietor that we would be leaving early in the morning to
catch our train to Innsbruck. On checking out of our hotel at
7, the proprietor told us he could only accept cash. We had
spent almost all of our lire so Chris had to run around Bressanone looking for a bank machine while I stood holding Nico
on my stomach in his baby-carrier. Forty-five minutes later,
Chris came running in, breathless, with enough cash to pay
for our week's stay.

At that point, we had only 10 minutes to get to the train
station, a distance we might have been able to make on foot
if we didn't have a heavy backpack, a baby and if I had been
able to run. So we asked the hotel proprietor to call us a taxi,
which he promptly did. It was fortunate, he explained, that
the one taxi in town was actually available at that hour of the
morning. The taxi driver arrived seven minutes later, her hair
in disorder and her shirt hanging out of her skirt. "You must
be foreigners," she said. "Anyone else would have called for a
taxi the night before." We barely made the train but we relaxed,
thinking that we could sleep at last for the two-hour ride to

Innsbruck. Unfortunately, Nico, who had slept through our nervous first morning hour, decided he had had enough sleep and was wide awake. We were very tired and a bit grumpy, but we consoled ourselves by thinking that our train would get us into Innsbruck in plenty of time to catch our plane to Amsterdam. Then, we detected a strange chemical smell.

It persisted during the rest of the trip throughout Italy. Just after crossing the border into Austria, the train came to a full stop. We craned our heads out the windows to see if we could see anything. There was a thick black smoke pouring out of the car in front of us. A few people wandered by that car, but nobody seemed particularly excited by the black smoke. Was the train on fire? Should we perhaps get off the train while the fire was extinguished? Nobody came by to tell us anything.

About 20 minutes later, with the black smoke still coming out of the car but not quite so fast, the train left again, going very slowly. We finally arrived in Innsbruck with only 30 minutes to catch our flight, but, we thought, at least we had arrived before our flight left. When we walked into the airport, the place was absolutely packed. The lines to the airline desks were at least 50 people long and moving at a snail's pace. Thinking there was nothing to do but wait, we got in the shortest looking line and waited. Occasional announcements in German were given, but we couldn't hear them and, even if we had, we wouldn't have understood them.

We got more and more nervous as the time for our flight approached and we had barely moved at all toward the desk. Five minutes before the flight was to go, the airline opened up two other desks and people started moving up. But one minute before our flight was to leave we were still five people away from the desk. The woman in front of us overheard us and explained that the German announcements had told passengers on our flight to go to the head of the line. So we pushed ahead and the man at the desk tagged our bags and sent us running for the plane.

Looking out the window as our plane rolled down the runway, we saw that it was snowing big, thick flakes—it looked like one of those snow globes. In Canada, we would have considered ourselves lucky to be leaving on a plane with only such light snow. But the weather proved too much for the Austrian air controllers and our flight was delayed for half an hour while the wings were de-iced again and again and the pilot checked ahead on the weather. We started to worry again. We had only an hour layover in Amsterdam and we had already used up 30 minutes of that. We spent a lot of that time discussing where our luggage might be. Finally our plane took off and landed in Amsterdam only 25 minutes after its originally scheduled time. Nico was an angel on the flight. We rushed off the plane to find out where to catch our next plane, which was scheduled to leave in 35 minutes.

That was when we discovered our flight back to Montreal had been cancelled. An Air Canada representative managed to get us on the next flight, which was seven hours later but we qualified for a free meal and a hotel room. She sent us off to the airport representatives to collect our freebies. The desk to which she sent us (which seemed about two miles away) was closed. When we went back to get further directions, the Air Canada representative was also gone, with no directions about where we could go to get help. We stopped and asked for help at the closest ticket agent, who sent us three floors up and a terminal over. The people there explained that this wasn't the right place and sent us back to the same desk the Air Canada representative had sent us to in the first place. We were tired and hungry and grumpy. We went back to the desk, hoping that it would now be open. It was! But the airport representative explained that we qualified only for $10 in airport money that we could put toward a meal. We appealed to their sensitivities, pointing out that we had a baby and we hadn't slept in ages. At least we got a meal.

At last, our flight left (and on time). We were thinking that it was only another six hours till we were home and we were looking forward to the chance of getting a little sleep before then.

The huge man sitting next to us had other ideas, however, and would not stop moving around and sniffing. It was absolutely impossible for either of us to sleep with such annoying noises. About an hour into the flight, the man got up, presumably to go the restroom. We thought we could fall asleep quickly before he got back. However, there was soon an announcement over the loudspeaker requesting that any persons with medical training to identify themselves to the flight attendant. It turned out that the man next to us had had a heart attack and collapsed in the middle of the aisle, blocking the passage. We kept catching sight of worried flight attendants wandering by and could not sleep a wink. The pilot finally announced that he was turning the plane around to land at the nearest airport in Ireland. When the plane landed, there were ambulance attendants almost immediately on board to take the man to hospital. The plane refueled and we were off.

There were no mishaps after that and we arrived home a mere 13 hours later than planned (with our luggage). Needless to say, we slept well that night.

Bowled Over

by Diane M. McNaughton

OUR DREAM VACATION turned into a nightmare when I traveled with my husband, four children and in-laws to Phoenix to watch my alma mater, Penn State, compete in the 1997 Aloha Bowl.

My husband, Mark, and I struggled to entertain, amuse and otherwise harness the boundless energy of our two youngest children, Christian, 3, and Kelly, 1, throughout the pre-game festivities and the first half of the football game. By half time, I had had all I could take.

My husband and I decided that I should take Christian and Kelly back to the hotel so that they could be put to bed for the night. Mark accompanied me to the entrance of the stadium, where he was stopped by uniformed security guards who told him that, under NO condition, could he re-enter the stadium if he left. He explained that he was just walking the kids and me to our rental car, which was parked several miles from the stadium, and that he would then return for the second half. The security guards would not bend; no re-entry for anyone who left. When my husband continued to plead his case, police were called over and threatened him with arrest. Seeing how frightened the children were and knowing we were in danger of being arrested, I told Mark to be quiet. I would go to the car alone, and he would stay at the entrance and wait with the kids until I swung by to pick them up.

Reluctantly, he handed me the keys, and I headed out toward where we had parked. I embarked on this trek in near-total darkness and past many groups of rowdy, drunken fans.

I rapidly discovered that the sandy parking lots looked very different in blackness than when we had parked, in the shining light of day. Worse yet, all the makeshift lots looked alike. No signs, letters or labels were posted to help you locate your car. I wandered swiftly through row after row of cars, then continued over to the next lot, only to wander some more.

My heart rate gradually started to escalate as time wore on, with fewer and fewer carloads of screaming partyers whizzing by. The farther I moved away from the stadium, the more unreachable our car seemed. I began to run frantically among the cars, all the while picturing my husband and two terrified children stranded at the stadium entrance.

As I could have predicted, my husband, a feisty state legislator, continued his tirade against the guards, threatening to sue if his wife was harmed while walking alone in the dark through the streets of Phoenix.

After what seemed like weeks, I decided to give up my search and return to the stadium entrance. By this time, I was trembling from fear and fatigue. Miraculously, my husband and brother-in-law intercepted me on my way back to the stadium, having given the kids to their grandparents to watch. The three of us ran back to the acres of cars to search again.

After what seemed like an eternity, we found it! Mark and I climbed inside and nearly collapsed from exhaustion. He turned the key and tried to back the car up, but we soon discovered that we were going nowhere. The tires of our car had sunk into the sand, which we later learned was a riverbed during certain times and seasons. Several nearby partyers tried to push us out, rock us out and dig us out, but to no avail.

After many tries, and with our tires sinking deeper and deeper, we gave up. We walked back to the stadium. As we approached the neon lights, we heard the raucous cheering of the fans as the game ended, with Penn State emerging victorious after an action-packed second half.

Spectators started pouring out, and this time it was not our car that was lost, it was us. I longed to hug my kids, but I feared that I'd never see them again.

Finally, I found our precious children being carried by my in-laws down a stadium ramp. All, adults and children alike, were panic-stricken. I was so grateful, and enormously relieved, to be reunited with everybody. We had to be driven home by my in-laws, with their cars packed beyond capacity, and have our car towed out of the bank the next morning. We were only told then about the snakes and wild animals that roam that part of the desert after dark.

Trip of a Strife Time

by William A. Douglass

In March 1986 I was scheduled to give a paper at a meeting of the European Rural Sociology Association in Braga, Portugal. My wife, Jan, and I thought we would combine pleasure with business by continuing on to East Africa for a photo safari, followed by a visit to the Pyramids.

Flying from Reno, Nevada, to the East Coast is a stultifying experience. To arrive in New York by early evening you leave at 7 A.M., which means up and at 'em time is about 5, before joining other zombies in the waiting area of the Reno airport. It was in such a mood that I fished for something in my wallet and then inadvertently left it on a chair or table at the airport. When I realized it was missing in New York, frantic calls to United Airlines initiated the search. Fearing the worst, I canceled my credit cards. It was therefore small consolation when the folks at the airline not only found the wayward wallet but also managed to get it to me before our international flight the next evening. I at least had my driver's license, but our financial backup was reduced to Jan's two credit cards, each with a $1,000 limit.

Matters were not helped by the fact that we were staying at the new Times Square Marriott Hotel, where the ecstasy of zooming 50 stories up the atrium in a glass elevator is surpassed only by the exhilaration from the rarified total of one's bill. But then by checkout time my predisposition toward the place was already soured by the pitched war cries of the University of Wyoming boosters and the conga-dancing of their

Florida State counterparts, both of whom were bent on dismantling the Big Apple when not at Madison Square Garden to cheer on their respective gladiators contesting the NIT basketball championship. We boarded our uneventful flight to Lisbon with relief.

It was Holy Week and the city was crowded, not with residents, most of whom seemed to have used the holiday for their own travels, but with fellow tourists. Luckily, we had reservations at the local Sheraton. Not so fortunately, we arrived there along with two busloads of Spaniards. After an hour of chaos it was our turn to check in. Our generally frayed physical and mental states were not improved by the news that the hotel was full, as were all the others in the city. The fact that we had a reservation seemed to be more of an irritant than an advantage in the negotiations. When Jan announced that she was not leaving and simply plunked herself down in the lobby in the midst of the luggage, the assistant manager softened his position. He speculated wistfully that there might be a last-minute cancellation or no-show. Two hours and several cups of tea in the lobby bar later we were shown to a room.

After three enjoyable days in Lisbon we rented a car for the trip north to Braga. It was the day before Easter and the roads were crowded. The plan was to travel leisurely, taking a couple of days to see the sights along the way. We began by driving the short distance to Sintra. A narrow, winding road above the town led to the Palácio Nacional da Pena, a summer residence of Portuguese monarchs. We were delighted to find the place practically deserted and spent about an hour exploring the many levels of an extraordinarily beautiful botanical garden before returning to the parking lot, only to find that our luggage had been stolen.

In a twinkling, all of our preparations for Portugal, Kenya

and Egypt evaporated, leaving behind the punched-out lock on the rental car door, the clothes on our backs, and about $80 in cash. The only good news was that Jan was carrying her purse, which contained both of our passports, her credit cards and a list of the serial numbers of our traveler's checks (gone, too, since they had been in my briefcase, also stolen from the car).

I automatically pointed the car in the direction of Lisbon. Our only vaguely familiar landmark, it seemed to harbor some sort of ill-defined assistance. As we drove along, exchanging self and mutual recriminations, we realized that we had failed to inform the local authorities. While it was likely a futile exercise at best, it seemed vaguely un-American not to become embroiled in a legal hassle given the opportunity. Back in Sintra at midday, we located the local commissary, which was conveniently hidden behind a castle and accessed by a twisting alley that became a descending staircase that ended in the vegetable garden and chicken run of Sintra's finest.

The officer, seated at the kitchen table that served as counter, desk and typewriter stand for an ancient manual Olivetti, nodded in sympathy, volunteered an occasional missing word and conjugated some of my verbs as I struggled through an exceedingly one-dimensional portrayal of our pratfall.

We were told that we had to fill out a police report; unfortunately, it was now the lunch break so we would have to return in two hours. It was not until late afternoon that we managed to extricate ourselves after working through a painfully detailed list of our losses. The officer was not at all nonplussed by the fact that we couldn't supply him with a Portuguese address at which to notify us should something turn up. He simply shrugged and acknowledged candidly that nothing ever did.

In retrospect it was not an entirely sterile exercise, since back in the States our homeowner's insurance paid in full on the strength of our copy of the police report. For the moment, however, we seemed to have simply compounded our woes. Gone was the glimmer of hope, however slight, that the authorities might do something. Rather, we had frittered away much of the day and were no better off than when we first discovered our breached car. As we drove to Lisbon we pondered the irony that the thieves had removed my reading glasses and a guidebook to Portugal from my coat pocket and left them on the seat before stealing the jacket. Was this a small act of kindness, a minor apology or salt in the wound?

When we arrived in the city we went straight to the American Express office. Only then did the full extent of our predicament begin to sink in. It was late Saturday afternoon, the day before Easter. A call to the closed office from the small hotel next door failed to rouse anyone. Another call to the American Embassy rattled around until reaching the private residence of a startled minor official. She tried her best to be sympathetic, but her suggestions that we go to Braga if we had contacts there or stay over in Lisbon until things opened on Monday seemed too obvious to merit verbalizing. The owner of the hotel announced that he was full, as were all of the other hotels in Lisbon on such a weekend.

It was 5 in the afternoon and there was no room at the inn. We pointed the car north into the incredible mishmash of short stretches of freeway, construction projects and truck-plagued, two-laned hills and curves that pass as Portugal's National Highway No. 1. It took three hours to travel the first hundred miles from Lisbon, impeded as we were by holiday traffic jams.

By 10 P.M. we had still not found a place to stay, while drizzle and fog worsened the driving. We faced the prospect of spending the night in the car, numbed by the late winter's chill. Our enthusiasm over the neon sign blinking "Motel" that beckoned in the gloom caused us to overlook the fine print beneath heralding a "Discoteca." We had no plans to go dancing.

The motel was of the Fresno, California, '50s variety, complete with bedraggled palm trees and phony Spanish colonial architecture. The one inexplicable difference was the aluminum garage door that covered the entire parking lot side of our room. We showered, dined and retired, too exhausted to be more than mildly annoyed by the lack of toothbrush or pajamas. Just as we were about to drift off into the slumber that promised to afford the day's only relief, someone turned on the lights—or so it seemed. I bolted upright to find myself staring into a pair of headlights. The parking lot quickly filled to capacity with jovial youths shouting greetings and challenges to one another while staging short drag races around the perimeter. Biding my time for a moment of darkness to hide my near nakedness, I dashed to the control and shut our garage door. Unfortunately, our newfound strength was also a weakness, since it had the effect of converting the sanctuary into an echo chamber. The point was underscored when, promptly at midnight, our assaulters opened a second front. Indecipherable music, piped out-of-doors at maximum decibel level, caused our room to reverberate.

Somehow, we had decided that I was due at the Braga Congress on Monday evening, when in fact registration was Tuesday and I was not to lecture until Wednesday. This opened new possibilities. The only American Express office was in Lisbon and we could possibly resolve our predicament with a full day there. We had been told that by Easter night there would be vacancies in the hotels. Once again we doubled back.

Easter Sunday actually turned out to be a thoroughly pleasant experience. There was plenty of time to take a circuitous route back to the capital and thereby avoid obnoxious Highway 1. We headed east into the mountains and worked our way through a series of semi-abandoned, yet starkly beautiful, peasant villages.

Next morning we opened the American Express office. Yes, they could replace the traveler's checks that same day, but first it was necessary to call the Madrid regional office. Meanwhile, it was off to the department stores to use up the remaining credit on Jan's Visa and MasterCard.

Braced by our renewed resources, once again we headed for Braga. The journey was uneventful (if such adjective could ever be applied to a trip up National Highway No. 1). While the overall quality of our Africa gear had definitely been downgraded, we were at least functional. The only two casualties were the photo equipment (which we simply could not afford to replace) and our prescription medicines.

Braga is a quaint provincial town set in a lovely countryside. The organizers of the Congress had a copy of my paper, so I was able to do my bit. Jan spent the days on organized tours of the city and surroundings, while my colleagues and I rehashed what each of us has been saying and writing for some years now and pledged to do so again in the future in some other exotic setting. In short, it was a success.

My only difficulty had been convincing the proprietor of the ancient inn at which we were staying of my need to call my brother in the United States to have our medicine sent air express to Madrid. He kept insisting that such calls were charged by units and that it was outrageously expensive. Convinced that the problem was semantic, regarding our differing views of what constitutes "expensive," and having little choice in the matter, I insisted. After two evenings of objections he reluctantly consented, and I made my five-minute call.

The Congress ended at midday. I had sagely told Jan not to convert dollars into escudos so as not to pay another commission when converting them into the pesetas of our next country of destination. By controlling the escudos myself I felt we could run out of Portuguese money just about the time we ran out of Portugal. There was, however, a snag. Our hotel bill included a $200 charge for a phone call to the United States!

Before I was able to protest, the proprietor exploded with a self-righteous, "Did I not warn you? Four thousand units, senor, four thousand!" With an eye roll to heaven and general gnashing of teeth, I acceded to the inevitable. Through some combination of traveler's checks and escudos, I ransomed our luggage. Our decent road map of Portugal had disappeared with our bags in the earlier caper, but I had a city map of Braga that clearly showed the road leading out of town to Spain. The gas tank was full, and I knew that it was only about an hour's drive to the border. The fact that we were down to 43 escudos seemed incidental.

The lack of a bridge at the riverine border crossing was but a minor irritation for the affluent, since a mere 50 escudos purchased a place on the ferry boat that for us represented the flight to freedom. As budding veterans of the travel wars, we were not to be denied. We scouted the routine of the ferry and noted that the first car on went straight to the front of the boat and was then blocked by all the others. The money was collected from each driver *during* the trip across the river. A piece of cake! The ferryman flashed only a modicum of irritation as he accepted our last 43 escudos.

Santiago de la Compostela is surely one of Europe's greatest, if somewhat lesser known, treasures. Its geographical remoteness shields it from the usual onslaught of tourists, at least for parts of the year. Our stay there was blemished only by the weather, which took a turn for the worse. It was, therefore, with a budding case of the flu that I drove toward Madrid through the snow-dusted landscape. I was to see colleagues in the Spanish capital but was essentially bedridden instead. Our only foray of any consequence was to the British Airways office, where my brother had been instructed to send our medicines.

It inspires confidence in neither your travel agent nor your carrier when you stop by the latter's place of business on the Gran Via only to find that it is gone. One's apprehension deepens when the forwarding address on the front door leads to an abandoned apartment building. After a call, we secured a new address that was considerably removed from Madrid's business district. Our curiosity grew when we passed through a security check and were whisked up to the fifth floor where we had to talk our way past another security man.

My name caused quite a stir among the three or four employees in the outer office. I was ushered into the assistant manager's inner sanctum and greeted by a visibly shaken Englishman. Yes, he had a package for me and thank God I had turned up when I did. An hour before it had arrived by courier and someone had accepted it despite orders to refuse all parcels. Six months earlier the airline's head office in Madrid had been bombed. For our part, with our anti-malarial drug and other prophylactic wonders of western science in hand, we were now ready to brave the wilds of Africa.

The night flight to Nairobi was surrealistic. As lightning crackled in distant thunderheads, I savored my first sense of real adventure in many a year. It made me realize that my frequent foreign travel had become highly routine, consisting of repeated trips to the same destination or at least always to places where I had some competence in the local language. At the same time, I was apprehensive about possible disappointment. We were anxious to see the animals, yet there were so many mixed signals coming out of Africa. Poaching, encroachment on the reserves of a growing human population and drought portended the demise of Africa's wildlife heritage. Particularly vivid in my memory was the image in an African television special of a starving mother and baby elephant, too weakened to flee, surrounded by vans of ecstatic tourists gaily clicking photos while oblivious to the reality. I was prepared to dislike or repress the Kenyan experience, and even began to look beyond it to our scheduled float trip down the Nile.

My African reticence disappeared immediately during the drive into town from the Nairobi airport. The left-hand side of the road has a game fence that separates it from Nairobi National Park. I was truly stunned to spot ostriches, gazelles and giraffes in the faint glow of dawn.

Nairobi's Norfolk Hotel is a time warp, a surviving island of colonial society. How Nairobi *a nuit* stacks up against the zestier districts of the average American city after dark I am unable to say, having been cowed somewhat by the admonition in our guidebook to avoid its "panga-wielding gangs" (whatever a panga is). However, our daytime experiences certainly reinforced a garrison mentality. To step foot outside the hotel was to run a gauntlet of university students requesting donations for a panoply of causes. The rest of the short route downtown was an obstacle course of street vendors selling crude wooden carvings and merchants exhorting you into their shops (many of which contain an amazing array of truly appealing carvings, masks, and items of clothing). You learn quickly never to lock eyes or respond in the slightest to the incessant spiels, if only in the interest of negotiating more than a city block in an afternoon's excursion.

There were exceptions. At one point I languished against the outside of a building to escape the other pushy salespersons in the store where Jan was making a purchase. A nice young man approached and said that I looked American and that, judging by my beard, I was probably not prejudiced like most of my countrymen. This sophisticated appeal to my liberal nature could neither be ignored nor denied. Could he buy me a beer since he needed my advice? It seems that he was on his way to Penn State University and wanted to know if an African black could possibly survive in small-town America. He had aroused the mentor that lurks inside most professors. What luck, a student to advise just when I was beginning to need a fix!

In the gloom of a nearby bar the plot thickened. It seemed that my new friend was actually a Ugandan student who, in the company of other university dissidents, fled the country in fear for his life. On the back of a napkin he drew a map of his escape route. He had been awarded a scholarship by a Christian fellowship group to study at an American university. However, there was a catch. He and his friends had to reach church headquarters in Dar-es-Salaam on the coast. They were broke and, to make matters worse, the Kenyan authorities had given them but a few days to leave the country or be deported back to Uganda.

By story's end I felt way in over my head. The tale, which fully elaborated takes about an hour to tell, was too implausible to be disbelieved and its teller was never out of character. I stared down at the King Solomon's-mine map on the table, with its arrows leading from central Uganda to the sea, and struggled with the conflicting impulses to either flee or to spring for 10 train tickets. My less than satisfactory compromise was to offer $20 to the cause (with the bar bill thrown in for good measure, of course). As we parted my Ugandan friend promised to write me from University Park one day.

The next morning we gathered in the lobby to await our Land Rover and traveling companions. I was filled with a certain amount of trepidation as I contemplated the regimentation implicit in a guided tour. James, our Kikuyu driver, was a delight—good humored, talkative and knowledgeable. Greg, a computer specialist from the East Coast who was treating himself to a photo safari after completing a work assignment in Australia, proved equally enjoyable. The ripple on an otherwise smooth surface was supplied by a couple from a Midwestern city that I will refer to simply as Bonnie and Clyde, since that came to be their private nickname. Clyde was a former machinist who now had his own small manufacturing business. High school sweethearts, they were celebrating their 25th wedding anniversary with their first trip abroad.

The first stop on our itinerary was Mountain Lodge, a hewn-wood, Swiss Family Robinson tree house built high on the slopes of the foothills of Mount Kenya. Upon going to the dining room for lunch we had failed to notice the small sign warning visitors to close the balcony screen door when not in the room. A roomful of startled monkeys is quite a sight. While we failed to get an accurate head count, several scurried over the balcony rail when we opened the door. The stouter hearts continued their task of unpacking our bags. Our precious medicines were strewn about the floor, interspersed with the candy wrappers that once held our supply of sweets. One shameless exhibitionist danced about draped in Jan's nightgown. Finally, all retreated except for the smallest, who began to shriek. Being a son of the Wild West, I was not about to let such a challenge go unanswered. I let out a loud "heh" and stomped into the room, at which point my adversary became all teeth and proceeded to chase me back into the hall.

One evening at Samburu Lodge we had another extraordinary experience. Each night the staff would hang a goat's hindquarters on a spotlighted pole across the river. The guests would sit at the bar and wait to see if an elusive leopard would appear. On our side of the river, meat scraps were strewn on the bank to bait crocodiles that would crawl out of the water, separated from the guests by only about 30 feet and a waist-high retaining wall. On land they seemed slow and cumbersome, and the proceedings were presided over by a massive 18-footer that kept the others at bay.

At nightfall on the evening in question, the president was resting its snout within inches of the choicest morsel when a huge leopard appeared out of the darkness. It seemed oblivious to the startled guests and began to circle the enormous saurian, causing some of the smaller crocs to scurry into the water. The game of wits proceeded for 10 minutes. Whenever the leopard got too close the crocodile let out a frightening hiss. Finally convinced that it was futile, the cat evaporated slowly back into the darkness.

Greg and I lingered over our drinks, savoring the moment. It was then that he began to tell me an extraordinary tale of a Ugandan student on the lam. I maintained a poker face until he produced the familiar map that had cost him only $80. I have since run into yet another American who took the tumble. However, on that wondrous evening at Samburu Lodge my consolation was that I was four times smarter than Greg!

Confirming our earlier suspicions, Bonnie declined to go on most of the game drives, preferring instead to sit by the pool. This was fine with all of us, since on our first foray she asked James to find her an elephant turd and then proceeded to photograph it "for the folks back home" while shrieking in amazement at its size.

There were other ways in which "Bonnie does Africa" became a bit wearing. At times we had to travel considerable distances over poor roads that she was simply not up to physically. She would ask James monotonously, "How much farther?" in the voice of a child nagging her father to make a pit stop. Her enthusiasm peaked only when we paused for gasoline.

Flanking every petrol station were several curio shops selling essentially the same merchandise. She would disappear into their maws and emerge sometime later with arms full, while James tried to hide his exasperation over his deteriorating schedule. The van was designed to carry nine passengers and their luggage, a capacity that we came close to exceeding, particularly when Clyde purchased a near life-sized statue of a Masai warrior.

The problem with space was further exacerbated by Bonnie's habit of stealing an object as a souvenir during each of our meals. Jan, Greg and I took to leaving the table early so as not to be a part of some ugly scene should it occur. The one exception was our dinner in the famed Kenya Safari Club. Upon our arrival Bonnie asked that her room be changed since it was the very night of her 25th wedding anniversary and she had expected better.

Although the standard issue was quite luxurious, complete with quaint fireplace, the management switched her to the bridal suite, with its wonderful view of the grounds. That evening we were escorted to a private dining room and served a sumptuous meal. There was an anniversary cake and the staff presented the beaming couple with a beautiful book detailing the history of the establishment. As they left to attend to their other duties, Bonnie slipped silverware into her purse.

One morning I found James seated in the van listening intently to a radio broadcast. He informed me that U.S. jets had just bombed Libya. For the next two days we hung on every newscast as we completed our itinerary and headed for Nairobi. By then we knew that a British diplomat had been killed by angry Muslims in Khartoum and that Westerners were flocking into Nairobi from the Sudan and Ethiopia to await flights to Europe and the States. When we reached the Norfolk Hotel we had conflicting messages from the Cairo Sheraton, which said that all was fine and we should proceed as scheduled, and our tour company in New York, which advised us to cancel. We opted for prudence. The first available reservations were on a KLM flight to London that was to leave at 2 A.M. three days later.

Airborne and flying over the turbulent Middle East, we assessed our muddled prospects. Once again we were all but destitute. We had managed to book our Nairobi to London flight only by calling our travel agent in Reno to arrange for direct ticketing from there. It was unclear how much could be salvaged from our prepaid Egyptian itinerary. (The loss turned out to be $2,000.) Furthermore, any rebate would be at some time in the future and could not to be entered into present calculations. Our first impulse had been to simply return home. However, our tickets from London were nontransferable. Any change of date invalidated them and our transatlantic reservations were still 10 days off.

In London we received an infusion of funds from our home. We decided to rent a car and head north. A student of other people's ethnic heritages, I had never taken the time to explore the Scottish dimension of my own. In the ensuing days we seemed to have Scotland's frozen countryside to ourselves as we explored the lochs, searched out a Gaelic-speaking inn in Sloat on the Isle of Skye and delighted in the occasional view of the improbable Scottish Highland cow.

After a few days we were thoroughly relaxed and enjoying a respite from the tribulations of the previous month, or so it seemed. Our reverie was interrupted by the BBC newscast that Swedish scientists had detected an unexplained dramatic increase in the radiation count and that something might be headed our way. For the remainder of our stay all eyes were focused upon the Soviet Union's Chernobyl disaster. Maggie Thatcher sought to assure us periodically that nuclear death was not imminent, but just in case we were also treated to large doses of pipers playing *Amazing Grace.*

At Heathrow as we boarded our aircraft, Jan asked, "Don't you think it only fair to warn the other passengers?"

Car Trouble

by Kimberly Robinson

MY HUSBAND, JOHN, and I and our two children, Anthony and Linda, were going to ring in 1999 in Pagosa Springs, Colorado, and spend a few days skiing at Wolf Creek. Accompanying us on the trip were our friends Dave and Jenny and their daughter, Brook, who was in town for a visit. We took off in our small convoy, Dave, Jenny and Brook in their Ford Ranger and us in our '91 Chevrolet Celebrity station wagon, and we were sure everything would go just right.

Our home outside Colorado Springs is about 4½ hours from Pagosa Springs. Ninety minutes into our trip, we turned west toward Pagosa Springs. There was a knocking sound—we'd thrown a rod and the engine was toast. After some discussion, the women and kids were left in Walsenburg to cool their heels while John and Dave drove back to Colorado Springs to get our other car, a Buick Skylark, which we hadn't taken in the first place because we couldn't fit all our skiing equipment and luggage in it. The women and kids ate lunch, went to the library, walked around town and waited. About 3½ hours later, the guys got back. We loaded what we could into the Buick from the station wagon. The rest was crammed into Dave and Jenny's Ranger. We left the station wagon at a garage and headed out once more.

We were going over Wolf Creek Pass and had just crested the summit, cruising on the downhill side into Pagosa Springs, when we saw a boulder in the middle of our lane. It was a small boulder, as boulders go, but definitely bigger than a bowling ball. This was a four-lane highway. We were going 60 miles an hour, a cliff face on our right, a car right behind us and another car in the lane next to us. John had time to say, "Hang on!" We ran right into it, and bounced up and over. Nobody was hurt, and miraculously the brake lines weren't damaged so we were able to pull over and stop. It wasn't pretty, but we survived. We found out a few days after the trip, when the car was put up on a rack, that the boulder had hit the transmission bell housing and cracked it, broken both half shafts, badly dented the gas tank and ripped out a few other things that made the car basically immobile. Dave and Jenny pulled up behind us; they had been far enough back that they hadn't seen what had happened. Evidently, we had walloped the boulder hard enough to knock it off the road so nobody else would hit it. None of us could believe that both disasters could happen to the same people all in one day. Since the brakes still worked, we coasted down from the 12,000-foot summit in neutral until we got to the flat lands, where Dave hooked a tow rope onto our car and towed us the rest of the way into Pagosa Springs. By this time, it was dark so we found our rooms, unpacked and drowned our sorrows with a few beers.

Determined that this wasn't going to ruin our vacation, the next day we rented a vehicle. When I arrived at the rental agency, they just happened to have a car that already had a ski rack on it, so I took it. As I was driving out of the parking lot, the ski rack fell off the top of the car. By this time I was kind of numb so I just picked the ski rack up off the road and took it back to the rental office, where they put it back on. We were almost afraid to go skiing but were determined to enjoy our New Year's Eve, so off we went, and amazingly, nobody broke a leg.

That night, all of us adults were going to party together to ring in the New Year and Dave and Jenny had a huge fight. They decided to drive back home on New Year's Day, cutting short their vacation by two days, and discuss a possible divorce. We wished them both the best of luck, but we decided to stay on. Now we had to figure out how to get ourselves and both of our broken vehicles home. We found a U-Haul dealer who was checking his messages that day even though it was a holiday. We rented their smallest moving van and a car dolly. Because John was a U-Haul dealer at his automotive garage back at home, they were able to strike a bargain and a token amount was exchanged for a vehicle "transfer". We turned in our rental car and used the U-Haul moving van to go skiing one last time. Now *that* looked a little strange in the Wolf Creek parking lot.

Dave had helped us get the Buick onto the car dolly in the hotel parking lot before he headed home, so all John and I had to do was hitch up the car dolly onto the moving van after we got back from skiing. We were all set to go in the back hotel parking lot so that the next morning we could just throw our suitcases into the moving van and take off for home. Well, best laid plans of mice and men. The next morning we got up and someone had parked their car right in front of our little train. The hotel was packed, so we had no idea whose vehicle it was and the design of the car dolly prevented us from backing it up to get out of the parking lot. John decided to roll the moving van a little forward and hit the brakes real hard so the car would roll off the dolly, but all we managed to do was get the Buick stuck on the car dolly and completely off center.

We almost cried. John called a tow truck driver in town who had two floor jacks. When he got there, he scratched his head and was wondering how the heck we had managed to do what we did. We just said, "Don't ask." He and John got everything straightened out, car on the car dolly, car dolly hitched up to the moving van. So ... $85 poorer we took off for home.

There were two adults and two kids (9 and 11 years of age) crammed into the cab of this small moving van, for a 4½-hour trip through the mountains. We didn't care. We didn't have another mishap, and I have *never* been so happy to get home in, relatively, one piece.

You Shouldn't Go Home Again

by Donna Feuerstein

I DIDN'T HAVE MUCH TIME to finish packing. In just a few hours we would head back to our former home in Tennessee for spring break. The premise of the vacation was to indulge our 7-year-old son, who lived the first three years of his life there. He wanted to experience the things he had seen in photographs, such as playing in our backyard surrounded by mountains, cave exploring, rattlesnake hunting with dad and hiking up into the hills. My choice of vacation was to go to the ocean, lay on the beach and get a tan, but I finally agreed to the Tennessee trip.

We decided it would be best to leave on the 12-hour drive during the middle of the night. Our boys, ages 7 and 3, would sleep most of the way, plus traffic would be minimal. Just before we turned in for a few hours of sleep, my husband decided to do some back stretches to limber up for the long drive. He complained to me that he was a little sore. Not thinking much of his comment, I went to bed. Several hours later, the alarm woke me and I realized I was alone. My husband had been in such pain that he had driven himself to the emergency room. He was diagnosed with a muscle strain and placed on muscle relaxers and pain pills. The doctor wrote specific instructions, bed rest and no driving! I suggested we call off the trip, but my spouse reassured me that he'd be better by morning. We removed the middle seat from the minivan and threw down a blanket, which is where he spent the entire trip flat on his back.

Thirteen hours later, blurry-eyed and exhausted, I pulled into the hotel parking lot in our old hometown. My husband limped into the room, flopped down on the bed and resumed his supine position for the next 12 hours. Meanwhile, I got to unload the kids and the van. Within 15 minutes of our arrival, I was ankle deep in a tiny creek running behind the hotel, which the kids joyously discovered. Before I could say, "I told you we should have stayed home" to my husband, I was climbing down the steep embankment with the boys, trying to scrape the dark, red clay off my brand new running shoes and wading through ice cold water pouring from a drain pipe. Holding onto rusty bottle caps and smelly crab claws, my jean pockets quickly became stuffed with the sharp remains of snail shells. I was the keeper of my oldest son's collected treasures. Realizing I was not prepared for three days of this, I sat down at the water's edge and watched the kids play.

I looked up at the window of our hotel room and could picture my husband lying there alone. I knew he was miserable and probably fast asleep from the strong medication. I wondered jokingly to myself, would he share his drugs? Day one ended as I bathed the children and tucked them into their beds. I collapsed into a hot bath, barely noticing the gritty, sandy bottom.

By day two, my husband was feeling a bit better. A good part of the morning was spent in the store picking up his prescriptions. I encountered long lines of mountain folk who'd come to town to buy their Easter frocks and clip-on ties. The woman in front of me was having trouble at the checkout. She was trying to enunciate "The sale sign said 75 percent off," but the cashier couldn't understand her. The problem wasn't her thick Southern accent, but rather trying to speak the words without front teeth (try it). I was able to translate, as I have a toothless first grader and was familiar with the dialect.

Later that day we went to see our old homestead in the country. We walked up to the house and were immediately recognized by the new owners. They were gracious enough to let us walk around the yard. I marveled at how the trees and landscaping had matured, yet I felt a bit sorry to see the lack of maintenance. My kids were then invited into the house to see some baby chicks. It was just two days before Easter, so I pictured a small cardboard box of fluffy, yellow, chirping fuzz-balls.

The man opened the sliding glass door to my once-beautiful dining and kitchen area. I stepped in with the boys, and there in the middle of the room was a towering mass of wired cages that housed at least a dozen, almost full-grown, ugly, smelly chickens. It almost broke my heart. I loved that house and I didn't want to see poultry in the kitchen unless it was stuffed and baked! I guess a person really *can* go home again, as long as you don't mind feathers in the kitchen.

Day three was warm and sunny so we traveled to a nearby lake. My husband and older son headed for the swimming dock. I walked with my younger boy back to the car to retrieve one of his plastic action figures. It seemed we had the whole place to ourselves when a small bus filled with young men and women dressed in their Sunday best pulled up next to us. The driver, an older gent, got out and approached me holding a small booklet. Before he had a chance to speak, I quickly chirped, "We're just visiting from Wisconsin, we're Catholic and very happy with our religion." He nodded politely and walked back towards the bus, then turned around suddenly and inquired, "Wes-con-son, huh? Isn't that in Minnesota?"

Early morning of day four we left Tennessee and headed back north. My husband was able to drive again and we took turns napping. The last leg of the trip was mine. I began to daydream about our next vacation. Ahhhh, the Gulf of Mexico, *I'll* be laying flat on *my* back, pass the suntan lotion. The exit for home just ahead, I shifted my mind back to the moment and thought to myself, "I've got to write about this trip." My husband glanced over at me and asked, "What are you smiling about?"

This Is a Test

by Priscilla Burgess

"ATTENTION, ATTENTION! This plane is going to make an emergency landing . . . "

Oh, no! I was going to miss my connecting flight to Rome. Then the message continued . . . "in water. Please put on your life vests . . . "

It was at that point that I realized there was little likelihood of surviving the emergency landing and that I probably wasn't ever going to get to Rome. Damn! I thought. Why does it have to happen on the way over? Why not on the way home after I had a chance to enjoy my trip?

A rush of adrenaline flooded my body while my brain was still playing catch-up. I was outwardly calm but every emergency warning system in my body was blasting: Do something! Don't just sit there! I reached down for my life vest because there was nothing else I could do. Meanwhile my mind kept racing along.

I was on a flight "over the pole." That meant that if we were going down in water it was going to be cold. A warning from the Coast Guard sailing class I'd taken at Fort Mason years ago ran through my mind: 20 minutes in the water of San Francisco Bay and you're unconscious; 45 minutes and you're dead. How much colder would the waters of the Arctic Ocean be? The last time I was on this flight I could see icebergs from the plane. I looked out the window. Pitch black, not one light flashing anywhere, no stars, nothing to give any indication of where we were.

A tug on my arm interrupted my racing thoughts. A young Frenchman on his way home asked me what the message said. I held up my vest and explained in halting French that we were going to land in the ocean and he should put his vest on. I didn't bother to tell him that if we did hit the water, putting on the vest would be an exercise in futility. I've heard that there is virtually no difference between hitting water and hitting ground.

As the French kid reached for his vest, I listened to the plane humming along. The flight had been incredibly smooth, not even a bit of turbulence. I hadn't felt it losing altitude but perhaps I just hadn't noticed. But then, wouldn't my ears have been popping? If we had to make a landing so urgently, why did everything feel so normal?

An enormous man blocked my access to the aisle. High seat backs blocked my vision but I was sure there was no cabin crew in the vicinity. And while I could now hear other passengers stirring, it was uncannily quiet. The vest lay limply in my lap while I waited to hear instructions for assuming the emergency landing position.

I didn't want to die. Every ounce of energy in my body was resisting the reality of it, I wanted to fight it, do something, anything! I felt a raging frustration that I had no control whatsoever over what was happening. At the same time, thinking about my life and what I'd already accomplished gave me an odd sense of closure. I had spent a joyous 20 odd years with my two sons watching them grow from sweet and funny little boys into interesting and attractive men, found the passion I'd been searching for all my life in writing and experienced a delightful melange of people coming in and out of my life, leaving behind the gift of knowing them.

There were still things I wanted to do. I hadn't published the book I just finished. I was heading to Rome to see about working with the United Nations, to perhaps fulfill a life-long dream of working abroad. My sons were grown, they'd be fine without me, but then I wouldn't get to see my grandchildren.

It was while I was making my peace with myself that I heard an impatient male voice: "Disregard that message. It was a mistake. There is some problem with the automatic warning system. Again, please disregard that message!" Click.

Screams, where before there had been an eerie silence, erupted from the back of the plane. As I watched the cabin crew race by carrying emergency gear, I wondered why those passengers had waited for the "all clear" to panic. I wasn't sure what to believe: that the smooth flight and impatient steward were correct and nothing was wrong, or that the message announcing the emergency landing was true and the steward was trying to avoid panic.

More tugging at my sleeve. The young Frenchman was peering at me anxiously through his glasses, his brown hair sticking up, his oversized clothes making him look like a worried scarecrow. Very politely, in careful French, he asked me again to tell him what was going on. I think the screaming passengers finally convinced him that we were indeed crashing, so then I spent a considerable time assuring him that the message was a mistake and that everything was fine.

He settled down to sleep again but I was too wound up to rest. I thought about *The Occurrence at Owl Creek*, a story about a man who in the last seconds of his life lived a lifetime. I thought I was living the last minutes of my life, but I certainly didn't have that experience. There had been enough time to face and accept my death and now that I knew I wasn't going to die, I felt a flash of disappointment that I wasn't going to get a nice long rest after all. But that was quickly replaced by thoughts of the adventures awaiting me in Europe, of the fun of meeting new people in Rome and visiting old friends in Paris.

A soul-searing experience such as that should have some effect and of course, it did. I mentioned the experience to others at my hotel in Rome and they exclaimed in horror and told me they had seen the story on British TV. They were so upset I felt I had to assure them that it hadn't been as terrible as reported. Then I raced for the phone to call my sons and discovered that the San Francisco papers had indeed carried the story. They knew I was safe but my younger son had called the airline to find out what had happened and why. They told him it was a mystery, no one knew why that particular tape had been played, especially since the plane was flying over land at the time.

Then as I traveled across Europe, I found a level of patience with the world I've never before known: The taxi driver robbed me of $200? No problem! At least I'm not dead. What? My train left an hour ago? Okay, I'll wait for the next one because I'm alive to do so. And unlike Scrooge, when faced with death, I didn't see the error of my ways because I still want to do exactly what I was already doing: I still want to write, I still want to work abroad, and I still hope to meet my grandchildren some day.

It's just that when I really do have to die, I would like to participate in the process and not have it sprung on me by strangers. I would like to have some control over when and where it occurs and I would like to share the experience with my loved ones. And I certainly don't want some rude jerk interrupting the event, broadcasting over an anonymous speaker: "Attention, Attention! This event has been postponed. Please disregard your invitation and make an orderly exit to the rear. Again, please leave. The announcement of this event was a mistake!"

Exchange Student

by Joel Thurtell

ON JUNE 1, 1962, Israeli jailers let a balding, middle-aged German man swig half a bottle of wine, then led him a short way to a platform where they hanged him. This was Adolf Eichmann, who helped deport three million Jews to German death camps in World War II.

When Eichmann was hanged, I was barely 17 years old, just finishing my junior year of high school in Lowell, Michigan. Lowell was then a farming community of about 2,000 people on the west side of Michigan's Lower Peninsula. Despite the relatively new inventions of television and radio, it was still a rather insular town. For most of us, a big trip was a day spent shopping in the department stores in nearby Grand Rapids. My church once held a contest and gave a prize to a man who had stayed his whole life within 15 miles of Lowell, and was proud of it. When I started high school, the choice of foreign languages in my school was the dead one, Latin. No French. No Spanish. Least of all, no German.

I didn't think of myself as being connected to the outside world, let alone to events that happened in Germany when my parents were kids in the U.S. Nor did I connect myself to events in Israel. Who would think that the execution of a German war criminal in Israel would affect a Midwestern American boy?

On June 1, 1962, I was busy. Besides studying for my final exams, I was getting ready for a big trip. I was going to be an exchange student. Despite my lack of even minimal training in the German language, I had been selected by an exchange program, called Youth for Understanding, to live with a German family that summer.

It was a big deal. We heard a lot about international understanding and how the youths of various nations could bridge the cultural gulf between them and maybe with time bring the people of the world closer together.

It was a big expense, too. My parents were not rich. Our church helped raise some of the money. As I recall, the summer was to cost $700—a big sum in 1962. There was lots of support for international understanding. The owner of a small factory that made automatic door closers gave me a pneumatic door closer to present to my German family. The owner of a bean elevator gave me a couple bags of navy or kidney beans to give away. I was told that Germans love classical music, and Germany being the native land of Beethoven, I bought a record of his Violin Concerto to give to my family.

Not long before I left for Germany, I learned that I would be staying with a family of dairy farmers in the northern German State of Schleswig-Holstein, not far from the old town of Lübeck. I was very excited. Germany was so old, compared to Michigan. Later, I would earn a B.A., and almost a Ph.D. in history. My fascination with things historical worked all sorts of fantasies into my head. What I really knew about German history was very little. The bibliography would have taken in Caesar's *Commentaries on the Gaelic Wars,* some historical novels set in the Roman Empire and maybe a bit of medieval lore from *Classics Illustrated.*

I considered myself more knowledgeable about recent German history. Twice in the 20th century Germany had entered into our U.S. History classes by way of two world wars. My father and uncle had served in the military during World War

II, as had most of the dads of kids in my school. All of my grandparents had lived through both world wars. I'd read sporadically among the war literature, mostly tales of submarine and anti-submarine battles and yarns about the air war. My father was an Air Force pilot, and through his love of flight I picked up a keen interest in the aviation history of World War II. It was that interest in the air war over Germany that would create a big, big diplomatic problem for me, as it turned out.

In the waiting area of Detroit Metropolitan Airport I found a bookstore and on its racks was a paperback volume called *Black Thursday*. It was a historical account of the British and American effort to bomb the ball bearing plant at Schweinfurt, Germany. The cover showed a color painting of B-17s raining bombs with German fighters aimed upward in pursuit. I read *Black Thursday* on the long plane ride to Amsterdam. Having finished the book, I couldn't bear to toss it out, so I hid it in the inner pocket of my blue zipper-sided suitcase, and forgot about it.

What a summer. On the return trip, when dozens from Youth for Understanding were talking about their experiences, I felt weird. I'd never brought myself to call the German parents "Vati" or "Muti." I felt I had not made my summer work, either for me or for the cause of international understanding. For most of the returnees, international understanding was a fact and they had done their part in furthering the ideal. I, on the other hand, had done my part in damaging that understanding. Yet I could not help myself. I am who I am. And my German family was who they were.

The German "father" was a former German Army officer who had commanded a huge farm in the Soviet Union when the Nazis were at their high point in World War II. My standard high school American history class didn't go so far as to explain that 25 million Russians died in World War II, many of them exterminated by the German occupiers. That would have been a depressing, even sickening fact to know on the farm in Schleswig-Holstein. And this guy's hands may well have been clean. He was an administrator, a farm manager.

On the other hand, Eichmann was an administrator, wasn't he?

The father picked me up at the Lübeck train station. I think he was flustered to find that I couldn't understand him unless he invented on the spot sign language. He had a little Opel, I recall, with windows that wouldn't roll down. The men in the family were heavy smokers, and the tiny car stank of sweat and tobacco smoke. From the train station, we raced along cobbled streets and I was leaning down for a glimpse of the tall spires of the seven big churches for which Lübeck is famous. We didn't stop for a view of the churches but raced on, past the Holstentor, which is the great medieval gate that once was part of a wall that ringed the old trading town. We didn't stop to look at the Holstentor, either, but suddenly were zipping along country roads, narrow cobbled lanes, passing houses with thatched roofs attached to long barns.

I remember catching part of one thing he said. It was in English: "international understanding." He said it with a grin.

My family's house was unusual in that it was separate from the barn. It was a big, two-story house. The father beckoned and I followed him inside, where I met the mother and their daughter, who was about 20. Both were hard at work in the kitchen, baking. I followed the father into a corner room, the Stube, or living room. There was a desk with a small typewriter, 78-RPM record player, black and white TV set, Blaupunkt radio, tile-sided wood burning stove, straight-backed chairs and a stuffed easy chair. The father left the room and I was alone. I set my suitcase down and sank into the easy chair. It had been a long train ride from Amsterdam, I was tired, and almost immediately I was asleep.

Suddenly I was awake when the father returned and angrily motioned at me to get up. "Op! Op!" he shouted. I was sitting in his chair. Verboten!

This could be a long summer.

Now the sister motioned for me to follow her. She would give me a tour of the farm. In the barn, she pointed at the floor. There was cow dung there.

"Scheisse!" she laughed. "Scheisse!"

Shit. It was one of the few German words I knew. My friend, Michael, a German boy who lived in Lowell as an exchange student the previous year, had taught me a few words because he suspected people would try to trick me into embarrassing myself. Same thing happened to him in Lowell.

He was right. I recall when a policeman came to the house to deal with the father on an insurance matter; the father was an insurance agent as well as a farmer. The two sons in the family, one 16 and the other 25, tried to persuade me to tell the cop, "Du bist ein Mors," Low German for "You are an ass."

Well, we're all having fun, I thought.

Sinister things began to happen. Soon after I arrived, the father proudly took me upstairs to a closet where he kept his old green Wehrmacht uniforms. It was illegal to keep it, but he didn't care. I suppose you could excuse that—I'd seen the dads in Lowell dress up in their old Army or Navy uniforms, those who could still fit into them, and march in the Memorial Day parade. This father had also served, but he had to hide his uniform. A hard-working farmer, his uniform still fit.

He also wasn't supposed to have kept his service Luger automatic, but one afternoon he pulled it out. The two brothers and I followed him to a field, where we took turns shooting at cans. I remember being amazed that there was no kick because it had an anti-recoil mechanism.

The father loved to shoot. There were tiny deer called Rehbock living in the forest near the house. The dad would take his rifle with a telescopic sight out at dusk and come back with a dead deer no bigger than a cocker spaniel draped around his shoulders. He was quite a hunter. But hey, no different than many people who hunt around Lowell.

But showing me his uniform was his way of starting an argument. He said the Americans came in on the wrong side. The U.S. should have sided with Germany, not with Churchill. But what could one expect, he said—that Rosenfeld was a Jew.

My ability to understand this guy, to begin with anyway, was nearly nonexistent. I didn't speak or understand German. Even had I known German, the Plattdeutsch spoken in this area would have been a challenge. But I had my pocket Langenscheidt's German-English dictionary, and I had sign language, and when people were willing to repeat things in different ways, I could understand. The father was willing to repeat over and over his views on World War II because like me, he was dedicated to furthering the cause of international understanding. That is how I was made to understand his interpretation of Second World War history.

It was really very simple. Hitler was a great man who raised Germany from the depths of the Depression, built the Autobahns, recreated the national war machine and made Germany once again a power to be reckoned with.

"What about the killing of Jews? Was that a good thing?" I said. I recall the mother's explanation: "We had no idea that was going on."

"But what did she think about it?" She didn't answer my question.

I thought I knew the answer, and it made me sick.

One evening when several neighboring farmers paid a visit, I got the answer. Long-necked brown beer bottles were brought up from the cellar. Green bottles of Mosel wine were broken out. There was lots of Gemütlichkeit in the Stube that evening, and the father turned on the record player. The sound was scratchy—a voice, high-pitched, rising up, shouting. I didn't understand a word, but I knew who it was.

Hitler.

A farmer sitting next to me explained the situation. Hitler was a good man with wonderful ideas for bettering mankind. One of his most important goals was the eradication of inferior races. The worst of these people are the Jews, a pernicious race of subhumans who have managed to gain control in all walks of life. It's not a problem just in Germany. In the U.S., you people have Jews running your industries, your banks, even your newspapers. Your country made a big mistake by coming into the war on Britain's side. With the help of the U.S., Germany could have finished the work of exterminating the Jews.

That answer made a lie of the stock response of the Germans that they didn't know Hitler was killing Jews.

In my own family back in the States, we talked and argued a lot about politics. So I thought nothing of trying to argue with my hosts, though my German was pretty crude.

Pretty crude, but getting better. My arguing provoked great outbursts of anger. In this patriarchal family, authority was in the father, and nobody had ever challenged him. Till now.

My duties on the farm included mowing the lawn and fetching the eggs twice a day—they had 1,000 hens laying eggs.

When they were cutting hay, all of us turned out to pitchfork great mounds of hay onto tripod racks, like teepee frames, which made the big hummocks, called Reuters, or haystacks. I would also work in the strawberry garden weeding or picking berries.

When I wasn't doing chores I'd read. I had one book, *To Kill a Mockingbird,* by Harper Lee. I bought it at an English-language bookstore in Lübeck on a trip with some family friends. It turned out that this family was not much for traveling or sightseeing. Occasionally I made day-long excursions with friends of the family. They lent me a bike, which I used in good weather to explore the countryside.

One day I came back from biking around the neighborhood and found people looking very serious, especially when they looked at me. The dam broke at coffee time. Usually, this was a merry break from farm work. But today the father confronted me with the big discovery. While I was out, they had searched my suitcase. And guess what they found. Not *To Kill a Mockingbird.*

Bleck Toorsday, they called it. The father sat across the table from me and waved the book, showing its color cover with B-17s raining bombs on Schweinfurt. He was livid that I should have smuggled such a piece of propaganda into his house. I was livid that they'd searched my suitcase.

(I should have been thankful that's as far as they went. The wife of a colleague at work tells me she was a YFU exchange student in 1967. She stayed with a family in northern Germany who seized her passport and money, doling out a paltry weekly allowance.)

By this time, my German was good enough that I could express my anger. But once more I was treated to the full lecture on American complicity in Germany's failure to solve the

Jewish Problem.

I was a fairly skinny kid, not very muscular. My two "brothers" were heavy-muscled farm boys. However, I was on my high school wrestling team one year and I knew something about the moves and about leverage. My "brothers" didn't know this. One day, they led me to the back yard, where there was a set of clothesline posts. These posts were fat pipes in the shape of an upside-down U. First the elder son grabbed the overhead pipe and began chinning himself. Then the big one started pumping himself up and down. Very impressive. Then it was my turn. I grabbed the pipe. My hands would not come close to encircling the pipe. My palms sat more or less arced along the side and a bit of the top. I couldn't get a grip. But I tried to lift myself. I could barely get my toes off the ground.

Having failed the strength test, the brothers led me into the barn, out of sight of the house. I didn't know what they had in mind. Inside, the younger one, the big one, spun around and took up a wrestling stance. He was reaching his long arms out, trying to grab my hands, my legs. To his surprise, I quickly had him down on the floor and pinned. After the count of "drei," or three, I released him. As I was standing up, his long arm snaked out and grabbed me around the neck. Next, I was on the floor and he was choking me. I could feel myself running out of air. I couldn't breathe. I tried to shout that he was killing me, but I couldn't speak. I was just about to pass out when, at the command of his older brother, he relaxed his arm and let me go.

By now, with the Hitler evening and *Bleck Toorsday* and this attempted strangling behind me, I wonder why I didn't leave. The tension, the mutual dislike, I mean the real nasty hostility from the male members of this family were so evident that I wonder why I didn't just toss my clothes, my *Bleck*

Toorsday and all into my suitcase and split. I had my traveler's checks and my passport.

Is it possible that Eichmann's execution just days before I arrived helped kindle the virulence of these people? I think it may have been involved, though I don't recall anybody speaking directly about Eichmann. Recent scholarship about the Holocaust suggests that my suspicion developed that summer is correct—that many, many Germans were involved in the mass killings. There may have been some uneasy consciences in that community.

Anyway, to go home before the end of the summer would have been a huge declaration of failure. I had worked hard to go on this exchange program. My community had supported me. I was writing occasional columns for the Lowell Ledger, bland reports that never mentioned the turmoil in this family.

There was another reason. As awful as these people's ideas were, they were real. They were part of what helped Hitler get into power and stay in power. Possibly through an error in placement made bureaucratically by the exchange program, I had been assigned to a family whose views reflected the ideas that drove Germany into World War II. In 1962, I could not know that I would study for years to become a professional historian and eventually would become a journalist. I was observing that summer. I was seeing and hearing things no history book could ever make clear.

I was, above all, a witness. Seventeen years after the war ended, I was living among people who still had not grasped that Germany had lost that war. Nor had they given up on Germany's vilest war aims.

International understanding—I'm all for it.

Puppy Love in Playa

by Cameron M. Burns

Editor's Note: Can't you guys ever say anything nice? It's a question often heard here at RDR Books. After publishing over 100 trouble travel horror stories, we've finally found one with a happy ending. Trips do work out sometimes, as this story demonstrates.

WINTER DRAGS A BIT when you live in the mountains. It's good to get out and find some warm sun and sandy beaches come April and May.

But when my wife and I booked a plane and hotel package ticket to Tahiti for a week-long spring vacation in 1998, we had no idea that we'd end up running a cafe for stray dogs and cats in Playa Del Carmen, a small fishing village on the Yucatan Peninsula.

Our oddly misguided adventure into the canine/feline culinary arts began when we booked a one-week trip to Moorea, a small island in French Polynesia, through a company called Tahiti Vacations. Our travel agent, a wonderfully traveled and like-minded soul named Marilyn, encouraged us to visit the exotically beautiful South Pacific and made all the reservations. She never once mentioned how hungry the dogs of Playa Del Carmen, Quintana Roo, Mexico, might be.

Thus, in mid-April, brimming with excitement and anticipation, we boarded a Los Angeles-to-Papeete flight on a French airline called AOM (Agence Ouvert a la Mer, or some such name that six years of secondary school French couldn't quite decipher). We crushed our bodies into square, coffin-like seats that had no rival in any airplane, anywhere in the world, and after a back-busting, butt-numbing eight hours, we awoke to feel a shudder as our plane banked into the final turn for Papeete's Faaa Airport.

The water was a deep blue. The mountains sprang from the islands as majestic green spires. The beaches were small and personal. Tahiti was going to be a week of pure paradise.

We uncoiled from the seats and hammered our joints back into place with the heels of our hands. Then, we were led toward a line of French customs agents who processed everyone ahead of us without a hitch. But when I stepped up to the window, handed the stern gendarme my passport and smiled politely, our meticulously planned little hiatus in the lush South Pacific was brought to a screeching halt. My wife was allowed into Tahiti, she being an U.S. citizen and all, and I was not.

I am a citizen of Australia, even though I've lived in the U.S. for 22 years. And, as we were to learn in the weeks and months that followed, I am a citizen of a nation that had recently been dumping French wine out in the streets of Sydney in protest of France's nuclear testing in the South Pacific.

"Hey," my dear and all-too-Australian father told me in a conversation some months after I was rejected from Faaa Airport. "Didn't you hear? They recently burned down the French Embassy in Perth."

I was politely shuffled into a small, ugly, dirty office inhabited by dozens of sweating French policemen and customs agents where I was to wait until the next flight back to Los Angeles.

"I em zorry, Monsieur," He told me in his thick Gaullic. "We cannot ah-low Australeins eento Frensh Polyneesia today." Ten depressing hours later, in a hotel in Inglewood, California, I went to sleep, praying for a better day on the morrow. It came, and I made some fast calls to Marilyn, begging her to get my wife and I to a beach, anywhere, immediately. Marital bliss would become a kick in the balls, I told her, if she didn't hurry. Ann had been wanting to spend a spring week on the ocean for the past five years. In my cunning, I'd talked her out of it every time by convincing her that adventurous road trips throughout the western U.S. were a far better expenditure of time and cash. Nineteen-ninety-eight was to be her year. We'd be sifting sand between our toes somewhere, "or else."

Marilyn came through, and within 20 minutes of waking up that day, my wife and I were inside a taxi bound for the Mexicana desk at LAX. We hopped on the four-hour flight to Cancun and counted our blessings. The beach was not far away. We immediately found a cab that would take us to Playa Del Carmen.

We booked a cheap beachside room at a local institution, the Blue Parrot Hotel, and within a few hours, were out strolling along the beach, sun in our eyes, wind in our hair, and most importantly, grains of sand sifting delightfully between our toes.

It didn't take too much strolling and sifting before we noticed that there were a lot of dogs in Playa Del Carmen. Dozens and dozens of the things. Everywhere. Big dogs, little dogs, thin dogs, fat dogs, dogs with strong bodies, dogs with limps and injuries, dogs with healthy coats and dogs with mange.

We first noticed the dogs at the south end of town, down near a dock, where the ferry to Cozumel departed every couple of hours or so. There, the Hounds of Playa Del Carmen congregated on the sand in an area that wasn't being used by people, a spot where the dogs could sit, sleep and hang out with each other and not be hassled by any humans who might want them out of the way.

These dogs, we soon observed, exhibited amazing social sensibilities in that they knew what not to do. They knew not to bark and fight, not to chase cats through the streets, not to beg food from the locals, not to poop in the streets, and not to sniff the tourists' crotches. Their happy, calm, well-ordered existence seemed a role model for all creatures that live in man's domain. In short, these dogs were smart.

At the beach-side bar that night, one of the healthier looking mutts we'd seen near the dock roamed past several times, stopping here and there to wag his tail and have his ears scratched by tourists. A young Mexican waiter, Wilberth, explained to us that that particular dog was named Silver and that he had formerly belonged to the bar's manager. Silver, apparently tired with having a master, had taken to a life of living on the beach. Wilberth called Silver over and introduced us.

How Silver ever got his name is a mystery. He was a medium-sized, light brown dog that appeared to be a cross between a boxer and a Labrador. The only thing I could ever guess was that the bar manager had thought "silver" meant brown, or something else dog-related, in English.

Despite our fears of mange, rabies, gout, gall-bladder infections and whatever else this friendly pooch might've been harboring, Ann and I tentatively scratched his ears. He wagged his tail and gave us a coy, submissive look. You know, the butter-melting kind. We were in love, and we spent the rest of the evening alternating between petting Silver and running to the nearby bathroom to wash our hands.

Of course, when midnight rolled around, and we decided to turn in, Silver followed us back to our beachfront bungalow. He slept on the front porch that night and wagged his tail maniacally when we arose the next morning.

We wandered the streets and beaches of Playa Del Carmen for the next few days, and everywhere we went Silver tagged along. When we went into a cafe for breakfast, Silver would sneak in and sit underneath our table. When we ventured into a shop selling souvenirs and Mexican trinkets, Silver would wait patiently just outside the front door. And when we snorkeled in the cool, azure Caribbean, Silver would carefully guard our belongings on the beach.

About midway through our beach week, I decided Silver might be hungry so I trekked to the nearest grocery store for a couple of cans of dog food. That evening, as we enjoyed a beer on our beachside verandah, I emptied a can of Alpo into a dish and set it down. Silver sniffed, licked and tasted the food. Then, tentatively, he took a few bites. After finishing only a third of the proffered meal, Silver returned to his nook under one of the beach chairs. Silver, obviously, wasn't hungry. He was, we surmised, well fed by all the local restaurant owners in Playa, who knew the animal affectionately.

The evening drifted into night, and my wife and I curled up in the beach chairs reading cheesy novels. Then, another dog came wandering up the beach. This dog, a black and healthy-looking male, smelled the Alpo and ventured over. He sniffed and licked Silver in a sort of doggie greeting, and then set to work finishing up what was left of Silver's dinner. The black dog seemed extremely hungry, so I opened the second can of Alpo. He polished that off, then wagged his tail as if asking for more. Having none, I hiked off to the grocery store—Silver in tow—and purchased five more cans of Alpo. When Silver and I returned, the black male had gone, but a very timid black female, who obviously had a litter of pups stashed somewhere judging by her sagging teats, was licking the dish. She ran off when she saw Silver and me coming.

I loaded up the dish with three cans of dog food and went into the bungalow. When I peeked out the window, the small black female was chomping down the entire meal. Silver sat quietly nearby, watching her eat.

The night drifted by, and dogs of all shapes and sizes wandered up to our porch, eating if they were hungry, and greeting Silver with licks, sniffs and wagging tails. Perro Cafe was born.

The next day, as my wife and I passed the grocery store, I bought 15 cans of Alpo.

I explained in broken Spanglish to the curious clerk that the dog food was "Para los perros a la Playa." We returned to our bungalow around 5 P.M., and I immediately set out the old dish with Alpo, and found three more plates which I loaded down with two cans of Alpo apiece.

"Perro Cafe is now open, huh?" my wife said, shaking her head in both wonder and disbelief. "What's on the menu tonight? Any dinner specials?"

Admittedly, she had a point. The menu was rather bland. My "Bifsteks de Alpo," "Alpo Loaf" and "Alpo A La Mode" were all pretty much the same thing: a pile of cheap, gross dog food on a plate. But what Perro Cafe lacked in culinary delights, Silver and I made up for in atmosphere.

We placed water bowls around the periphery of the verandah within easy reach of the clientele, and even took a couple of bowls of dog food down a nearby side alley for the more timid dogs and cats of Playa. We turned off the music inside the bungalow and set the exterior lights down so that passing dogs could see Silver sitting happily near the front of the bungalow. I even made barking sounds at passersby on the beach to let them know the cafe was open.

The night was a resounding success for Playa's newest dining establishment. Fifteen dogs and five cats had been served, and there was not a scrap of dog food left.

Silver and I celebrated by ordering a plate of ribs at the hotel restaurant and shared the entire meal on a lounge chair on the beach. That we didn't actually turn a profit on the cafe didn't matter to Silver and me—no one was keeping the books anyway.

As the second half of our seaside sojourn drifted by, Ann and I spent our days taking in the sights, swimming and wandering the quaint streets of Playa. But by night, we became an efficient culinary machine, dolling out 20-plus cans of Alpo to the hungry canine and feline residents of the small beach town the way McDonald's shovels up hamburgers to the huddled masses. As business grew, the menu evolved. Not only did we offer the old standbys, but Ann and I also created an "Alpo Soufflé," "Creme D'Alpo" and Silver's favorite: "Alpo A La Orange," which actually had tiny pieces of lime in it as a result of my fears about the dogs catching scurvy. (I figured the disease might run rampant near the ocean.) Of course, all these fabulous dishes were nothing more than plain old dog food slapped on a plate, but our customers didn't mind my queer, gourmet fantasies. They were just happy for an easy meal.

As Perro Cafe flourished, Ann began to question whether or not it was such a bright idea to feed Playa's strays after all. The animals, she pointed out, might become habituated to eating at the Blue Parrot's room No. 17. And once we left, what would they do for sustenance? Eat small tourists?

I felt a pang of guilt. She was right. Was it fair to lavish the dogs and cats of the village with Romanesque banquets, then take it all away in a blink of an eye?

Carefully, I pared back the size of the servings and the number of plates being offered each night so that no one single animal could fill up at Perro Cafe lest he forget how to scrounge out of a garbage can. I even chased off animals who were eating more than a specially allotted number of calories per day.

Finally, our last day arrived.

With the exception of Silver, none of the dogs or cats of Playa hung around our room as we humped our luggage over to the front desk. Indeed, we spotted several dogs down the beach, relaxing near the dock, scratching fleas and sniffing the coastal wind. They seemed to be thinking little of food.

I scratched Silver's ears, then climbed into an awaiting taxi. "Bye-bye, Silver," I said, leaning out the window and offering a weak smile.

Silver grinned and wagged his tail, aware that our partnership had come to a sad end, aware that the most successful dining establishment on the Yucatan coast was now just a mere memory. He watched the cab back out into the street and, as we pulled away from the Blue Parrot, he trotted off down the beach.

I don't know how many dogs inhabit the beaches of French Polynesia and how happy they are, but at least in one beach resort I know of—Playa Del Carmen, Quintana Roo, Mexico—the resident dog (and cat) population lives a happy and healthy life. And, when the occasional oddball tourist comes to visit, they even score a few free meals.

About the Contributors

Brian Abrahams is a writer and marketing consultant living in Chicago. Prior to that he was in senior management with an "Inc 500" computer memory chip company until a disastrous European assignment derailed his career and left him a shell of his former self. He does have a lot of good travel stories, however.

Janet Barton is the married mother of three grown children, has three grandchildren and has worked for 20 years as an administrative/executive assistant for a CPA firm. She enjoys reading, gardening, photography and other crafts projects, as well as volunteering for a local charity organization, and, of course, traveling.

Ralph A. Bolton lives in New York with his wife of over 50 years. He has three grown children and 11 grandchildren. In addition to his writing, Bolton has worked in the consulting field for almost 20 years and has written several systems contracting books, including *Systems Contracting: A New Purchasing Technique,* as well as articles for a number of professional magazines. He compiled some of his more memorable times in *Away and Far Out* for his children and grandchildren.

Marius Bosc is a painter who specializes in color and light in San Francisco.

Christine A. Brady is married to David Bell and has four grown children. She has worked as a speech pathologist, then as a school administrator in special education, for the Rochester City School District for 27 years. Currently she tracks down truant students, bringing their cases to family court when necessary. Brady enjoys writing personal essays, generally humorous, chronicling the joys and "disasters" of everyday life.

Loretta Graziano Breuning is a professor of international business in the Department of Management and Finance at California State University, Hayward. She developed a sister city relationship between Piedmont, California, and Cuneo, Piemonte, Italy. Breuning spent a year in Africa working for the United Nations Development Program. Two international management issues capture her attention — the management of reproductive health care and the management of family-owned businesses.

Breuning dabbles in foreign languages, and in college practiced Japanese by working as a waitress in a Japanese restaurant. She had a heavy travel habit for many years, but now she is thinking that she really should stay home. Her home is populated by a cuddly new husband and some teenagers.

Priscilla Burgess divides her time between writing and managing Web projects. She lives in San Francisco.

Cameron M. Burns was born in Canada and is a Colorado-based writer, climber and adventurer. He has authored both magazine and newspaper articles about rock, ice and mountain climbing, as well as essays and articles about adventure travel. He has also written several mountain climbing guidebooks, including *Kilimanjaro & Mt. Kenya, Colorado Ice Climber's Guide, California's Fourteener's: A Hiking & Climb-*

ing Guide, Climbing California's Fourteener's, Maroon Bells: A Climbing Guide and *Selected Climbs of the Desert Southwest.*

As a photojournalist, Burns has been a staff writer/correspondent for over two dozen publications and has won awards for his writing and his photography. Much of his work has focused on either environmental issues or outdoor activities, but he has also written hundreds of stories about politics, art, music and literature. He has done photography assignments for *Newsweek* and *GQ Magazine,* among others.

Claudia R. Capos' ever-changing career as a magazine editor, publisher, newspaper correspondent, travel writer, photographer, importer and communications consultant has created her dynamic life style and taken her to more than 50 different countries. During her 10-year stint at *The Detroit News,* she received 21 regional and national writing/editing awards and was a three-time Pulitzer Prize nominee. Currently, she is the president of Foreign Accent Inc., an international trade corporation, and the owner of Capos & Associates L.L.C., a full-time communications firm, based in Brighton, Michigan.

Brooke Comer lives in California and New York but spends little time in either state because she is always traveling. She is the author of *The Secret Caribbean: Hideaways of the Rich and Famous* and numerous short stories, most of them set in foreign countries. Comer is a contributing editor at Rudy Maxa's *Traveler,* and her articles have appeared in publications including *Playboy, Men's Journal, Hollywood Reporter* and *New York Magazine.* She is particularly fond of Cairo but also feels very much at home in Bangkok, Istanbul, Jerusalem, Rangoon, Rio de Janeiro and Venice, in alphabetical order. She would like to go to Tehran.

Jan DeGrass is a freelance writer with many years' experience in non-fiction writing and editing for newspapers, women's magazines and trade publications. Her credits include *The Globe and Mail, The Vancouver Sun* and *Province* and such magazines as *Chatelaine* and *Canadian Living*. She is a major prizewinner for a travel memoir, "Loving in Leningrad," based on her experiences in the former Soviet Union.

Dorothy Ciminelli Delmonte is a field rep for a major food corporation, as well as a freelance writer. She has been married for 36 years and has two children and two grandchildren. Her work has been published in local, regional and national publications including *The Buffalo News, Western New York Family Magazine* and *Capper's Magazine*. Delmonte enjoys biking, reading and writing, as well as traveling and hiking with her family, and is active in various organizations for the blind.

Carole Dickerson grew up in Denver, moved to the Pacific Northwest and graduated from Evergreen State College. She worked for the State of Washington and retired in 1996. Dickerson now owns a part-time business called Away You Go driving people in their own cars to the airport. She has three children and three grandsons, loves to travel and is involved in several hobby groups.

William A. Douglass is a social anthropologist and author of 14 books and more than 100 articles. His noted publications include *Death in Murelaga: The Social Significance of Funerary Ritual in a Spanish Basque Village* (1969); *Amerikanuak: Basques in the New World* (1975); *Emigration in a South Italian Town: An Anthropological History* (1984); *From Italy to Ingham: Italians in North Queensland* (1995); *Terror and Taboo:*

The Follies, Fables and Faces of Terrorism (1996); and *Tap Dancing on Ice: The Life and Times of a Nevada Gaming Pioneer* (1996). His works have been translated into several languages. He was the founder and, for 33 years, the director for the Center for Basque Studies at the University of Nevada, Reno, where he is currently professor emeritus.

Douglass is widely traveled, both for professional reasons and as a fly fisherman. He is currently completing a book on his fishing adventures in places like Brazil, British Columbia, the Bahamas, Australia, China and Mongolia.

Burt Dragin teaches journalism at Laney College in Oakland, California. His freelance articles have appeared in *The Los Angeles Times, USA Today, San Francisco Chronicle, San Francisco Examiner, Image Magazine* and other publications. His favorite traveling companion, after his wife, is a competent pharmacist.

Ann L. Egan is a retired professor and administrator at the State University of New York at Buffalo. She has five children, three grandchildren and has authored texts on statistics and research. Ann is an avid reader and herbalist and has traveled extensively in North America, Europe and the Caribbean.

Julia Niebuhr Eulenberg is a writer and historian, as well as a wife and mother of three children. She has a Ph.D. in history and is a former member of the University of Washington faculty. Eulenberg writes in a variety of fields and genres and is currently working on a short story, some poems, a memoir and a review of new historical writing. Her many hobbies include gardening, cooking, sewing and traveling.

Donna Feuerstein is happily married to a sweet, gorgeous man who is the inspiration for many of her stories. She has two beautiful sons and a slobbering St. Bernard. Feuerstein has a B.A. in writing and has had several short stories published by her local newspaper. Besides holding down the fort at home, she works part time as a medical transcriptionist and teaches fitness classes.

Matthew Fike is an English Professor at Winthrop University in South Carolina. "Where Sins Are Forgiven" will appear in the forthcoming anthology *Lessons on the Road: Stories of Teachers Abroad,* edited by Diana Renn.

Kent Foster has had severe chest pains in Zimbabwe and Uruguay, giardia in Nepal, food poisoning in Indonesia, Burma, Spain, Syria and Mexico and has suffered through three operations: one in Hungary, one in Denmark and one in Vietnam.

Foster usually works in the San Francisco Bay Area to compensate for lost money from a pickpocket in Turkey, speeding tickets in Australia, Canada, Costa Rica, the Czech Republic and Hungary and for really minor infractions in the Netherlands, Ukraine, Norway, Poland and Israel.

He is single. Email: otabe@yahoo.com

Stephanie L. Freid is a San Francisco-based freelance writer/television producer. Her future plans include volunteer work in Tanzania and living on an island off the coast of Honduras.

Anne Hagen is a happily married woman who started at RDR Books as an intern and had the exquisite privilege of taking care of the project *I Really Should Have Stayed Home.* She would like to thank all the writers for their great cooperation and fantastic work.

Robert Holmes is an award-winning travel photographer. His work has appeared in several major magazines and books around the world. He lives in Sausalito, California.

Kim Klescewski is a writer and editor. She has been happily married for 20 years and has three wonderful teenagers. Her hobbies are quilting, reading and Bunko. She resides in San Ramon, California.

Eva Mansell is currently on sabbatical to write travel tales and short fiction stories. Mansell has traveled throughout Europe, Latin America and Southeast Asia. She has had a variety of jobs including actress, waitress, file clerk, salesgirl and teacher. Her hobbies are yoga, Flamenco dancing and her cat.

Ruby E. McCreight was born in London and came to Canada in 1946 as a war bride. She has four children, 11 grandchildren, and four great-grandchildren. Although Ruby has been deaf since age 19, she was a teacher for a short time and then began writing seriously five years ago. McCreight has had several poems and a weekly column called "They Went Thata Way" published by a local newspaper.

Diane M. McNaughton is a part-time communications specialist for the Dauphin County Commissioners and a substitute language arts teacher for sixth through eighth grade. She is married to Mark, a Pennsylvania State legislator. McNaughton earned her M.A. degree in journalism from Penn State and her undergraduate degree in English from Elizabethtown College. She is the proud mother of four children and currently works as a newspaper reporter, a college writing instructor for Elizabethtown College and Penn State and Pennsylvania Senate speechwriter.

Charles Nevi recently retired from teaching and school administration after 36 years. He spends his time playing golf, traveling with his family and freelance writing. Nevi has been published several times in educational journals. He is married, with two sons and three grandchildren.

Elena Nicoladis is a post-doctoral fellow at the University of Alberta. She is married and has two children. The family plans to stay firmly in North America while the second child is young.

Larry Parker is a househusband in the Great Pacific Northwest, is happily married and has three children that make his life a delightful disaster. His hobbies are reading, music, movies, hiking, politics and his family.

Nadine Michele Payn is a clinical psychologist with a practice in Albany/Berkeley, California. She hosted a popular psychology call-in show on KGO radio in the early '80s and was a contributing editor to the *Berkeley Insider Magazine* in the mid '90s. Payne began traveling at the age of 15 and loves to write about her many adventures and misadventures around the globe.

Randy Pruitt, born in Bakersfield, California, and raised in Oklahoma, is an assistant professor of journalism at Midwestern State University at Wichita Falls, Texas. He has worked as a reporter for the *European Stars and Stripes,* covering events in Eastern Europe and the Middle East. He has taught at the college level for nine years and worked in the newspaper business for 12. In 1984 he spent a year living in a Volkswagen camper in Europe and North Africa with his wife and two dogs.

Roger Rapoport, publisher of RDR Books, is the author and editor of numerous books including *After the Death of a Salesman, I Should Have Stayed Home* and *The Getaway Guide to California.*

Kimberly Robinson is happily married and lives with her husband, Dennis, and their two children in Fountain, Colorado. Robinson works for the Air Force Reserve as an aircraft mechanic supervisor.

Zona Sage has traveled the seven seas and especially loves Paris, Asia and wild jungles. She has published in *Salon, Traveler's Tales, California Lawyer* and *Tokyo Family Law Journal.* Sage currently lives in Oakland, California.

Neal Sanders is an executive with a Boston-area high-technology company.

Dorothy Thompson is public information manager at the University of Wisconsin campus in Richland Center, where she lives with her husband, David, and their Yorkshire terrier. Thompson, who has an adult daughter, enjoys travel, especially international. Other interests include blues music, women playwrights, theater, ballroom dancing and reading, which she is addicted to. Ouidah, Benin, is Thompson's favorite place to visit. She loves to drink coffee and hates driving in snowstorms.

Joel Thurtell is the author of a forthcoming novel, *Schützen-fest.* He is a reporter with the *Detroit Free Press.* After his summer in Germany, he studied German and history at Kalamazoo College and the University at Bonn. Thurtell was a Peace Corps volunteer in West Africa. He lives in Plymouth, Michigan.

Pete Wiley has entertained friends and business associates with his encounters on the road for the past 20 years. Finally, long-time friend and colleague **Carol Nicholas** corralled Wiley long enough to capture all those tales in print—from his first winter tour where he was ceremoniously christened the Sauerkraut Cowboy—to his legendary victory over the kamikaze grasshoppers of Blaine County. Nicholas resides in Olympia, Washington, and Wiley lives in Portland, Oregon.

Docia Schulz Williams is a professional writer, lecturer and certified tour guide. She lives in San Antonio, Texas, and has conducted tours throughout the U.S., Europe, Canada, China, Africa and South America. She has authored several travel books including *Ghosts Along the Texas Coast, Phantoms of the Plains, When Darkness Falls, Best Tales of Texas Ghosts* and most recently, *The History and Mystery of Menger Hotel.* She is also a published poet.

Jennell Woulf is a senior at the University of Washington in Seattle, majoring in creative writing. Woulf, who is single, has traveled extensively. In addition to writing, she is also a bookseller for Barnes & Noble and an aspiring photographer.

I Should Have Stayed Home

The Worst Trips of Great Writers

Edited by ROGER RAPOPORT AND MARGUERITA CASTANERA

In this hilarious anthology, 50 top travel writers, novelists and journalists, including **Isabel Allende, Jan Morris, Barbara Kingsolver, Paul Theroux, Mary Morris, Dominique Lapierre, Eric Hansen, Rick Steves, Tony Wheeler** and **Helen Gurley Brown**, tell the stories of their greatest travel disasters. Most of the writers of these original essays are contributing their royalties to Oxfam America, the international relief organization. Guaranteed to whet your appetite or make you cancel your reservations.

ISBN: 1-57143-014-8

$16.95 (CAN. $21.95)
PAPERBACK
256 PAGES

I've Been Gone Far Too Long

Scientists' Worst Trips

Edited by MONIQUE BORGERHOFF-MULDER *and* WENDY LOGSDON

Here are the stories of 26 research scientists who go off the deep ends of the earth. Travel with a young researcher in Dian Fossey's camp as she is handed a gun and told to go out and shoot a gorilla poacher. See how a scientist reacts when he discovers a poisonous bushmaster in his bidet. From bush pilots and endangered species to Land Rover nightmares, this hair-raising book will keep you up past dawn. This book is a tribute to the courage of an intrepid band of researchers who have risked all to bring home the truth.

ISBN: 1-57143-054-7

$15.95 ($21.95 Can)
TRADE PAPERBACK
296 PAGES

After the Death of a Salesman

Business Trips to Hell

By ROGER RAPOPORT

In this sequel to bestselling *I Should Have Stayed Home* and *I've Been Gone Far Too Long*, business people tell of their greatest travel disasters—from the emergency room to the paddy wagon. Read this book and you'll be happy you weren't traveling with: oilman Jack Howard, cruise scout Marcia Wick, bookseller Monica Holmes, conductor Murray Gross, investor Jack Branagh, or publisher Cynthia Frank. Dedicated to the memory of Willy Loman, this tribute to corporate road warriors offers an amusing view of everything they don't want you to know in business school.

ISBN: 1-57143-062-8

$15.95 ($21.95 Can)
TRADE PAPERBACK
224 PAGES

I'll Never Get Lost Again

The Complete Guide to Improving Your Sense of Direction

By LINDA GREKIN

Millions of people including Ann Landers, Joan Baez, Beverly Sills and Dr. Kenneth Blanchard have a poor sense of direction. In this groundbreaking book, Linda Grekin explains why some people never get from point A to point B and what, if anything, they can do about it. Based on original research and talks with top scientific experts, this book offers a provocative and lively examination of the seventh sense—the sense of direction. Written with wit and wisdom, *I'll Never Get Lost Again* is the perfect traveling companion

ISBN: 1-57143-069-5

$12.95 ($18.95 Can)
TRADE PAPERBACK
128 PAGES

THE GETAWAY GUIDES

Each of these guides is an ideal itinerary planner for short or long trips. Organized with daily trip schedules, each book gently guides you to well-known and off-the-beaten-track destinations with helpful directions, recommended schedules and convenient lodging and dining recommendations. Written by experts who visit every one of the places they recommend, the Getaway Guides can be used for long weekends, week-long trips or grand three-week tours. Perfect for budget travelers and those who prefer luxury, each Getaway Guide is years in the making to insure that your trip is a winner from beginning to end. Selective and fun to read, each book reveals the secrets travel writers usually reserve for their closest friends.

The Getaway Guide to Agatha Christie's England

By JUDITH HURDLE

ISBN 1-57143-071-7

$17.95 ($21.95 Can)
TRADE PAPERBACK
192 PAGES

The Getaway Guide to California

By ROGER RAPOPORT

ISBN 1-57143-068-7

$17.95 ($21.95 Can)
TRADE PAPERBACK
256 PAGES

The Getaway Guide to the American Southwest

By RICHARD HARRIS

ISBN 1-57143-073-3

$17.95 ($21.95 Can)
TRADE PAPERBACK
232 PAGES
JULY 2001

The Getaway Guide to Colorado

By ROGER RAPOPORT

ISBN 1-57143-072-5

$17.95 ($21.95 Can)
TRADE PAPERBACK
192 PAGES
DECEMBER 2001

Our books are available at your local bookstore, or contact RDR Books at 4456 Piedmont Avenue, Oakland, CA 94611. Phone (510) 595-0595. Fax (510) 595-0598.

Email: info@rdrbooks.com.

See our books on the Web at www.rdrbooks.com.